"Ruslan Feldman ha[s a refreshing] writing style. His m[emoir shares] his dreams, thoughts[, feelings,] and writing style wit[h ... drawing] us into his world of r[eality.]
Pilgrimage to Wisdom will help us see Ruslan sometimes as clay being molded by the personalities and incidents of his life and sometimes as the master craftsman molding the clay into his perception of reality. In both cases we will come out ahead--richer, more spiritually aware, and 'alive.'"
Saleem Ahmed, Ph.D., author, *Beyond Veil and Holy War: Islamic Teachings and Muslim Practices with Biblical Comparisons* (Moving Pen Publishers, 2002) and *Islam: A Religion of Peace?* (Moving Pen Publishers, 2009); founder, the All Believers Network, Honolulu

"Ruslan is an engaging storyteller with an open heart, sense of humor, and vision. A capacity for detail and a passion to share draw us into his story—a search and appreciation for wisdom. He gives the reader a sense that it is possible to raise existence to something fine and meaningful. I highly recommend *Stories* to your reading list." Lynore Banchoff, poet, Menlo Park, California

"In these times when the boundaries among religions, churches, temples, and mosques are falling, it is a treat to read Ruslan's wisdom pilgrimage intersecting all the world's major religions. Ruslan finds value in each of his religious experiences and builds upon them. He has the gift of gleaning the wisdom of all his first-hand personal spiritual experiences, weaving them into a golden chain embracing them all. For those interested in encouraging interfaith dialogue and understanding to create a more peaceful world, this is a must read. Perhaps his pilgrimage can be a model for uniting people of all faiths and beliefs into one spiritual family." Rev. Sam Cox, UMC, Coordinator, The Interfaith Open Table, Hawai'i

"In Reynold Ruslan Feldman's autobiography, he has the magic to combine the best of both worlds--the realm of imagination and the realm of action--in his quest for spirituality. I strongly commend his book to your attention." Ramon Cuencas-Zamora, Ph.D., President, Prima Behavioral Health Providers, Dallas, Texas

"Many people give lip service to ecumenical and interfaith 'dialogue.' Ruslan Feldman is another kind of seeker. He has given himself to a deeply intuitive search for meaningful experience—what he identifies as wisdom. Through his memoir, tinged with the mystical and leavened by humor, he takes the reader on a journey through the 'varieties of religious experience' that have shaped his life. It's a wild and exhilarating ride." Janet Ray Edwards, Ph.D., senior adviser emerita, National Endowment for the Humanities

"Ruslan's spiritual autobiography is fascinating. It proved enjoyable reading for even someone like me who is not usually interested in spiritual topics. I particularly liked the early chapters, above all the description of his relationship with his father, and found the final chapters and epilogue very moving. I recommend this powerful book broadly, even to readers not ordinarily interested in the less conventional aspects of personal development." Michael Field, Professor of English Emeritus and former Provost, Shawnee State University, Ohio

"Reynold Ruslan Feldman embodies the truth of the adage, 'Seek and you shall find.' He has been an eager seeker all his life and has found fulfillment sequentially through several religions and continuously through the spiritual practice of Subud. He loves stories and people and finds friends wherever he goes, more friends in more places than anyone I've ever met. The story of his lifelong search for wisdom is enlightening and also fun to read." Marianne Gilbert Finnegan, State University of New York - Empire State College, Saratoga Springs, New York

"Reynold Ruslan Feldman's autobiography is simply a delight. Beautifully narrated, it is a collection of inspiring stories about his journey in quest of love and wisdom. There is a superb flow to the writing; it seems almost effortless." Scherto Gill, Ph.D., Executive Secretary, The Guerrand-Hermès Foundation for Peace, Brighton, England; and co-author, *Narrative Pedagogy* (Peter Lang, 2010); and editor, *Exploring Selfhood* (Centre for Research in Human Development, 2009)

"Ruslan Feldman is a masterful storyteller. He has led a life rich in worldly and spiritual experiences and shares it generously. In this book we meet family members, friends, colleagues, and especially Bapak Muhammad Subuh, the spiritual guide of Subud, who greatly affected Ruslan and many other people. I recommend this book highly and without qualification to anyone interested in personal or social transformation." Victor Margolin, Professor of Design History Emeritus, University of Illinois - Chicago

"Reynold Ruslan Feldman has never been one to 'color within the lines.' As a result, his life journey has taken him across boundaries of many sorts, not least national and religious boundaries, and has been enormously colorful. The stories in this engaging autobiography are the kind we need to hear nowadays when so many people live fearful and monochrome lives, afraid to 'cross over' into other people's worlds and encounter the full spectrum of human experience. In *Stories I Remember* all of us will find encouragement to lose our fear of 'the other' and, in the process, start to feel more at home on the face of the earth, where the One Light is refracted in so many illuminating ways." Parker J. Palmer, author, *A Hidden Wholeness*, *Let Your Life Speak*, and *The Courage to Teach*

"Reynold Ruslan Feldman's delightful *Stories I Remember - My Pilgrimage to Wisdom* is a deeply moving account of the ongoing inter-religious dialogue for world peace. Through his association with the All Believers Network in Honolulu and a life-long membership in Subud (a movement open to all faiths, dedicated to finding the Absolute inwardly), Ruslan describes his journey from a Jewish childhood, a Lutheran adulthood, to Roman Catholicism later in life, and a respectful acceptance of all religious-spiritual encounters as a part of the human journey to inner peace. The inspiration derived from Subud (its central practice is called '*latihan kejiwaan*,' literally 'spiritual exercise' or 'training of the spirit') has meant for Ruslan that the meeting with holy men and women from Jewish, Protestant, Catholic, Islamic, Buddhist, and other spiritual traditions has brought peace and inner wisdom. These well-told tales, including the death of his beloved wife, suggest a clear path to peace for today's war-torn society." Father Michael Saso, Ph.D., Kyoto, Japan

Stories I Remember

My Pilgrimage to Wisdom

Dear Philip,

Thanks for your example of wisdom unquenchable by the dead hand of authoritareanism. Blessings as you continue on your pilgrimage.

With love and admiration,

Reynold Ruslan

Boulder, Colorado   XI.25.2009

Dear Philip,

Thanks for your comprehensive note of the two inequalities — they look so nice, I am afraid of their applicability.

Thanking you for everything and your pilgrimage with love and admiration

Raphael Robinson

Berkeley, February 14, 1988

Stories I Remember

My Pilgrimage to Wisdom:
A Spiritual Autobiography

By

Reynold Ruslan Feldman

Wisdom Foundation Publishing

STORIES I REMEMBER, MY PILGRIMAGE TO WISDOM: A SPIRITUAL AUTOBIOGRAPHY

Copyright © 2009
Reynold Feldman

All rights reserved.

This edition was printed in the United States of America. No part of this book may be used or reproduced in any manner whatsoever without written permission from the publisher, except in the case of brief quotations embodied in critical articles and reviews.

ISBN 1-932590-00-5

Published by
Wisdom Foundation Publishing
PO Box 61599
Honolulu, Hawaii 96839
USA

Phone: +1.808.754.6960
Fax: +1.808.942.7885

www.wisdomfactors.com
info@wisdomfactors.com

Please contact the publisher for organization bulk orders of *Stories I Remember*.

1 2 3 4 5 6 7 8 9 10

" . . . Our destiny as human beings is to work in partnership with the Great Life Force."

Adrienne Campbell
Lewes, East Sussex, England
February 2008

This book is dedicated, with gratitude and love,

to Simone Zimmermann Feldman,

the best storyteller I know.

She's now telling the angels

a tale or two.

RRF

Table of Contents

Preface i

Introduction iii

1. The Opening 1
2. My Parents 13
3. Florine 29
4. Other Special People in My Youth.................................... 39
5. Junior Year in Germany 47
6. Graduate School, Marriage, and Early Subud Experiences 61
7. Queens College and Subud New York 79
8. University of Hawai'i and Subud Honolulu....................... 89
9. The Subud World Congress, Indonesia 107
10. University of Maryland (Europe) and Subud Germany 113
11. Northeastern Illinois University and Subud Chicago 123
12. Metropolitan State University and Subud Twin Cities 135
13. Simone 141
14. Back in Honolulu 157
15. New Worlds 173
16. Denmark Again and Ireland 183
17. The Beginning of Wisdom 191
18. Judaism 207
19. Lutheranism 217
20. Catholicism 229
21. Universalism 241

22. Wisdom Gained 251

Epilogue 257

Acknowledgments 261

Preface

ONCE WHEN I was six years old, I remember being unable to fall asleep. My mother had tucked me in and prayed with me as usual. "Now I lay me down to sleep. I pray the Lord my soul to keep. If I should die before I wake, I pray the Lord my soul to take. God bless Mommy, Daddy, Natalie, Florine, and everybody. Amen."

She turned off the light, left the room, and closed the door. Suddenly I was terrified. "What if I ready *should* die before I wake? I'm only a small child six years old. I haven't done anything yet. God, please help me. I want to live!"

Then a voice that wasn't mine, that belonged to a male adult, said inside my head, "Don't worry. You'll live to be a very old man, till you're 96."

After that I fell asleep and wasn't afraid of death again for a long, long time, though scary movies did a good job of keeping me awake in the later years of my childhood. "Mommy, please leave the door to the hall open a little and the hall light on." Just in case.

I'm now 68. I don't know if that voice back in 1945 was prophetic or not. I do know that a similar voice, not mine, has visited me again from time to time. As a result, a widower of 18 months, I find myself today in the middle of a three-month visit to Denmark. My Danish friend, Aisha, aware of my still-unprocessed grief, suggested I keep a dream journal and start writing about my life—especially those aspects that took me from being a secular middle-class Jewish kid in Great Neck, New York, to a contemplative Catholic and long-time follower of an interfaith spiritual practice called Subud. I have taken her advice. The result is this book.

I hope reading it will be as pleasant and useful for you as writing it has been for me.

May your life be rich in stories.

Reynold Ruslan Feldman

Copenhagen, March 2008

Introduction

I'VE NEVER considered myself a storyteller. One day, however, I was asked to address about 500 people. The occasion was a meeting of my spiritual association, Subud, at the Stevens Institute of Technology in Hoboken, New Jersey. The topic was my recent trip to São Paulo, Brazil, where I had represented Subud's North American Zone at an international Subud meeting. The year was 1981. I remember describing to the Hoboken gathering some things I had experienced in Brazil. One was how our Muslim spiritual guide, Muhammad Subuh, had greeted the line of blue-clad Catholic nuns belonging to the convent where we were meeting. They were all smiling, and so was he—his big, friendly grin. This was a foretaste of a desirable future, I thought, where devoted Christians, Muslims, and people of other faiths could greet each others with smiles, not distrust, insults or bullets. Yet what also struck me was the feeling that Bapak, as we called our spiritual guide, was parading the troops—a metaphor that tickled both me and the audience because Bapak was no general and these nuns were certainly no soldiers.

The other story took place a few days later at another convent during the same trip. There were about 16 of us, Subud representatives from all over the world in a kind of great hall. Bapak arrived, sat down in an easy chair on the dais, and made an unusual request. He wanted us to pair up and dance a Viennese waltz for him. A tape player and appropriate music were quickly found. As it happened, we were exactly eight men and eight women. The next thing I knew, a Mexican woman and I were whirling around the room along with the seven other couples. Bapak smiled his big smile for us, too.

Anyway, after I told my stories, an actor who was also a Subud member and a friend of mine, Raymond Owens, came up to me and said that, as far as he was concerned, I was right up there with Francis von Kahler and Varindra Vittachi, two of Subud's top storytellers. Another New York member, Walter Siegel, a concentration-camp survivor as a child, joined me a few minutes later with a present. It was the lapel pin with Subud's seven-circles logo that had belonged to the above-mentioned Francis von Kahler—you'll hear more about him later. Walter wanted me to have it, one of his prized possessions, he said, because I had now taken up Francis's mantel as one of Subud's notable storytellers.

I have called this narrative of my spiritual life *Stories I Remember*, since for me the practice of Subud, I'm certain, has caused me to remember less and less over time. I think of that toy writing tablet I had as a kid. When you wrote with a special stylus on the hard cellophane sheet, you would see your words. But as soon as you lifted the sheet, the words would instantly disappear. Still, I have also experienced that when I truly *needed* to remember something, like a word in a foreign language I hadn't used for a while, it would miraculously come to me. Just-in-time delivery, you could say! The stories I'll share are thus only the ones I remember—that come to me as I am writing. *Stories* is also the account of my pilgrimage not just to personal wisdom, a work in process, but to helping the world become wiser. In the later part of the narrative you'll learn how I became interested in the concept, co-founded Wisdom Factors International, and am working in the field. In any case, I hope these stories will be useful to you, the reader, in reflecting on your own spiritual development. Perhaps they will even help you embrace the wisdom of your best self. *Inshallah*, as the Muslims say. May God make it so.

1
The Opening

I WAS born in New York City on November 6, 1939. But the first story I want to tell comes 21½ years later, in Chicago: My Opening in Subud.

May 22, 1961. I arrived a little earlier than usual so that the men helpers could sit with me and I could become quiet before my opening. Like others before me, I was feeling a certain performance anxiety. Would I get it? What would happen if I didn't? Was the *latihan* really from God? I felt it was, but was it really? Stuart told me in his soft Southern accent that everything would be fine and that I should just relax and prepare for whatever God had in mind for me. All I had to do when I got into the exercise room was stand there and wait. "Waiting for Godot" was the phrase that went through my nervous English-major mind.

We walked into a spacious room, perhaps 50' by 20'. Chairs were arranged around the sides, leaving a large, empty area in the middle. There were perhaps 20 men standing around, waiting for things to begin. The three Chicago men helpers—Harrington, Lee, and Stuart—stood in front of me, while the others had deployed themselves around the room. Everyone, including me, had taken off our glasses and watches and put these along with our wallets and loose change in our shoes, which we placed under the chairs lining the four walls. Then we all stood at ease, although I'll admit I felt the way I always had in prep school just before beginning a 100-yard butterfly race. The butterflies were in my stomach, now as then.

Harrington began to say the four or five sentences of Bapak's Opening Words: "We are helpers in the Spiritual Brotherhood [now "Association"] of Subud and are here to witness your wish to worship the One Almighty God. We hope that your wish is truly based on sincerity. As you know, God is almighty, all-present, and all-knowing. Therefore it will not be right for you to concentrate your thoughts, self-will or desires but you should simply relax your thoughts and surrender everything to the Greatness of Almighty God. So that you will not be disturbed by the exercises of others, we ask that you close your eyes, stand quite at ease, and have no worries. Now please begin."

As Harrington slowly spoke these words, I felt myself relax. At first, maybe for four or five minutes, I stood there. Nothing appeared to be happening. No movement. I was simply aware that others in the room, including the helpers, were going about their business of walking, singing, invoking God's name, whatever. By this point I began to think nothing like that would happen to me. Then, as in a fairy tale, no sooner had that thought crossed my mind when I "saw" within me that someone was standing behind me with a gun pointed at the back of my head. "*Nein! Nein! Warum?!*" I said out loud in German. "No! No! Why?!" Then I "died."

Being killed happened so fast I didn't feel anything. I sang a high note that went down to the lowest note in my register. Then I dropped to the carpeted floor and lay on my back. Being "dead" was fantastic. I have never, before or since, felt so peaceful or quietly happy. Then after perhaps ten minutes, a voice inside my head said, "Now you have to be born again." I objected. "No. It's much better here. Why must I go down there again?" But the voice insisted. So I stood up and starting dancing all over the room. I felt happy now. Then in my mind I saw a slowly turning globe. First I noticed Russia and said the Hebrew word *Adonai*, Lord, with what struck me as a Russian accent. Then I saw Germany and said *Adonai* in a more German way. Finally, I noticed that I was now looking at New York City, where I had been born in this life. As I started to feel myself being drawn down, I said *Adonai* one more time with an American accent. Immediately thereafter, Harrington said "Finish," and everyone including me moved to the chairs where our shoes were placed and sat quietly for five or ten minutes. After that, the helpers and most of the other members came up and hugged me. "Welcome to Subud," Harrington said. "You're a Subud member." And with an echo of the Catholic priest he once had been, he added, "May God bless you."

When I left the *latihan* room and walked into the waiting room, a girl my age, Trudy, a fellow probationer who would be opened a few weeks later, gave me a questioning look. "So how was it, Steve [my name then]?" "Unbelievable," I answered. But what had struck me were her eyes. Unlike those of the Subud members, which appeared clear and deep, hers seemed muddy, as if a thin film were covering and somehow obscuring them. Then, the Biblical line crossed my mind, "And the scales fell from their eyes and they could see clearly." For whatever reason, I had never understood that sentence. I kept thinking the *scales* were miniature weighing balances and couldn't figure how they could get into anyone's eyes. But now it struck me in a flash—as many other things would over the course of my nearly 50 years in Subud—that these were fish scales. Some of Jesus' disciples had been fishermen. A fish scale over the pupil would mimic a cataract, being translucent but not transparent. With such scales obscuring one's vision, one would see human beings as "trees walking" and reality, in the words of the King James Version, "as through a glass darkly."

Now the scales had fallen from my eyes. In the well-known verse of "Amazing Grace," "I . . . was blind but now I see." It was a new beginning, a brand new birth. From now on, my inner life would take on an entirely different meaning and direction. I was now opened.*

How did I get to this point? After graduating from Yale in June 1960 with a Bachelor of Arts in English, I couldn't decide what to do next. Initially I had planned to spend a year teaching English at San Andres, a bilingual Scottish private school in a suburb of Buenos Aires. I knew that twelve months in a Spanish-speaking country would do wonders for my conversational Spanish, not to mention my tango. My sister Natalie, married to an Argentine businessman, lived in Buenos Aires as did Aunt Ruthie, my mother's youngest sister. Natalie had taught at San Andres before. So it was only a matter of doing the paperwork and I was in. Plus I would have several free places to stay. Then my sister wrote that she was pregnant with baby number two, which she planned to have not in Chicago, as her first child, but in Buenos Aires. My mother, who didn't trust Argentine doctors or hospitals, decided *she*, not I, would go to Argentina to oversee the situation and that I would stay in Chicago with my father. So much for *español* and the tango!

Because I was 1-A in the draft, no one wanted to give me a job, my *magna cum laude* degree from Yale notwithstanding. On top of that, I would usually tell the interviewer I planned to go to graduate school soon. My commitment to honesty at all costs generally led to a friendly handshake and a "Thank you for your time, Mr. Feldman. I wish you well in whatever you decide to do." So, I ended up staying at home, listening to Studs Terkel and classical music on WFMT,

---

*"Opening" is a literal translation of the Indonesian *pembukaan*. Frankly, I was not crazy about the term when I first heard it. In graduate school, the year following my opening, I learned that George Fox, founder of the Religious Society of Friends (Quakers), referred to all his spiritual insights as *openings*. Frequently he would say, "The Lord opened it to me. . . ." Later, I found out that the introduction to the Qur'an is called the *Fatihah*, Arabic for "opening." A common Muslim prayer is *Yah Fatah*, in which one praises Allah as the One Who opens the way and takes away all obstacles blocking one's progress.

reading books, and writing in my journal. Finally, out of boredom, I started working at my father's grain-brokerage business at the Board of Trade. I basically typed contracts, did gopher work, and had lunch with my father and his colleagues at nearby restaurants. I didn't learn much about the grain or any other business, nor, to my father's dismay, did I have much interest. One of his friends, Joe Nugent, called me "The Brain." Joe was an Irishman from New York City, where he and my Dad went back a long way, as he often said. "So what does The Brain recommend for lunch?" He would ask. Lunch with Joe and my father was the highpoint of my day.

After a month or so downtown, I decided to start my own language-tutoring business. Thanks to my junior year abroad in Heidelberg, my German was fluent. My French and Spanish were passable. And with six years of Latin under my belt, I could tutor that too, not to mention English. As it happened, I taught geometry, my worst subject in high school, to the 15-year-old son of one of my father's friends and German to my mother's beautican and another person I'm sure was a Mafia hit man. (Why in the world was he learning German? I wondered.) Here and there I got some work teaching French and Spanish as well. Since all my basic expenses were covered by living at home, my $5 per-lesson-per-person income went to vinyl records and the occasional date. Five bucks was useful if not exactly serious walking-around money back in 1960.

I first learned about Subud that year from a taxi driver named Raymond, later called Luscian. It was at the Bon Ton Restaurant, on the Lake side of State Street, just south of Division in the Near North area called the Gold Coast. One March day I was there enjoying a Napoleon and a cup of coffee when an intense-looking young man approached my table. "Haven't I seen you here speaking German with the waitress and French with another woman? Tell me, are you German or French?" "Neither," I replied. "I'm American." With my permission, Raymond brought over his coffee and sat down. He had parked his cab outside and was taking a break, he explained. He asked me about myself; then told me he was reading philosophy books while earning some money driving his taxi. Specifically, he was studying the work—The Work—of George I. Gurdjieff, a Greek mystic from the Caucasus who had died in Paris in 1949. Had I ever heard of him? No.

Over the next weeks we would meet from time to time. Usually it was a planned coffee at the Bon Ton. Several times, though, a taxi would pull up, discharge a passenger, then honk at me. Freaky! It was Raymond. We'd go have coffee somewhere nearby and talk more Gurdjieff. By this time I had read Dr. Kenneth Walker's introduction and P.D. Ouspensky's classic, *In Search of the Miraculous.* I had learned about Gurdjieff's Octaves, the Law of Three, Personality versus Essence, and the technique of Self-Remembering. Most people, per Gurdjieff, were asleep; a much smaller number were aware; and a very few were awake. Not only that, but there were seven levels of human being. Level 1 was the Man of the Body. (This was 1960, so there was no inclusive language yet.) Then came Levels 2, Man of the Emotions, and 3, Man of the Intellect. What struck me as a Yale sophisticate was that all three types, according to Gurdjieff, were subhuman—even the intellectual. It wasn't till Level 4 (of 7) that one encountered the harmoniously developed human being. People at the lower three levels were living partially, not fully. They were stuck in their Personality, their outer persona. The point of the Work was to learn to live in one's Essence, one's real self, not the self imposed by one's family or society (Personality). This was possible through Gurdjieff's rigorous training program of Self-Remembering. The Law of Three meant that two opposing forces would eventually lead to stasis. That was why, according to Gurdjieff, so many people where stuck in their Personalities. By intervening, a third force would dislodge this blockage and lead to movement and progress. That third force was Gurdjieff's program, The Work. Among other things, the concept of Octaves suggested that outwardly two people might appear quite similar. But one could be much more advanced spiritually than the other, on the same note, so to speak, but a full octave higher.

Gurdjieff and his instructors would have people walk at speeds and in ways different from their ordinary walking, or do things with their non-dominant hand. Soon the trainees would fall back into their usual ways of doing things. In other words, they'd fall *asleep* again. My favorite example of self-remembering from the Walker book was having English ladies use fancy silver teaspoons to dig up a tree stump. They were even required to keep their pinkies turned out. Gurdjieff's approach seemed a kind of spiritual shock therapy. If one could be successfully shaken out of automatic actions, of sleep-walking through life, so to speak, there was a chance one could wake up, integrate body-heart-mind, and become an essential, not superficial, human being.

All this interested me. But what really got my attention is that one day, as I was practicing an exercise described in the Walker book, I seemed to lift off the floor of our living room just a little. Whether I was deluding myself or not, I can't say. But I vividly remember the feeling of starting to levitate. (I was lying on my back.) When Raymond and I met the next day, I told him about my experience and said I was ready to go to his Gurdjieff group and begin The Work. Then he told me about Subud.

As I recall, it was a rainy April afternoon. Raymond had taken the day off so he could tell me about this new spiritual practice from Indonesia. He had been doing the Subud spiritual exercise for six months or more, well before we met, but had felt to tell me about Gurdjieff first. An intellectual like me, he figured, would find Gurdjieff much more approachable with its principles and set techniques than Subud, which was comprised of spontaneous mystical experiences. He was probably right.

Anyway, as Raymond went on to explain, Subud was started by an Indonesian named Muhammad Subuh Sumohadiwidjojo. Bapak ("Father"), as he was called by his followers, was born in Central Java, volcanically fertile ground for mystical practices of all kinds, on June 22, 1901. So he was now 59. Although descended from the Sultan of Surakarta (also called Solo), his family was not wealthy. His father had been a lower official for the Dutch Colonial Rail System; his mother, a housewife who went on to have a number of children.

When Bapak was born, his parents—actually his grandfather—named him Soekarno. Ironically, he was born a few weeks after and not far from the birthplace of his namesake, the future co-founder and president of Indonesia. In later years, he was in fact often mistaken for the president, even by Indonesians, because of their unusual height for Malays and a striking facial resemblance. But he did not keep the name. Within a few weeks, the baby fell ill. A wandering Arab, dressed in black, stopped by the house one day and warned that unless the child's name was changed, it would die, since the name was dangerously incorrect. The Arab then recommended the name "Muhammad Subuh." Muhammad was of course the name given many male children throughout the Muslim world. As for Subuh, it was the Indonesianized form of the Arabic *subh*, the Islamic pre-dawn prayer and standard Arabic for "morning."

Once his name was changed, Subuh, as he was subsequently called, grew strong. He also turned out to be very intuitive. For instance, when his parents took him as a boy to weddings, he would comment in a loud voice if he felt the bride and groom were incompatible. Since he generally proved correct, his parents stopped taking him to these occasions. It was just too embarrassing for all concerned. Also, the boy seemed unable to lie and became incensed when others did. Moreover, as a tall, strong child, he would take it on himself to defend smaller children from schoolyard bullies.

The itinerant Arab, who was never seen in the village again, had also predicted that Subuh might die at age 24—something his parents felt duty-bound to tell him so that he could take whatever steps necessary to become physically and mental strong or, as a good Muslim, to prepare himself internally to accept God's will, even if that meant an early death.

As a teenager, Bapak lived in a nearby city with his uncle so he could attend the Dutch-language high school. Fluency in Dutch was a precondition for natives to get any of the white-collar positions that were starting to be available to them in the early 20th Century. Through family connections, Bapak got a job with the regional railway while studying at night to become an accountant. As the story goes, one evening in his twenty-fourth year, Bapak finished his homework late and took his usual walk to clear his head before retiring. It was a cloudless, moon-free night as he passed the site of a new hospital under construction near his house. At that moment, he said, it was as if a bright light or ball of fire dropped from the sky and entered his head. (Later I was to learn that St. Hildegard of Bingen had had a similar experience as did John Travolta's character in the movie *Phenomenon*.) He started shaking and got home as quickly as he could. As he explained, he thought he was dying. He knocked on the door, which his mother opened. "What's wrong, son?" She asked. "You look terrible." "Nothing," he replied, and went upstairs to his room, where he laid himself out on his bed, said his prayers, and prepared to die.

What happened instead was that he saw his hands as if with x-ray vision. Then he felt moved to get up and do his regular Muslim prayers. For the next three years, various automatic exercises, not just traditional prayers, came to him and sometimes went on all night. Not only was he moved to walk and dance, but he also sang songs he'd never heard before and did a variety of spontaneous martial-arts-type exercises. Surprisingly, Bapak didn't feel especially tired in the morning and was able to do his work as usual and even got a promotion.

He was also shown a variety of things during these long nights. Once a large folio book with blank pages dropped onto his table. Whenever a question occurred to him, the answer would appear spontaneously in a kind of video format on one of the pages. He was also sometimes shown "videos" without asking a question. For instance, he saw in the late 1920s how in the future the Japanese would occupy his country, drive out the Dutch colonists, and eventually leave themselves, after which Indonesia would be free. He also saw how he would travel the world one day and find himself in the midst of people of different races, religions, and nations, all of whom were worshipping God together.

Eventually, the book disappeared into his chest, and from then on he could ask questions and receive the moving-picture answers inside his mind. Finally, at the end of this three-year process, an Arab-appearing man showed up one night in his room and thrust a dagger into Bapak's chest. Bapak felt the pain yet miraculously was not wounded, let alone killed. As the man withdrew the dagger, Bapak noticed a clot of blood on the tip. The man spoke in Arabic, which Bapak could recognize from having memorized portions of the Qur'an as a boy. Surprisingly, Bapak could also understand the gist of what he was saying, that the blood on the dagger represented the last of his impurities that needed to be purged before Bapak could begin his mission. For anyone familiar with the life of the Prophet Muhammad, a similar thing happened to him at the hands of an archangel.

But what was that mission? The man had only told Bapak that he would know when the time came. Meanwhile, he was not to go anywhere nor speak to anyone about what he had received until he was specifically asked. Bapak was puzzled. Still, he had experienced so many unusual things by that point that he felt confidence in what the man had said.

I should mention, Raymond continued, that as a young man, Bapak had consulted various well-known gurus and spiritual guides then active in Central Java. They invariably told him they could not help him with his inner development and that, when the time came, he would be guided directly from above.

So how did these spontaneous exercises of Bapak become available to others? I wanted to know. Not long after the Arab with the dagger had appeared to Bapak, Raymond answered, two young men showed up at his door. They had been sent by their master, they said, to receive some kind of spiritual contact from him. They became the first Subud members, although at that time Bapak's spiritual exercises had not yet been named.

I looked at my watch. My father would be at the Bon Ton in half an hour for dinner. Then we were planning to go see a foreign film at the theater across the street.

"How did Bapak's exercises get out of Indonesia and to Chicago?" I asked. I wanted to bring the discussion up to the present before my father arrived. Raymond obliged. At first his exercises, eventually called the *Latihan Kejiwaan*, Indonesian for "spiritual training," spread slowly to spiritual seekers in central Java, including members of Bapak's family. It wasn't until 1951, when Bapak was living in Jogyakarta, the revolutionary capital of Indonesia, that an English Muslim named Husein Rofé, who was teaching English to officials of the first Indonesian government, heard about Bapak, met him, and was opened. Actually, as the story goes, Bapak had predicted to his followers that a foreigner with roots in Syria who spoke many languages would join the spiritual exercises one day and become the vehicle for taking them out of Java and eventually to the West. Rofé's father was in fact a Syrian Jew who had been raised in Egypt and then moved to Manchester, England, where he ran a profitable textile import/export business. Husein himself had studied Near Eastern languages in London and proved so talented that the British wartime military had recruited him and quickly taught him Japanese so that he could monitor enemy shortwave broadcasts. By the time he reached the newly formed Republic of Indonesia, he had taught English in a number of countries and already understood, spoke, read, and wrote more than 20 languages.*

Since it was not possible in the early 50s for Bapak to travel in Indonesia, let alone overseas, he authorized Rofé to go first to Sumatra, then Japan, Hong Kong, and Cyprus, in all of which places he started groups. Finally, in 1956, he traveled to England, where he opened John Bennett, a physicist who was also a leader of the Gurdjieff Work in the U.K. In 1957, Bennett and some of his wealthy associates raised funds for Bapak, his wife Siti Sumari, and two spiritual assistants called "helpers" to travel to England, where they stayed for eight months. Hundreds of people, including Gurdjieff members from the Continent as well as the U.K., were opened during that visit. There was even a miraculous healing of the Hungarian movie actress Eva Bartok which the European tabloid press was quick to pick up. This notoriety brought many people to Coombe Springs, Bennett's Gurdjieff school in the countryside outside London. Some of these also joined what by then was called

---

*When Rofé moved to Hawai'i in the late 1990s, he told me the number now stood at an even 70, and he was currently working on Tibetan and Georgian. He died in winter 2008.

Subud. After, Bapak was invited to go home by way of a half dozen countries, where he and his party opened many more. He also gave explanations about the aim, nature, and potential results of following the Subud spiritual exercise, especially if one followed them consistently over time.

What did that mean? I asked Raymond. Basically, one would do the exercise twice weekly—men with men, women with women—for approximately thirty minutes. Then, one simply lived his or her regular life. There was no requirement to do anything special. Over time, the *latihan* would purify the practitioner so that the individual's life would become peaceful, harmonious, and focused on drawing on his or her true talents to support him- or herself and family and to contribute to the needs of others and the world. Still, as with anything else, a person had to stick with the process for a while to see the benefits. Why do men and women do the Subud exercise separately? I continued. For one thing, he replied, so people could receive honestly and not edit their receiving to impress the opposite sex. Also, Bapak explained how the vibrations of men and women differed, and that men might "drown out" the receiving of women. A third reason was that because individuals were very open and relaxed while doing the spiritual exercise, there might be sexual attraction between certain men and women, and that would not be appropriate to the Subud exercise.

Was there a Subud group in Chicago? "I'm going tonight," Raymond replied. "Want to go?" At this point, my father arrived and bought the three of us dinner. After eating, he begged off from the movies since he had a headache and wanted to go home. That was fine with me, since now I could accompany Raymond to the Subud meeting in the Loop.

Subud-Chicago met in those days on the eleventh floor of the Fine Arts Building, near the present downtown campus of Roosevelt University and not far from Orchestra Hall, the home of the Chicago Symphony Orchestra. I remember that the first floor of the building housed an arts film house which specialized, as I soon discovered, in the soft porn available in the early 60's. Ironically, the film playing that first night was "Naked Apollo," featuring the renowned Eva Bartok as the female lead. Upstairs in Subud's waiting room—the members "exercised" in a large, empty room next door, first the women then the men—I found the book *Worth Living For* by the very same Eva Bartok, in which she described her encounter with Bapak, her opening, the resulting cure from cancer, the healthy birth of her baby, and her subsequent year or so in Subud. There were also two books by Husein Rofé about his experiences in Subud plus the major introduction to Subud in the early days, *Concerning Subud* by John Bennett. At that point there were not yet many writings by Bapak himself. The translated talks I found were mainly for opened people, since those who had not yet experienced the *latihan* might find his clarifications for practitioners more mystifying than useful. I did notice, though, that the Indonesian, printed on the left-hand pages, looked interesting and not too difficult. So I decided on that first visit that if I ever became a Subud member, I would learn Indonesian so I could understand Bapak in the original and even talk with him if I ever had the chance—all of which would happen later.

The ladies were doing their *latihan* when we arrived. Raymond introduced me around to a half dozen or so men in the waiting room. As the time got closer for the ladies to come out and the men to go into the big adjoining room for *latihan*, another five or six men showed up. There was a former Catholic priest with the ur-Irish name of Harrington McDonald, a German-American voice teacher called Lee von Hohenstein, a University of Chicago staffer and sometime Shakespearean actor from North Carolina named Stuart Moody, an East Indian accountancy grad student at Northwestern University, Kasi Ramanathan, a German clerk at the American Medical Association named Rolf Rattay, and an elderly Jewish businessman called Sam Wolf. When the ladies came out, I met and was most struck by a beautiful elderly Scottish woman named Sarah Gordon. She had large blue eyes, silky-white hair, a creamy complexion, and an incredible smile. I guessed she was around 70. Somehow she among all the others reminded me of the early Christians in the Roman catacombs, where they had all things in common as they supported one another in facing the hostility of the Empire above. As it happened, her presence helped give me the courage to join Subud some weeks later.

When Subud first came to England, Bapak permitted interested people to be opened on the spot. After six months or so, he thought better of it and decided it would be preferable for "probationers," as they were then called, to wait three months while deciding whether or not they really wished to join Subud. Although the exercises are simple—you just do whatever you feel moved to do for a half hour—the process could occasionally lead to "heavy purification." Bapak explained that if people waited three months before being opened, they would be more likely to persevere if the going got rough until they could break through to a better place in themselves.

I attended the meetings regularly three times a week and read everything available as I sat outside in the waiting room. I was hooked. I loved the people and felt something different and winning in them. Even Sam Wolf, a Jewish businessman like my father, had an entirely different feel even though he was outwardly like the friends and relatives of my parents. I couldn't quite put my finger on it. There was a quiet joy, a sense of peace. Whatever it was, I wanted it.

One evening—it was Friday, May 19, 1961—I was sitting outside the women's *latihan*. The doors were closed, but anyone passing by could hear the singing and other noises. That night the sounds were especially harmonious, I thought. As I sat there, my torso started moving rhythmically in a circle—gently at first, then stronger and stronger. I was of course aware of the movement, but "I" wasn't the one who was causing it. It was happening all by itself. Then I heard that the ladies had become silent. Their *latihan* was over. My body stopped moving, and I felt a warm, tingly sensation all over. Then, when I opened my eyes—they had been closed—I saw Lee, Harrington, and Stuart looking down at me and chuckling. "Okay," one of them said. "Come back Monday evening, and we'll do the *official* opening." And that was the beginning of everything else.

2
My Parents

MY FATHER was the oldest of the three sons of Grandpa Paul and Grandma Ida. He was born, in Brooklyn if I'm not mistaken, in July 1905. He always celebrated his birthday on July 5 even though his birth certificate declared him to be born more than two weeks later. The certificate was wrong, according to Dad. Apparently he had been born at home, and by the time my grandparents understood how and where to get a birth certificate, what with language difficulties and all, the clerk simply put down the date they showed up in the office, July 21. His younger brother, Murray, came along three years later, while Uncle Alan was a kind of afterthought, not arriving on the scene till 1920—just in time, once he became of age, to join the U.S. Army Air Corps as a side-gunner in Flying Fortresses over France and Germany in World War II. When I was growing up, Uncle Alan, dark-haired, handsome, and laid back like the soldiers I saw portrayed in the war movies, was a real-life hero. These days he looks like the elder President Truman. He is the last living child of Grandpa Paul and Grandma Ida—Uncle Murray having died in 1960 and my father in 1986.

Anyway, to get back to my dad, he was a talented musician. So, in the Jewish tradition of his day, he received piano lessons from I believe age five. By the time he graduated from Central High School, Philadelphia, at age 15 or 16 with a straight-A average, he had been good enough to win an all-expenses-paid piano scholarship to the city's renowned Curtis Institute of Music. Alas, it was not to be. Just when he was planning to enter the conservatory, Grandpa Paul decided to take one of his periodic sabbaticals from married life and fatherhood. With Murray still in high school and Alan either an infant or on the way, Dad was forced to decline his scholarship and, as the eldest child, begin working to support the family. Grandma Ida and the boys moved back to Brooklyn to be closer to Grandma's siblings, and through family contacts, Dad got a job as a Western Union runner at Number Two Broadway, as he always called it, an old, square, dirty-red building which housed the New York Produce Exchange.

My father didn't deliver telegrams, as one might think. Instead, he was busy carrying around buy and sell notices to offices in the building confirming various wholesale grain deals. Clever, articulate, and quick to learn, he impressed the managers of some of the big grain houses—Cargill, Bunge, Dreyfus—and by the time the Depression hit nine years later when he was just 24, he was already making $25,000 a year in salaries and commissions—huge money back then—as a hot, young grain dealer. That was the year he married Mother, not long after Black Tuesday, and after a honeymoon at the still somewhat fashionable Fifth Avenue Hotel near Washington Square, they moved out to an apartment in Far Rockaway, Long Island.

According to my mother, Dad was among the fortunate few who maintained their job and income during the Great Depression. As a result, my parents usually found themselves playing hosts to some out-of-work *mishpuchah*, a family member or friend, who would sleep on the couch in the living room or come by regularly for meals. Mother herself was a flapper, long-legged and good-looking, who had to suffer from the fact that she was too busty in an era that preferred women with willowy, girlish figures. She didn't simply grin and bear it, though. She bound her chest up tightly to make herself seem less well endowed and apparently did harm to her breast muscles. By the time I was consciously on the scene in the mid-40's, when my mother was in her early 40s, the damage had been done, and her bosom hung low like that of an old granny.

In the 20s Dad like to hang around with the fast crowd, go to jazz clubs and speakeasies, not that he was much of a drinker, and take in the latest Broadway shows or Off-Broadway plays. One of his colleagues at the time and a fellow man-about-town was a young, well-to-do Englishman who had been sent by his father, a successful grain merchant in the U.K., to learn the business in the States, presumably to come home later on and take over the family business. Instead, he went on to be a well-known actor, eventually joining Orson Welles as part of the Mercury Theater repertory. Several generations later he became known to American movie and TV audiences as the austere but charismatic law professor in *The Paper Chase*. His name was John Houseman.

When I saw *Guys and Dolls* on Broadway as a young teenager, one of the main figures, good old reliable Nathan Detroit—a kind of Broadway character who always had an angle, knew everyone, and had a solid lock on what was happening—reminded me of my father. Dad was clearly an urban original right out of a Damon Runyan story, *New Yawk* accent and all. He referred to me as Kid or the Kid and would tell his friends that my mother, who spoke like the radio, was a "classy broad." I think he identified himself with Nathan and must have seen *Guys and Dolls* a half dozen or more times.

He did have an eye for theatrical talent and in his 50's was often named to produce the Board of Trade's annual show, which was a pretty big event in Lower Manhattan. I remember meeting Dianne Carol, whom Dad claimed he had picked from obscurity and gave her first big break, as well as Eva Marie Saint, the Academy-Award-winning actress, with whom we once ate lunch in Atlantic City. He had used both of them in shows. He would often end up hanging out with famous entertainers. It just seemed to happen. Once, for example, as he was crossing the Southwest on the Santa Fe *Chief*, he spent two nights and days drinking and joking around with Dean Martin and Jerry Lewis in their compartment. On another occasion, it was Danny Kaye. According to Dad, they all encouraged him to leave his career as a grain merchant and go into show business. He was a great storyteller who could deliver a punch line with panache, and I guess when he had a couple of drinks, he must have gone tit for tat with the pros.

One story he told which I especially liked had to do with an experience he had during a grain convention in Galveston, Texas. It was during the 40s or 50s when the city was still dry, and Dad and some of his buddies were passing the time after their sessions in a speakeasy. Apparently, the piano player got sick and had to leave early. So my father, who could play just about anything by ear, sat down at the piano and started hammering out the standards. Requests came in thick and fast, but Dad never missed a note. In the wee hours, as he and his associates were getting ready to leave, the owner came up to him and offered him $75 a week plus tips and all the free food and booze he could handle. He paused for a moment; then said no. Later, some of his friends told him, "Jack, you just turned down the best job offer you'll ever get." Whenever he told this story, it seemed he might have felt that way sometimes himself.

As a father, he was essentially laid back and permissive. On the rare occasions when I provoked him past his level of tolerance, however, look out. But he was full of good surprises too. For example, he might call on a stifling hot Friday afternoon in summer and tell Mother to pack and get us ready to leave as soon as he got home from town. We were going to Atlantic City for the weekend. We didn't have air conditioning in the house or any of the rooms; very few people did back then. And I remember well, 60-plus years later, how wonderful the first cool breezes and the salt air felt when we turned off U.S. 1 and headed across the causeway—a word I still like—to the famous seaside resort. Arriving around 10 p.m. at the Traymore or the Claridge, we'd drop our bags in the room and head for the boardwalk. Many people apparently had had the same idea, since, late as it was, the boardwalks were full, and of course, all the arcades and lemonade stands were doing plenty of business. The only other times I saw such vibrant late-night street life were in places like Morocco and Indonesia. The feeling of a street carnival was palpable. And if we'd had a relatively smooth drive down, my dad would say something Nathan Detroitish like "Here's a sawbuck [a five-dollar bill, for the uninitiated], Kid. Go have a good time. Don't spend it all in the same place, and make sure you're back in the room by midnight." I was in heaven. Soon I was inspecting my favorite haunts between Million Dollar and Steel Piers and seeing if I was still an ace at my favorite pinball games or in Skill Ball bowling, or whatever it was called. The whole time, of course, I was trying to seem cool and act older—at least twelve. I wasn't trying to impress girls yet; it was more a matter of impressing myself. Years later when I saw the French film *Atlantic City*, I remember my sadness and shock at the opening scene, which showed the destruction by a giant wrecking ball of the Hotel Traymore. There I had spent hours playing pool, billiards, and ping pong in the game room; getting to know kids my age, older kids, and even a few adults; and passing some of the most enjoyable hours of my young life. And now all that was irreparably gone.

Another favorite experience at home was when on weekends my father would sit down at the piano and play old favorites. I got out the *Fireside Book of Folk Songs*, and he would dutifully play my choices too, items like "On Top of Old Smoky" and "The Bob-tailed Nag." For my part, I tried to sing them with the twangiest pseudo-Southern accent my elementary-school self could muster. The most fun was when Uncle Joe Lustgarten, the Socialist liquor salesman married to my mother's sister Lilly, would visit, stand next to me, and intone the songs with all the gusto of a barroom baritone. Sometimes, though, if left to his own devices, Dad would play his own composition which I dubbed "The Wall Street Rag." It had a sad, Jewishy feel to it, which may have expressed whatever sadness he felt in his life. I was too young to know the details or even the bigger picture, as far as that went, but playing that piece seemed to give him some kind of release. He would also do a pretty decent job with Debussy's *Clair de Lune*, which he knew by heart. I'm half-guessing it might have been the bravura piece which got him his forgone scholarship at the Curtis Institute. I regret now that I never asked. It was my dad in fact who got me interested in classical music, a love which I have been loyal to, and it to me, my whole lifetime. Dad had some old classical 78 records—things like Chopin's *Military Polonnaise* and Schubert's

Unfinished Symphony, which always sounded pretty finished to me, and my special favorite, *Peter and the Wolf*, with Boris Karlov doing the speaking part as only he could. I would spend free time daydreaming while listening to these pieces over and over again. In this way, they began to fill in the background of my inner landscape and give me a feeling of connection to something bigger and more comforting than I knew in everyday life.

Another thing Dad liked to do was read. He could go through a fat book in a night, it seemed. There he would sit in the living room on the couch or in an easy chair zooming through anything he happened to get his hands on, from pulp fiction to the classics. One day it might be Turgenieff's *Fathers and Sons*, the next Mickey Spillane's *My Gun Is Quick*. Inevitably, he would run his hand through his thick, brown hair as he read—something that drove my mother crazy. A regular evening refrain in our house was "Jack, leave your hair alone." "Jack, can't you read without doing that?" All in vain. He was somewhere else, in a world made up of letters and the pictures and sounds those letters evoked in his imagination. The best she could get out of him if she stuck to it long enough was an unconscious "Wha?," after which she would leave the room, defeated once again.

One of our special father-son treats was going to the barbershop together—something we did well into his 70s. It was there, in the banter between him and the barber, inevitably an older man in my childhood, and occasionally with other male customers, that I began to learn bad words, shocked at first but also somewhat proud that my father would use them in front of me, a mere child. Back then parents made efforts not to argue, let alone use foul language, in front of their children.

Another of my father's practices was reading aloud from the *New York Times*. Not only that, but he would add his own commentaries in full-out New Yorkese. "How do you like that? That son-of-a-bitch _____ got caught with his hand in the cookie jar again! You'd think in today's world they'd find a way to get rid of crooks like that from Tammany Hall [New York's City Hall]." My dad also had a sliding scale when it came to financial crime. He would say, "If you steal $10 you're a thief; if you steal $1,000 you're a crook; and if you steal a million you're a big businessman." It would be interesting to hear what he might have to say about some of our latter-day tycoons in the era of President George W. Bush.

Dad was less funny, however, when he used derogatory terms for other minority groups. I won't give any examples here, but he used them all. Wasn't he aware of the others out there, just like him but not Jewish, who were using the same kind of negative terms about us? I guess he was, and maybe that's how he justified his own practice. No doubt he had heard himself as a kid on the New York streets or in public schools referred to as kike, heb, or hymie more often than he cared to remember, and now, from his perspective, it was pay-back time. I experienced anti-Semitism much less, I am sure, than he did, but I none the less felt that if we expected others to respect us, whether they in fact did or not, we had to practice self-restraint ourselves and use only good words about people of other racial, cultural, or national groups. But I was from another generation and already two away from the original immigrants in our family. Moreover, I had received all that fancy private education, much of it with more than a hint of Christian background. It was certainly easier for me to take the position I did.

I remember one example of Dad's racism when he and Mother came to visit Simone, Marianna, and me in Hawai'i in 1968. He was in his early sixties at the time. We went out to eat at our favorite Chinese restaurant, the old Hong Kung in the Kaimuki District of Honolulu. It was a fancy place with red-decorated walls, golden dragons and elegantly carved Chinese characters everywhere. The food was good, too. Plus there was a large bar with sexy Caucasian bar girls in revealing costumes. I couldn't believe it when my father in a normal, maybe even slightly raised voice commented, "Why can't these Chinamen get their own women to serve drinks?" For him it was all right for Caucasians to have Asians and other people of color in subservient positions, but having things the other way around seemed to go against the laws of nature, as far as he was concerned, and was intolerable. Again I thought, "Why was it okay for us Jews, a widely criticized and even despised minority, to make our way in the world and achieve positions of wealth and influence and not for Chinese Americans or anyone else?" That kind of thinking remained totally lost on my father until he died.

Dad was also no internationalist. When it came to languages other than English, he was hopeless. I can't speak for his Yiddish, which he learned as a child to communicate with the older, non-English-speaking members of his family. But when he took his solo trip in the 1950s to Argentina to visit my sister, who was living there at the time, he found himself forced to learn a few words of Spanish in self-defense. On his return, he would love to tell about his adventures in *Bone-yeeze Aye-reeze*, his best approximation of the phonetic Spanish pronunciation of the city's name. His attitude toward the way foreigners talked their language was like that of the Texan in his joke. Apparently a wealthy Texan and his wife wanted to take a taxi from the Paris Airport to the Georges V Hotel. The Texan, however, was having trouble communicating his wishes to the cabbie. Finally, he turned to his wife in frustration and said, "If English was good enough for Jesus Christ in the Bible, I don't know why these damned Frenchmen can't speak it!"

Dad did tell one cute story from his two weeks in Argentina. Apparently missing his regular weekly appointment at the barber's, he decided to go to Uncle Arthur's (my mother's brother-in-law's) barber. No one could go with him, but full of his usual New York bravado, he determined to go on his own. He had rehearsed the word *poco*, "little," to indicate he wanted just a trim. The barber, however, thought Dad wanted only a little hair left and started giving him a military cut. In desperation, my father tried to save his hair by speaking Yiddish. It turned out that the man was a Jewish immigrant from Eastern Europe and understood—just in time!

Jacob Newton Feldman, whom everyone called "Jack," was a short man, not more than 5' 1". In this he took after Grandma Ida, who was 4" 11". Grandpa Paul was perhaps 5' 6", though maybe he had been taller in his younger days. As a child I learned that my dad wore elevator shoes to make him, per their radio commercials, "taller . . . taller . . . taller than she is." It didn't quite work, since Mother at 5' 4 ½" always stood taller than Dad. When he would take me in to work with him Saturday mornings, he seemed such a shrimp compared to most of the other men. In some cases, his belt buckle would reach only to the mid-thigh of his taller colleagues. I took to calling him Shorty Pants, which he generally overlooked. But sometimes it got his goat, and he would say, "Shut up, Kid!"

Like many short men, my dad had a bit of a Napoleon complex and felt the need to assert himself. This he frequently did, to my sister's and my endless embarrassment, in hotels, causing us to change rooms once and sometimes twice until he got something that came up to his standards as a top grain merchant from Wall Street. In restaurants it was even worse, since there were so many others around, and he sometimes played to the audience. He would tyrannize maître d's, send back dishes all the time, and ask us to do the same. "How can you serve crap like this and call it food?" He would storm and then demand to speak to the manager. Sometimes at his command we would all walk out of the restaurant together, with Dad aiming a few well-chosen parting words at the management while everyone looked at us. My sister and I must have died a thousand deaths back then. My sense is that she occasionally invokes his memory and practices this technique herself, abetted no doubt by her years of living in

Argentina, where customer-imperiousness may be standard operating procedure. As for me—not necessarily to my benefit—I eschew making a fuss in a restaurant or hotel, sometimes with the patience of a martyr. The memory of those scenes from childhood is still too painful.

On the good side, Dad would pay for whatever activities I became enthusiastic about, from Scouts to clarinet lessons to summer camp. Eventually he in effect paid for college twice over by underwriting my four years and two summers at the Peddie School, my boarding high school in New Jersey, followed by a costly undergraduate education at Yale, including my junior year in Heidelberg. All that, stretching from 1951 to 1960, must have set him back substantially, and it is an investment for which I am eternally grateful. He could have used that money on plush vacations and Mediterranean cruises for him and Mother. Instead, he generously put it toward the Kid's education, as he would explain to others. What I didn't get from my father, though, was any kind of religious instruction or the role modeling of what it might mean to live in the world as a believer, a person of faith. The Talmud says that a father who doesn't teach his son Torah is worse than a thief. Still, I don't judge my dad for this lack, since faith isn't something one can conjure up or pretend to have for the sake of one's children. You either have it or you don't. As Catholics say, it's a charism, a gift. My father had been permanently scarred by the form of Judaism his mother had imposed on him. He never found a better substitute. So, while he remained a self-identified Jew all his life, his Jewishness was always social, never religious. He was a secular, patriotic American and a New Yorker through and through. He could see the benefits of religion in some of his non-Jewish acquaintances or co-workers. But as far as he himself went, it must have been a bridge too far and not one he necessarily wanted to cross. Fortunately, God had other things in mind for me.

My mother, Estelle Potash Feldman, was an entirely different person. Whereas Dad was an extrovert and a populist, she was reserved and ladylike. She was also elegant. At parties she would sit demurely and silently on the sofa, her long, slender legs daintily arranged next to each other, in a tasteful, expensive-looking dress she had recently acquired from Bonwit's, Bergdorf's, or Sachs. Mother would tell how, after dropping out of Ohio State upon finishing her sophomore year, she had made her pilgrimage to New York City, where she entered the Macy's Basement training program, and, by the time she married Dad in the fall of 1929, had become an assistant buyer for ladies' foundation garments, i.e., bras and brassieres. During the War she also worked at the Lord & Taylor store in Manhasset, Long Island. As a result, department-store trips with her would usually include a certain amount of shop talk with the sales ladies—with other women she was not so reserved—thereby taking even more time. Finally, I would become so impatient and obnoxious that I could sometimes get her to take me home earlier than she had intended. And sometimes, if I was really lucky, she would leave me at home with Florine, our maid, so she could go shopping in peace, as she put it.

From the end of World War II until she was in her 70s and Dad had announced that the family was in financial trouble, Mother did not work outside the house. Also, since Florine took care of all the cleaning and cooking, Mother didn't have much to do except on Florine's day off, when we would often eat out. As a seventy-year-old, Mother lied about her age and got a half-time job at Sachs Fifth Avenue on Michigan Avenue in Chicago. She did as much as she could to help keep the family afloat financially. This she continued for a year or two until one day, as she was looking for something in the back of the family's storage closet, she stumbled on a collection of credit-card receipts for purchases of expensive women's items my father had bought, none of which Mother had received or had even known about. This is when she found out about his long-standing girl friend, whose maintenance to a considerable extent had caused the family's financial difficulties. Mother was incensed and hurt. She quit her job and after some 40-plus years of marriage told my father she was going to sue for divorce. Simone, the girls, and I must have been living in Evanston, a near-north suburb of Chicago, at the time. I remember being physically between my parents as they threw the worst kind of language back and forth at each other. Already an adult and the father of two children, I was shocked to hear Mother use some of the words she did that day. She had always been so lady-like. She was the one who spoke Standard American English, while my dad spoke New York dialect. They were each saying I sided with the other. For my part, I tried to stay quiet, both inside and out, since, for one thing, I didn't have a clue what to say. Also, I had known about my father's philandering for some time but had resisted the temptation to tell my mom. Now I felt like the accomplice I was in this breach of family trust. When they calmed down a little or possibly had exhausted themselves with their anger, I simply said that after all these years I hoped they could find a way to work out their differences and stay together. I don't know if they ever did the former. For whatever reasons, however, my mother never did file for divorce. All I know is that at my father's interment, or rather, at the enclosure of his urn in its final marble resting place, my mother took a trowel full of dirt and virtually flung the contents on my father's enclosed ashes. I was right behind her so I could see the action clearly. My feeling then was that she had never forgiven him for his disloyalty coupled with in effect making her go to work as an older person to help support his philandering ways.

I criticized both my parents, at least within my head, for their focus on material things. Of course, given that they had lived as adults through the Great Depression, they had a sense of the importance of material things. What family of their generation did not have a healthy respect for the good things of life and how quickly, through forces outside themselves, those things could disappear? Still, I knew something important was missing in my life and wasn't sure what. After all, by American standards I had everything: a caring family, a nice house, a room of my own, good food, a safe neighborhood with nice neighbors, a friendly school with considerate teachers, and friends. Florine with her unconditional love and connection to something greater made up for a lot, but still I wasn't satisfied.

My father was all about business. Yet, as a kind of balance, there was his music and reading, both books and newspapers. My mother didn't work outside the house except during the War and, later, to help with the so-called family emergency. She shopped, and when she wasn't shopping, she read *Vogue*. When I heard my parents talking, it was all about people making money and doing all the wonderful things that you could only do with lots of it. When the conversation was directed to me, older children and young adults were trotted out as role models. The operative concept was that "they were doing very well." I usually got salary details as well as the fact that they had married into rich families. My mother's two favorite sayings were, "Rich or poor, it's nice to have money." And "It's as easy to fall in love with a rich girl as a poor girl." She herself had been the first daughter of eleven children born to dirt-poor immigrant farmers from some Jewish *shtetl* in northeast Central Europe. In short, she was warning me off from ever falling in love with someone like her when nowadays there were Jewish orthodontists, skin doctors, and lawyers, not to mention accountants and business people, all of whom, in the family parlance, were "stink rich" and most of whom had marriageable daughters.

My mother had only one hobby, and even it had a connection with money. She saved pennies and got books that told which years and issues were especially rare and valuable. One or two of them, she said, could bring in a small fortune. So Natalie, my sister, and I were instructed to give her all our pennies so she could look at them under the magnifying glass just in case we happened to bring home one of those rare coins. That never happened, but at least the pursuit gave Mother something to do.

She did have a caring side and might have made an excellent social worker. Her sister-in-law Jeannette, a Goucher College-educated banker's daughter from Maryland who had the figure, looks, and style of a middle-aged Jackie Kennedy, was a special favorite. Aunt Jeannette's health, though, was fragile, so my mother would often spend time at her house as a kind of companion. The same was true of her youngest sister, Ruthie, who was the baby of the Potash family. In 1939, the year of my birth, Aunt Ruthie had married Uncle Arthur Hirsch-Pels, a German Jewish Argentinean businessman, who took her to live in Buenos Aires. Cut off during the War from her family in America, Aunt Ruthie came back to the States for the first time in 1946 or 1947 with her son, Pablo, and daughter, Susana, my cousins. Wealthy all her married life, Ruthie began to have medical issues as she got older, so Mother spent time as the oldest sister taking care of Ruthie as a kind of live-in companion. This took place during several extended stays in Argentina and, later, on a long tour to Europe.

From her very first trip to B.A., as the Argentine capital was familiarly known in our family, on a small, passenger-carrying freighter, *The José Menendez,* Mother found she was a good sailor and liked the adventure of the high seas. From then on, she would travel by ship whenever she could. Later, after my sister became a travel agent, Mother would periodically go on a cruise, sometimes with Natalie. I have a picture of her in her early 90s, still slender and nattily dressed, standing next to a life-saving ring on board a cruise ship somewhere in the Caribbean. With her over-painted lips and dyed red hair, she looked like the older Lucille Ball.

One other thing about Mother: she had Gentile style. In mixed company, that is, one which consisted of both Jews and non-Jews, she was always reserved, well-spoken if someone addressed her, and never ostentatious. She never showed off or spoke about money matters in these circles. Also, unlike her fraternal twin, Helen, who had a strong Southern Jersey accent, mother sounded like she came from California or Oregon or some other part of the country where there was no distinguishing local accent. She was classy, all right.

When I married Simone, Mother was upset. I don't think Simone's being German bothered her as much as it did my father. For Mother it was more the fact that she came from a struggling refugee family and was the daughter of a mere elementary-school teacher. Okay, he was the principal of a school in the Bavarian village where they lived outside Munich. Still, she was clearly not the daughter of a lawyer, doctor, dentist, or other well-to-do person. Where was the appropriate result of all her and Dad's investment in my education— four years of prep school, an undergraduate education at Yale, and even a European year abroad? Had it come to this? A poor German girl and a *shiksa*, a Gentile, to boot!

From then on, Mother had a mission, to make sure Simone and I had no children. When we spent our first Christmas (1963) with my parents in Chicago, they rented us a room in the apartment hotel where they were living at the time, The Churchill on Chicago's Near North Side, at the corners of State Parkway and Goethe [pronounced *Go-eethee* in Chicagoland]. I was spending most of my days preparing for my comprehensive pre-doctoral oral exam that would take place at Yale soon after our return in early January. Basing her remark on that fact, my mother counseled us every evening before Simone and I went upstairs to our room that we go straight to bed—"no reading, no talking, no *nothing*!" Later, when we were living in Flushing, Queens, and I was a Lecturer in English at Queens College, Mother would call every Sunday from Chicago to remind us to practice birth control. "You know, dear," she would say in her sweetest tone, "it's much easier to get a divorce when no children are involved." She was hoping against hope that I would see the light before it was too late, divorce Simone and send her back to her parents in Germany, and then go on a serious hunt for one of the remaining daughters of a Jewish doctor, dentist, or lawyer. It was a hunt for which she was fully prepared to pull out all the stops, use not only her network but Aunt Jeannette's and Aunt Ruthie's as well, and get me married to a high-class, wealthy Jewish girl. She became so persistent with her advice that when the phone rang on a Sunday afternoon, Simone would start crying. "It's your mother again telling us to practice birth control!"

Once we had our first daughter, Mother gave up. A realist, she figured she'd make the best of it. To her credit, before she entered the senile dementia of her last years—she lived two months past her ninety-fifth birthday—she and Simone became friends. For our daughters Grandpa became Opa [German for *grandpa*] Honey, because he always called them that. So by natural process, my mother became Oma Honey. She also became proud of my career— she lived to see me a university dean and academic vice president—so when I was named a Fellow of the Society for Values in Higher

Education, she insisted on paying my initiation fee.

There are a few experiences I had with my mother in her last years that I'd like to share, since they show the transformation of our relationship into something sweeter and better than it had been when I was growing up or a young professional. I don't know whether it is true, but I've heard that when individuals fall into senile dementia, the nicest people can become nasty and the nastiest nice. Well, my mother was never nasty, but she could certainly be intense. I guess it takes one to know one, as the kids say, since I am pretty intense myself. In fact, one of the main reasons for our difficulty getting along was doubtless that we were too much alike. It can almost make one believe in astrology, since we were born a week apart, Mother on Hallowe'en and me seven days later on November 6, both Scorpios. (One might say that Mother and Aunt Helen, having been born on October 31, 1903, as twins were Grandma Sarah Potash's trick-or-treat.) In any case, as an elderly woman, Mother became funny, easy-going, even cute.

Once when I was visiting the family in Florida, I remember receiving strict instructions from my sister not to let Mother have any chocolate. Apparently it constipated her, and the doctor had forbidden it. Still, Mother, as she liked to say, was a chocoholic, with a special—to me, incomprehensible—fondness for milk-chocolate Hersey bars. (I am a fellow chocoholic, but since my junior year in Germany, my taste has tended to dark chocolate.) Anyway, as we were heading home to her apartment building, where she lived with my sister, I felt a pull as Mother, a frail 90-year-old at the time, all but lifted me from the sidewalk in her eagerness to enter the little drugstore in her building. At the time, I had been guiding her toward the apartment house's main entrance. Before I knew it, we found ourselves before the counter with the Hersey bars. Mother gave me one of those "You've just got to let me have one of those!" looks, and I knew the battle was over. If she wanted to have her chocolate that much—arguably one of the few pleasures in her life at that time—who was I to stand in her way?

On another occasion, maybe five years earlier, Mother had been visiting us in Saint Paul for several months. She had arrived in late-summer, and every day she would come downstairs from her room, open the front door, and say, "I think it's going to snow." "But Mother," one of us would remonstrate, "it's 80 degrees outside and still summer. How could it possibly snow?" She would shake her head and with the conviction of a Sybil repeat, "I think it's going to snow." For Hallowe'en, her birthday, Simone dressed the two of them up as witches. In her mid-80s at the time, Mother didn't need too much make-up to look convincing in the role. She actually scared a few of the younger kids who came to our door trick-or-treating. That morning, birthday or not, she intoned her familiar refrain. And sure enough, the next day the Twin Cities sustained one of its worst snowstorms in recent history. To honor Mother's prophetic gift, we dubbed it "Blizzard Estelle."

During the same visit, she figured in a cute incident involving our "wise-beyond-its-species" black cat, Winston, who also contributed to the Hallowe'en spirit that afternoon by arching his back on our split-rail fence and scaring an old lady in the neighborhood half to death. Apparently, Mother too had been badly frightened by a cat when she was a child and therefore didn't like them at all. She had a problem, though, since she did like Winston. What to do? I'll never forget one morning at breakfast when she looked around, puzzled, and then asked, "Where's the dog?" Problem solved. As long as she thought of Winston as a dog—the fact is, he *was* a rather large cat—she could continue to like and not be afraid of him.

One of the nicest experiences with Mother happened at Simone's and my Silver Anniversary on November 30, 1988. Having purchased our beautiful house in Saint Paul the preceding July, we decided to throw a big party at home with catered Afghan food and even live harpsichord music by an artist who brought his instrument to the house. Mother was there representing the Florida family. Simone's mother, who had been living with us for some years and would do so until her death a year and a half later, was also on hand. My mother-in-law had been partially paralyzed in 1972 by two back-to-back strokes, and with the exception of one year, had lived with us ever since. Anyway, Oma, as she was called in the family, spoke no English, and my mother no German. Yet somehow the two elderly women got along just fine. Mother would trot out some of her childhood Yiddish, and in the privacy of our house, Oma would show she knew a lot more English—thanks doubtless to hundreds of hours of American TV—than she ever let on to. My mother in her dementia was still physically strong. My mother-in-law could walk slowly with her cane, but her faculties remained intact up to her death. So, how's this for a sight that would cause Hitler to roll over in his grave? My senile Jewish mother each day would make sure to help my partially paralyzed German Aryan mother-in-law up and down the stairs. This, I always thought, is how relations between people of different and sometimes mutually hostile groups should be, since in the end we are all just people, incomplete in some way and needing help from our fellows. It was during this visit, I think, that Mother was opened in

Subud by Simone and Renata Fitzpatrick, a helper originally from England. They were able to do perhaps a half dozen *latihans* with her before she returned to Florida. Once there, however, my sister, who was not a Subud member, was afraid to let her be picked up for *latihan*, so that was the end of Mother's active Subud life.

On another occasion I was in Florida for Mother's ninety-second birthday. She had had water in her lungs a month beforehand, so the actual occasion took place in a nursing home where she was spending a few weeks after the hospital before going home to be cared for by my faithful sister, Mother's principal caregiver in her later years. When Natalie and I arrived at the facility, Mother's bed was neatly made, and she was nowhere to be found. My sister and I looked at each other, suspecting the worst. As it turned out, she was in another room enjoying a little Hallowe'en party, which the staff was also using to celebrate her birthday. The next morning we returned and found her dressed, sitting in a wheelchair in her room. Natalie had some shopping to do, so she left Mother and me alone for an hour or so. A warm November 1st in South Florida, I wheeled Mother out onto the little porch in front of her room. There, for some reason I began to play children's games with her, the kind of kinesthetic games she had played with me when I was a little child. I remember specifically singing "Patty cake, patty cake, baker's man. . . ." while we both performed all the gestures. When it was all over—Mother was all smiles, something I was not used to seeing from her—, I gave her a big kiss on her forehead. "Oh, for kisses like that," she said, "I would dance the night away with you!" Suddenly I felt a happiness I couldn't remember ever feeling with my mother before. It was as if her slate with me, all my assembled grievances, had been wiped clean with a single stroke. Turning around I saw three round black faces with beautiful even-teethed smiles looking at me through the window. When I wheeled Mother back into her room, one of the caregivers—all were from the Caribbean—said, "You sure do know how to be with your mama!" Indeed, something in me did—a part of me that was better and higher than my ordinary self and which that day had been in charge. And for her remaining three years on the planet, our relationship remained permanently altered for the better.

A final story concerns Mother's death. It was January 1999. Mother had again been hospitalized with water in her lungs. At 95, she was not expected to make it this time. As the on-the-scene caregiver, my sister had granted the doctors permission to use a ventilator to keep her alive. Had I been there, I would have argued against this so-called heroic measure. Finally, the doctors decided to take her off the machine. At around this time, I called my niece Leslie on her cell phone. (I was at home in Hawai'i at the time.) As it happened, Leslie was at Mother's bedside. The latter was curled up in a fetal position and moaning. I asked Leslie to hold her phone to Mother's ear. Then I said, "Mother, this is Reynold. Thank you for being a good mother. Now you can relax and leave whenever you want. Lots of good people are waiting for you on the Other Side. I'm praying for your smooth passage and so is Simone. Goodbye, Mother. I love you." Then I handed the phone to Simone, who said something similar. When I got back on, there was silence on the other end. In a matter of seconds, I heard Leslie's voice. "Uncle Reynold, what have you done?" "Oh my God!" I thought. "I've just killed my mother." "What happened?" I asked. "Grandma stretched herself out, relaxed, and has stopped making that awful sound." Shortly thereafter, the hospital staff wheeled her down to the Hospice Floor and the next evening she passed away peacefully in her sleep.

When I arrived at the Miami Airport a few days later to officiate at Mother's funeral, my niece Leslie picked me up in her convertible. As we drove north on Interstate 95, she kept looking at me from time to time with a combination of curiosity and fear. Finally she said, "Uncle Reynold, what in the world did you say to Grandma that evening on the phone?" I told her. It was nothing special, just an ordinary sort of thing, it seemed to me, and I told Leslie so. "Yes, but how did you know what to say?" I replied, "You know I've been doing the spiritual practice called Subud for many years now. Well, one of the benefits seems to be knowing what to do and say in important moments like that." And it was true. Perhaps half a year after I was opened, I had accompanied my graduate-school girl friend, Jane Parry, to visit her mother's sister who was dying of cancer in a New York City hospital. It was my first time meeting Jane's aunt, but somehow I felt remarkably comfortable and seemed to know exactly how to conduct myself with the sick woman. What was more, I instinctively knew this unexpected capacity was directly related to my then fairly recent practice of Subud. Later I would spontaneously sing to and massage my Aunt Ruthie, who lay paralyzed and seemingly comatose after a stroke in Florida. And most importantly, this sense of comfort, even familiarity, and knowledge of what to do would return, as you'll hear, during the months I cared for my wife Simone, as she was dying.

3
Florine

IN GURDJIEFF'S autobiographical *Meetings with Remarkable Men*, the first three people he describes are his father, the local Orthodox priest, and a retired general living in his village. For Gurdjieff, remarkability wasn't a matter of public fame. People were remarkable in direct proportion to their impact on us as individuals. These three qualified as the first such people in his life. In the same way, my first teacher and spiritual guide was an African American woman named Florine Tolson Bond. She came to be our "maid," the term in use back then, in late 1940 or early 1941, when I was one.

Florine, or Flora, must have been 40 when she arrived. She was not new to the family, having served in my mother's twin sister Helen's Philadelphia household for some years prior to coming to us in Great Neck, a New York City suburb on Long Island. Unlike my mother, Aunt Helen had no children. Her husband, Uncle Sol, was the family dentist. This was no easy assignment, since my mother and Aunt Helen had nine other siblings, all but one of whom had kids. We were two, my older sister and now me. Natalie, born in March 1931, was nearly nine when I appeared on the scene. Apparently I was a kind of afterthought and not one my older sister appreciated. Now, all these decades later, I can better understand what she must have been feeling. In Jewish families, boys were princes. I was suddenly the only boy. So, after nine years, she not only lost her privileged status as only child but was demoted to child second-class. Her lot was especially hard, since as she was becoming a gawky pre-teen replete with braces, here came her little brother who had naturally curly platinum-blond hair, big blue eyes, and a precocious gift of gab. The neighbors were always telling my parents how cute or smart I was, sometimes in Natalie's hearing. That had to have hurt.

To get back to Florine, the deal between mother and her twin was that the latter would let Mother have Florine on lend-lease for a year—until I was two. Then she would go back to Philly, and Mother would carry on as best she could. As the family told the story, when Florine showed up at our door, I greeted her with a big "Hello, Floreen!" That was it—love at first sight. Florine stayed with us the next fifteen years, until I was sixteen.

Small as I was, I soon learned that Florine was the strongest, most trustworthy and loving person in the house. Jewish American literature has reserved a place of honor for the "Negro maid." So I was clearly not the only Jewish child in those days, or white Christian either, who was formed by their Florine. Later, when I read William Faulkner's *The Sound and the Fury*, I found someone familiar in Dilsey, the Compson Family's black housekeeper. She represented strength and sanity in the otherwise dysfunctional Compson household, haunted as it was by the family's earlier participation in a slave-owning society.

Not that the Feldmans were especially dysfunctional. My parents were in many ways wonderful, caring people. Later, I learned my mother had taught Florine to read and write, and my father, at her request, had invested some of her wages in stocks. As a result, she could have a pleasant retirement while paying for her nieces and nephews, not to mention the neighborhood kids, to attend college. She also helped underwrite the rebuilding of her Methodist church after it burned down. When she died in her late 80s, she was a wealthy woman.

Florine, by virtue of her race and generation, might have died in a nice house in an integrated neighborhood but ended her life instead in an all-black trailer park in rural Maryland. She was too old by the time places like Evanston, Illinois, and Scarsdale, New York, opened up to people of color. It was another world for her, one she doubtless believed was unjust. She nevertheless accepted her lot with the grace of the Christian she was. Life for her was more than a nice house.

And that was the point. Florine was a believer, while my parents were not. She listened to Bible programs on the radio and hummed hymns while she worked. She would tell me about Jesus, God, the church she attended every Sunday and the wonderful singing there. Sometimes we would sit in her kitchen (it was definitely hers!) when my parents were out and listen to George Beverly Shea's Bible Hour on the radio. She also introduced me to the popular black music of the day like the Ink Spots and the Mills Brothers, both of whom she would refer to as "the Boys." I might be playing in the backyard when she would call out the kitchen window, "Man, come on in now. The Boys are fixin' to sing." I would come running. Sitting next to Florine in her kitchen with all the good smells of dinner emanating from the stove while we listened to the Boys was as close as little Stevie Feldman came to a religious experience in the early 1940s. I remember wanting to go with her to church, but apparently my parents never let her take me. It's something I regret. Fortunately, I later attended African American services, in both the North and the

South, and can think of few places where I felt the Spirit moving more strongly than there—the Spirit of Florine and God.

She was of course much more than a maid. She was actually our housekeeper. She lived with us in the various houses or apartments we rented during her time with us, which coincided with her remaining years of fertility and beyond. I was the son she had never had. She called me "Man" or "my Man"; my father, "the Boss"; and my mother "the Miss." Natalie was the only one she referred to by name, though sometime she would say "Stevie's Sister." Once in a while—I don't remember the intervals—she would go to her niece's apartment in Astoria, Queens, already a black neighborhood back then, for a weekend off. I never liked those weekends. When Florine was away, the life seemed to go out of our house.

My father was an air-raid warden doing World War II. Periodically he would don his pith helmet and patrol the neighborhood to make sure all light was successfully blocked. We Americans were lucky we were never bombed like our European Allies or the civilians in the Axis countries had been. But occasionally a German sub would be spotted off Long Island, so everyone wanted to be careful. During the War years, my mother worked at the Lord & Taylor department store in nearby Manhasset. On certain days she and my father stayed late. During those nights and some others when I got scared, I made a beeline for Florine's bed. I knew instinctively if anything bad happened, the only safe place would be there, where I could snuggle against her for protection. The Nazis wouldn't dare do anything to Florine, since she had Jesus and God on her side and was the strongest as well as the nicest and most loving person I knew.

Once when I was perhaps four, I did something that really upset my father. He came after me with his belt. I bolted for Florine's kitchen and hid behind her. Red with anger, he ran through the swinging door. "Where's Stephen, Florine?" She responded with authority, "Now Mr. Feldman, don't you touch that boy! Don't you touch my man!" Then I remember my father leaving the kitchen without a word. Afterward, Florine turned to me and said, "Man, you shouldn't vex your daddy that way. Think of all the good things he's done for you. Now I want you to go in to your Daddy and say, 'Daddy, I'm sorry. I promise I won't do it again.'" And I did it. I knew she was right. She always was. She was connected. She had Jesus and God and black music and wasn't afraid of anybody or anything. She was the compass in my moral universe. She pointed to True North.

Florine had a voice as deep as mahogany. When she sang as she worked, even when she hummed, I always listened up. I was fascinated. Her singing and her voice comforted me. She seemed to know something no one else in the house did. I could tell from her singing. I was also sure I was the only one in the family in on the secret. She was truly magical. At some point I began to associate that magic with the way she talked, like Amos 'n' Andy on the radio, except she was a real person. Before I knew it, I started speaking like her. In my child's mind, I must have felt that if I learned to speak like Florine, I could gain some of her magic powers, her authority, her connection with something higher and stronger than whatever the rest of us had, even though our family was white and well-to-do and she wasn't. Presumably I switched back and forth, because my parents never noticed or commented on my speech. But one day, according to them, I brought a note home from Kindergarten that said, "Your son Stephen is suffering from a speech problem." When my parents talked with the teacher, it turned out their blond-haired, blue-eyed son was speaking Black English at school.

We lived in three different houses in Great Neck before moving for a year, 1947-48, to 502 West Vernon Avenue in Phoenix, Arizona. My father had a Jewish grain-broker friend, Alan Rosenberg, who lived in Phoenix and was constantly singing its praises. So one summer day, my parents, Natalie, and I piled into our new fire-engine-red Oldsmobile convertible and headed west. Florine would join us by train after we got there. My parents had spent a mini-vacation at the famed Arizona Biltmore resort the prior spring to check the area out. Eventually, with Mr. Rosenberg's help, they rented a white adobe house in a new residential district in North Phoenix. So that was that.

The road trip was an adventure for all of us, especially me as the youngest. Till then, the farthest I had been from Great Neck was to Aunt Helen and Uncle Sol's row house in Philly, with a side trip to visit Grandpa Max and Grandma Sarah, my mother's parents, in Woodbine, New Jersey. What I mainly remember from our trip west were the Burma Shave and Stuckey's signs, the changing landscape, the St. Louis Zoo with its great monkey show, and my first cowboy, replete with boots, a ten-gallon hat, and a holster with a real pistol in it, whom I saw in a small town near Oklahoma City. I was also struck not only by the new states that rolled by but also the different ways people talked as we moved west. Apparently, I had always been interested in accents, foreign and domestic, though most of my role models were from the radio. Why, I wondered, did some people say "ar-ange," like my parents and me, while others said "or-ange" for the very same thing? I was a good mimic too, although I sometimes demonstrated my talent at the wrong time, with the result that my parents shushed me with a warning not to show off. I also remember spending hours on end in the well of our car, where the cloth convertible top neatly fit when down. Stretching out, I filled the entire space. I felt I had a place of my own where no one else in the family was small enough to fit.

When Florine arrived in Phoenix, it was not by train. Instead, she came in a big black Buick, the proud possession of Charles, her new husband. Eager to keep Florine, my father hired him as the family chauffeur, albeit for our red Olds. Since Dad needed to spend blocks of time for business in New York City, he thought it a good idea to have a man in the house, even if he were a *shvartze* [Yiddish for "black"]. My only memories of Florine's husband were the smell of alcohol on his breath and his showing me a wooden model of a black man and a red woman that could be manipulated so that the black man put something long and cylindrical into a slot in the red woman's mid section. He would accompany this demonstration by saying "The black ant went into the red ant's hole." I didn't figure out till some years later what either the action or the words meant. Charles and I would also sing popular black songs together, and I said we should call ourselves "The Black and White Duet" and go on the road together.

Charles and Florine's marriage didn't last the year we spent in Phoenix. It turned out he already had a prior wife back East and had not bothered to get a divorce. After Florine left our family in 1956, she worked for several other families before retiring. In the early 50s she married again, more successfully this time, to a Mr. Bond (known as "Mr. B"), an older man and a supervisor at the Dixie Cup factory in Queens. After his retirement, his health failed, so Florine spent several years taking care of him before he died. A decade or so before her death, she moved back to her hometown in tidewater Maryland.

Our staying in Phoenix what with my dad's frequent, extended periods away didn't work out either. As he later would say, there were just too many cowboys, Indians, and other *Goyim* (Gentiles) for him in Arizona. My sister, who graduated that year from North Phoenix High School, had made friends, however, and liked Arizona. She had in fact applied to and been accepted at the University of Arizona in Tucson. So when we moved back to New York, she stayed behind.

I liked Arizona well enough myself. As a Gene Autry fan, I even had the chance to see him, his horse Tony, and his sidekick band, "The

Sons of the Pioneers," once in person. The latter sang my favorite song, "Water," which of course couldn't be more appropriate to bone-dry, sauna-hot Phoenix. I also got to go to a real rodeo, and Indians as well as cowboys were visible every day on the streets as were suntanned people speaking a foreign language I soon learned was Spanish. I did get into a fight one day at school. I still remember being pinned to the ground and hit as someone called me a dirty Jew. I was able to be on top and give some pretty good punches myself before a teacher broke us up. Otherwise I don't remember much about third grade.

One important incident in Phoenix involved Florine. One day my mother gave her money to take me to a movie. Although our house had what in those days was called an "air cooler," it couldn't do much against the 115 degrees Fahrenheit outside, and I must have been complaining. When Florine tried to get us two tickets in the mezzanine, she learned she could buy one there for me but had to sit in the balcony herself. When she said I was too young to sit alone, she was told that then we both had to sit in the Negro section in the balcony. The schoolyard fight had been my first personal encounter with anti-Semitism. Now this event at the movie theater made it clear to me that, cowboys and Indians notwithstanding and regardless of how good a person Florine might be, Arizona was a Southern (Southwestern) state where, in 1948, blacks were second-class citizens. After that, I was happy that Flora and I would soon be heading back East, where at least we could sit together in the movies.

Once I graduated from boarding school in 1956, Florine decided to leave our family. I would now go to college and didn't really need her anymore. My parents reluctantly let her go. I stayed in some kind of touch with her over the years but didn't see her again till the early 80s when Simone, our two daughters—one in high school and the other in elementary school—and I took a road trip East from our home in suburban Chicago. Along the way, we drove to Chestertown, Maryland, the seat of Kent Country, and asked at a gas station how to drive to Florine's rural community. "You don't want to go there," the sturdy, red-faced white attendant told me. "Yes I do," I insisted. "Well, I ain't gonna tell you how to get there," came the reply. I guess, the Civil Rights Act to the contrary notwithstanding, racism was still alive and well at that time in rural Maryland.

We finally found the village on our own. It was only twenty minutes outside Chestertown if you knew where you were going, but it took us a good three-quarters of an hour to get there. After asking a few people, we found Florine in a newer mobile home on a nice, shady plot of land. She was happy to see me after so long and was thrilled to meet Simone and the girls. She had a whole meal prepared for us—cooked by one of the younger women of the community—based on my childhood favorites: meatloaf, mash potatoes and gravy, fresh country baby corn on the cob, a mixed green salad, and her famous home-made lemon-meringue pie. After washing up, she presented me with the large glass bowl she'd used for the salad. "Do you remember this, Man?" She asked. It had belonged to our family, but my mother had given it to her before she left us. Now she was giving it back to me.

At some point prior to this visit, I'd told Florine on the phone about both Subud and my conversion to Christianity. Now she wanted to know if I had really accepted Jesus Christ as God's son and my Savior. I told her I had. She was satisfied. She also gave me the phone number of a certain Mary, a younger neighbor who looked in on her and helped her now that she was older and no longer as spry and mobile as she once had been. She was still able to work the old iron-handled well pump in the back, though—something Simone, the girls, and I all found challenging.

Several years later, the summer after our family's move to Saint Paul, Minnesota, in December 1987, I received a call from Mary to say that Florine's health was failing and that she had asked her, Mary, to call and let me know. I thanked her and said to give Florine our love and let her know we would pray for her. A few weeks later, another call came, and I made arrangements to fly to Baltimore.

I arrived in good time to make the visitation at the funeral home in Chestertown. The next day, back in Florine's hometown, I watched as the funeral director lined up the cars for the motorcade to the churchyard where Florine would be buried. I would not need to take my rental car, he told me, since Florine's family wanted me to ride in the limousine along with Florine's remaining brother and sister, the second of whom bore a striking resemblance to her. After all, as they told me, everyone there considered me Florine's "son." I was also the only white person in a crowd of over 100 African Americans who had showed up to honor her life.

Before we left for the interment, young George, the last person Florine had put through college, offered the invocation. He was slender, of medium height, perhaps 30, and—despite the killing heat and humidity—dressed to the nines in a gray sharkskin suit, with a sparkling white shirt, cuff-link-fastened French cuffs, and a beautiful silver-gray tie. His black patent-leather shoes looked brand new. He got up onto a two-foot-high tree stump and motioned for all of us to be silent. Mary whispered to me that, thanks to Flora's help, he was now a supervisor in the Campbell Soup factory in nearby Wilmington, Delaware.

In a rich baritone he offered an extemporaneous invocation that would have made Dr. Martin Luther King, Jr., proud. In the middle, out of nowhere, a cool breeze penetrated the stifling tidewater heat. It occurred to me that Florine was there, offering a little relief to all those who loved her and whom she had love. She had always been thoughtful and considerate of others, and her funeral would be no exception.

The little country church she had helped rebuild was not far, perhaps a ten-minute slow drive. As we rode through the shady green of August on the little country road, I caught sight of the white wooden church through the trees. That's when I started crying. One of Florine's hymns she would often sing in our kitchen in Great Neck was "Church in the Wildwood." Now her body would be buried outside just such a church.

In lieu of a traditional church funeral, Florine had requested a simple graveside rite. Before long we were back at the little community of mobile homes. A large canopy had been put up. Underneath were rows of folding tables and chairs. Older elementary-school boys had doffed their suit jackets and ties and had started a pick-up game of basketball at a nearby hoop till all the preparations were complete. It must have been 100 degrees Fahrenheit that afternoon, with the relative humidity not much less. The family invited two elderly ladies and me into one of the newer mobile homes. Like that infamous movie house back in Phoenix, it too had a good air conditioner—apparently the only house so equipped in the area. We were happy to go in.

The two ladies, both portly, and I sat down on a couch and an adjoining easy chair. One lady had a pink-tinted bouffant hairdo, the other a blue-tinted one. They must have been well into their 70's. Both were wearing elegant floral dresses that matched their respective hair color. They had been two of Florine's "younger" friends who went back decades with her.

"Now Miss Mabel," one of them said, fanning herself with a church fan. "Do y'all recall when young George was offering the invocation, how that cool breeze came up out of nowhere?"

"Um Hmm." The second lady was fanning herself too.

"Y'all know what that was, don't you?"

"Um Hmm!"

"Miss Florine was bidding us ado."

The hair stood up on the back of my neck. For that was exactly what I had been thinking at the time.

In the mid-1990s while on a business visit to Honolulu, my wallet had been stolen from my friend's parked car at Kailua Beach Park. Fortunately there hadn't been much money inside, $60 as I recall. We reported the incident to the nearby Kailua Police Station, but as the duty officer there had predicted, the wallet was never found. I didn't mind its loss or even that of the money. It took time, to be sure, to report the missing credit cards and have them and my driver's license replaced. What I regretted most, though, was the loss of the small 1955 photo I had of a smiling Florine in the white-tiled kitchen in our apartment on 91st Street and Central Park West in New York City. For me she was truly the mother of my soul—my first spiritual teacher, mentor and guide. She, not Yale, was my true *alma mater*.

4
Other Special People in My Youth

IN SUMMER 1952 two significant things happened: my parents moved from Westchester County to New York City, and I began what turned out to be two summers and four academic years at the Peddie School in Hightstown, New Jersey. In May 1956 I graduated from high school there and went on to Yale. Now I want to tell you about three formative individuals during those years, a teacher and a student at boarding school and a professor at college.

Without question my most important teacher at Peddie was a then-recent Yale graduate named Albert Leisenring Watson III, who was my sophomore, junior, and senior English teacher, my golf partner, the faculty advisor for the yearbook which I edited, my friend, and one of the most influential people in my life. Because of him more than anyone else, I decided to attend Yale, be an English major, take German as my foreign language, write poetry, smoke a pipe (that didn't last more than a few years), develop an abiding love for classical music, and become a teacher. He introduced me to Mozart, whom he loved with a passion and who became my lifelong friend for all seasons. When I graduated, he gave me his old stereo system for my graduation present.

My parents hated Watson, who was long-legged, slender, bespectacled, and balding, with thin, flaxen hair. He spoke with an upscale Gentile Long Island accent. His wealthy, Episcopal family, who were Scottish and Germany by ancestry, lived in Brookville, Long Island. His father was some kind of major corporate CEO—the Watson of IBM? Al himself was a Yale legacy, the third or fourth generation of his line of Watsons to attend that famous place. The Leisenrings were an old Yale family, too. I am sure my parents thought Watson was gay and buggering me and other members of his small group of young male protégés. Although such things happened at our school as at others, that was not the case with Watson. (Ironically, the main example while I was at boarding school was the super-macho Third Form football coach, a kind of Peddie legend, who one day was suddenly fired. Fortunately, I was never part of his swaggering, hard-ball crowd. You had to play football on his team to get in.)

I think the real reason my parents disliked Watson was that he turned me against the materialistic aspects of my Jewishness, something they intuitively picked up on. In this, I am afraid Al participated in some of the anti-Semitism implicit in his background—one of restricted country clubs and gated communities where Jews were discreetly excluded. "Make money, make friends, make connections, Stephen!" He would taunt. He would also tease me when I tried to seem more Gentile by calling myself "S. Michael Feldman." "Ah yes," he would say. "Here comes S. Michael Feldman, the famous poet." On top of all this, he apparently felt that Jews tended to be cowards, so he would wrestle with me and a shy boy one year my junior named Stephen Clark to try to toughen up us. "Go ahead, Stephen. Get mad. Let's see if you can pin me." Watson was tough, wiry, and slippery. It was nearly impossible to get him on his back, let alone pin him.

Above all, he was a brilliant teacher. It didn't hurt that our classes had fewer than ten students, one of the main reasons parents sacrificed to send their kids to boarding schools like ours. Students got personal attention. In addition, Watson knew a lot and was interesting. As a published poet, moreover, he encouraged all of us to write both poetry and fiction. One of my efforts even landed on the first page of a national high-school prize poetry collection, an achievement of which I am still proud. Later, I won the named prize for best senior essay, with a certificate presented at Senior Class Day. More than anyone else, Watson gave me the impression that, when it came to English, I was hot stuff—an excellent writer and a developing literary critic. This self-confidence lasted clear through Yale College, where I graduated *magna cum laude* as one of the top English majors of my year and was invited to join Phi Beta Kappa, the prestigious national honor society.

In class, Watson favored American writers like Emily Dickinson, Ralph Waldo Emerson, Henry David Thoreau, Walt Whitman, Herman Melville, and Robert Frost. His favorite English writer was the early romantic poet William Wordsworth. As I reflect on his selections now, I find that what unites them all is their nature mysticism, a kind of pantheism. These readings became an important source of spiritual nourishment for me at a time when I had neither a formal religion nor a regular spiritual practice.

To be sure, Watson's teaching was not confined to the Peddie classroom or even his faculty quarters where we would by turns wrestle or listen to Mozart. He owned a cabin on a generous piece of property overlooking Mt. Chocorua in New Hampshire. On at least three occasions he would drive several of us boys there for a long weekend like Thanksgiving. Once on location, we would chop wood and mend walls—New England skills he taught us—take hikes and climb the nearby mountains and hills, including Mount Chocorua. Actually, it was in doing the last that I had one of my early mystical experiences. The higher we got, especially after we passed the timberline, the lighter I felt. As silly as it may sound, I had the sense that as I got to the top of that mountain, a power place sacred to the native populations long before the white man had come, I had somehow gotten closer to God.

Watson was a Pied Piper—a magician of sorts with us boys, or at least those of us susceptible to his particular charms, with me perhaps the foremost in my class. He would read Edgar Allen Poe stories in the cabin by candlelight, with us under-aged sophisticates sipping from our snifters of Drambuie and slowly but surely getting scared out of our wits. (Al was an excellent reader.) Since there was no indoor plumbing in the cabin, going to the bathroom required trips to a nearby outhouse. I remember on one of those Edgar Allen Poe nights how I tortured myself by refusing to go to the outhouse till first light. The wages of cowardice in that case was a long, painful, sleepless night.

Of course we boys were absolutely captivated to be treated like adults, even to the point of being introduced to liqueurs underage. Especially that! Watson somehow knew that our 15- or 16-year-old bodies lodged adult longings and sensibilities which he was able to unlock just by addressing us as fellow grown-ups. Later when I saw the film *Dead Poets' Society* with Robin Williams in the leading role, I could easily identify with the situation. Watson's New Hampshire cabin was called James Hills. Apparently the property had once belonged to the famous Harvard psychologist and philosopher William James, brother of the equally renowned novelist, Henry James. Later in graduate school, when I decided to write my doctoral dissertation on the fiction of the latter James, I always thought that maybe my visits to James Hill had had some kind of subliminal impact on me that caused me to make that choice. Henry after all had doubtless visited his brother there on more than one occasion.

Two other trips with Watson were notable. The first was a magical mystery tour of the Yale campus on a damp, chilly late-October weekend night. Watson knew all the interesting spots and secret passageways. I felt I was wandering the gothic quadrangles of Oxford or Cambridge in some bygone era. Then Stephen Clark and I were taken to Al's tobacconist in a little shop across from the Shubert Theater. Although Watson had graduated four years prior to our visit, he and the owner were still on a first-name basis, with Al's private mix listed in some akashic record in the back of the store. At Peddie he would send in hand-written mail orders from time to time. We were introduced as "future Yale men," even though we had not yet applied, with Watson sealing the deal by buying us each a new briar pipe. "These boys will be back as your customers in a year or so," he told our new friend. Later that month, when I did apply to Yale, I decided it was Yale or nothing. (My back-up school, Trinity College in Hartford, Connecticut, was not even a real option.) Fortunately, I was accepted, and Yale became the institutional continuation of many of the interests and talents Watson had managed to awaken.

The second Watson trip occurred during senior-year spring break. Our class spent the first three or four days on the traditional graduation trip to Washington, DC. That spring of 1956, America was embroiled in the Suez Crisis. I remember we had speakers from the U.S. State Department (the person was a Peddie grad), the British Embassy, and the Egyptian Embassy. The high point was a field trip to the Israeli Embassy, where we were served freshly squeezed Haifa orange juice. One of my classmates, not noted for his wit, came up with a pun I've remembered for the last 52 years, long after having forgotten whatever the Israeli diplomat told us. "You go to the Israeli Embassy," Arthur said, "and what do you get? *Jewz*!"

Picking me up at the end of the class's visit to the Nation's Capital, Watson took me on a trip to Colonial Williamsburg, Virginia, followed by a tour of several major Civil War battlefields including Gettysburg, and ending in Charleston, South Carolina, followed by Savannah Beach, Georgia. I still recall the warming of the spring sun, the smells of the earth, and the feeling and heft of the South and its complex history. Watson of course added to the mix with snatches of history and poetry (Walt Whitman's Civil War verses among them) that made everything come alive and become memorable. Here and there he wrote poems of his own, but I don't recall that I did. It was a great trip, after which I cruised to the end of a triumphant senior year, in which I graduated third in a class of 94 boys. The four top students that year were all recruited by Watson for Old Blue and indeed all ended by going to Yale. We got our acceptance letters on May 1, 1956. It was just after the morning Peddie worship service, and the four of us future Yalies were talking together on the steps of Ayer Memorial Chapel. Suddenly a little Latin American kid, an eighth-grader, ran up to my Venezuelan friend, #4 in our class, and said, "I hear dis June you gunna congratulate and go to Jail!" Ah, the wonders of the American "Y" in the mouth of a Latin American.

Later, in memory of that experience, I would say that "Jail" gave me the third degree—as well as the second and the first.

※

My best roommate and housing arrangement were both parts of senior year. My roommate, a young man from a town in Delaware where his dad was mayor, and I had originally signed up to be senior monitors, what were called *resident assistants* in college, in one of the smaller freshman dorms. The faculty member who lived there concluded, however, that we were spending way too much time with Watson, so after a few weeks we moved to Wyckoff House, a large Victorian residence across the street from campus. If memory serves, there were eight of us seniors sharing four bedrooms on the second and third floors. The ground floor was where our master, Wild Bill Thompson, the athletic director, and his family lived. Thompson, a Peddie graduate and record-holder in several sports (who died only in 2007), was a terrific guy, funny and fair. He had a pretty blond wife, who was nice to us boys also. I know they had kids, but I don't remember any being at home. Every once in a while, on a Friday or Saturday night, Wild Bill would stand at the bottom of the stairs and shout "Fire drill!" in his authoritative bass-baritone. The first time he did it, we boys threw on bathrobes or jeans and hurried down the stairs. From then on we knew of course that the fire drill was really a party at his place with to-die-for pies or cakes fresh baked by his wife with lots of ice cream on the side and Cokes to wash it all down. Wild Bill was clearly a housemaster who knew what would win the hearts of late-teenagers like us. Unsurprisingly, Wyckoff was known as a consistently well-behaved house.

My senior roommate came from a rural Methodist family. I don't know what it is about Methodists—Florine was one too—but, as a group, they have been the nicest, most considerate, most Christian bunch of people I've ever met. About half the men were named James. I guess this practice was based on Saint James, Jesus' brother, who was careful in his Epistle to balance Grace (the Lutheran emphasis) with Works, just as the Wesley brothers, the sect's founders, did in their theology. Anyway, my senior roommate was a model of kindness, consideration, and patience—truly unusual qualities in a 17- or 18-year-old boy. Later, when I visited his home for one of our long-weekend breaks—I believe it was Thanksgiving—I was impressed after church and Sunday dinner, served at 1 p.m., by how the family gathered around the piano, which my roommate's mom played, while we all sang folksongs and hymns. There was a feeling of harmony and shared faith there that was notably lacking in my family, even though we too would sometimes gather around the piano, my father would play (no hymns, of course), and he and I and my eccentric Uncle Joe, the liquor salesman and Socialist artist, would sing.

My senior roommate had never considered himself much of a student until Watson got hold of him in sophomore or junior year. Then the country boy blossomed, started adding Mozart and Beethoven to his down-home records, and did well enough academically to go to Dartmouth after Peddie. Later he got into Columbia University's Physicians and Surgeons School of Medicine. He ended his career a few years ago as a well-regarded orthopedic surgeon specializing in hands at the renowned Cleveland Clinic. He was also the beloved father of a bunch of kids and a committed spouse. To quote Wordsworth, the child was father of the man.

My freshman English instructor at Yale disappointed me the first day of class. He was a slender old man with a funny Southern accent and strange way of speaking. Although he had the requisite tweed jacket with patched elbows and striped tie, he looked for all the world like a cross between a bullfrog and Scrooge McDuck. His name was Alexander McClarin Witherspoon.

I'm happy to report that my first impression proved totally wrong. Withy was an excellent successor to Al Watson. He was a fantastic reader who had an almost religious love of literature. He seemed to know everything worth knowing about English history, literary and otherwise, and was focused on our success as both students and human beings. It also turned out he was a dedicated Scottish American Presbyterian, who like President Jimmy Carter taught Sunday school his whole adult life and whose lineal ancestor had been John Witherspoon, the first president of Princeton University and the only clergyperson to have signed the Declaration of Independence. Decades later I concluded from a remarkable facial resemblance that he was also related to the Oscar-winning actress Reese Witherspoon, a point borne out by her saying in an interview that she too was a descendant of the Rev. John Witherspoon. I'm guessing that Withy may have been Reese's great uncle. (He himself never married and had no children. The campus rumor was that he was gay. After freshman year, he became my English departmental advisor. So I was around him a good bit. If he was gay, you couldn't prove it by me. He never did anything in my presence to verify the rumor.)

Later in graduate school, when I studied Plato's dialogues under

Professor Harry Berger, I found that Alcibiades's comparison in the *Symposium* of Plato to the nested Silenus dolls applied to Withy also. Apparently Socrates was homely, some said even ugly. The outer Silenus doll was that way too. But the inner doll was beautiful. That's how it was, per Alcibiades, with Socrates. Ugly on the outside, beautiful on the inside. And that's how it was with Withy. After a short time, I no longer saw his outer appearance nor paid attention to his unusual mannerisms. I later took his 17th Century Literature course as a senior and his History of English Prose in graduate school. I think I learned more about literature as a source of personal inspiration and reflection from him than from anyone else, including Al Watson.

In sophomore year I took a course in Chaucer from the renowned Chaucer scholar E. Talbott Donaldson, who had written the anthology we were using and later married one of my grad-school classmates. I liked Donaldson as a lecturer—he looked, by the way, like an older version of Watson—and I loved the works of Chaucer, which I had first met as a freshman in Withy's English 25. Unfortunately, no matter how much I crafted my weekly essays, his graduate assistant, who graded them, could never see her way to give me better than a C+. I was incensed. I never got grades that low—not at Peddie and not at Yale. I went to see Witherspoon who was by this point my advisor. As I remember, I was so angry in his office that I cried. He comforted me by say, "Now, now, boy. It will all work out. *Solvitur ambulando*—you'll walk your way to a solution. Why don't you make an appointment to see Professor Donaldson? He's a reasonable man. I'm sure you'll be able to work something out." So I followed his advice and spoke with Professor Donaldson. "Strange," the latter said. "I'll have to talk with my grader, Miss _____. Giamatti [the late A. Bartlett Giamatti, future president of Yale and Commissioner of Baseball] was just in here complaining about his paper grades too. I'll tell you what, Feldman. I'll raise your paper average to B+. How's that?" I was delighted and told him so. When I reported back to Withy, he was happy I had followed his advice and things had worked out.

By the time my wife-to-be arrived in the States in October, 1963, Withy was dying of lung cancer. (Yes, he smoked.) Several weeks after Simone came to New Haven, we visited him in the nursing home where he was staying. He was dressed in a suit and tie, and his room was filled with flowers, books, candy, and other presents from his many admirers and friends. I introduced him to Simone, whom he greeted cordially. We talked about this and that. I noticed that he couldn't finish his sentences. Probably his brain wasn't getting enough oxygen. He would start a sentence, then finish half way through with "You know what I mean." It was sad—that wonderful mind brought down by disease. We didn't stay long. As we were leaving, I knew without a doubt I would never see him again. He said to us, "I don't need all these things. Please take whatever you want." I think Simone took some flowers.

We had barely made it out of his room when I burst out into howls of emotion. We were on the sidewalk of a busy street. I didn't care. I couldn't contain myself. Withy died six weeks later in the first days of 1964. He was 68 years old. That spring I bought his annotated copy of the anthology of 17th Century English poetry and prose he and a professor from Amherst had compiled and edited. He had signed his name on the inside left corner, the signature resembling that of his famous ancestor. Although I have sold or given away most of my library, this is one book I have kept.

Alec Witherspoon influenced me very much as a college teacher. I too would read aloud to the students. I too was as interested in their personal development as in the literature we were studying. I too focused more on teaching than publishing and on the students' future versus my own. For that reason Withy never made it past associate professor. Being a great teacher was not what famous institutions like Yale wanted. They preferred faculty who were world-class names in their fields—professors who could add honor and glory to an already highly regarded institution. But for me, Alexander M. Witherspoon from Bowling Green, Kentucky, joined Florine Tolson Bond from Kent County, Maryland, Jim Culver from Bridgeville, Delaware, and Al Watson from Brookville, Long Island, as one of the major influences in my life.

5
Junior Year in Germany

HEIDELBERG, WHERE I spent academic year 1958-59, was a beautiful medieval town with no bomb damage. The taxi took me from the train station to Kettengasse 19, in a narrow cobblestone street not far from the mountain cable-car station in the heart of the *Altstadt*, or old town. One flight up, I met my new landlady, Frau Laupp, who showed me to my room. The rent was 60 Deutschmarks a month, approximately $14 at the time. Frau Laupp had several other students living there as well, all preparing to be Lutheran ministers. She informed me I was her very first non-theology student and thus an experiment of sorts. She made it clear that there was no drinking in her flat, I should be quiet if I came in after 10 p.m., and I was never ever to bring in female guests regardless of the hour. She also mentioned she was willing to do my laundry for a small fee as she was already doing for the theology students.

Frau Laupp was a small, portly woman with white hair and matching whiskers. She had a marked *Badenser* accent, wheezing and grunting a bit like a pig, but I was able to understand her well enough. I responded that I would be careful to follow all her regulations and happily accepted her laundry offer. She turned out to be a wonderful, caring human being. Never married, she had raised a daughter, Elrike, on her own. Fortunately, Frau Laupp had inherited this large apartment in town that had enabled her over the years to support herself by renting out rooms to Heidelberg students. She also did their and other people's laundry and occasional house cleaning to supplement her modest income.

Of the other seven Yale-Heidelberg exchange students, one was my fellow Peddie alum, Douglas. A German history major in New Haven, he was in Heidelberg to research his undergraduate honors thesis. After summer school, the two of us took a three-week tour of Southern Germany, Liechtenstein, Switzerland, and Austria that would include one of the formative experiences of my life.

Heidelberg's Summer Vacation School was pleasant and relaxed. One interesting experience was my class with Professor Dr. Munch. He was an inspired lecturer who introduced us to the mysteries of German culture. I wondered why such an obvious powerhouse was languishing here with a bunch of foreign students in the vacation school. A German student assisting him enlightened me. Dr. Munch had apparently been among the most famous Heidelberg professors during the Nazi period. Unfortunately for his post-War career, he had also been an active Party member. Only now, thirteen years after the War, had the Occupation Authority given him permission to teach again, and then only low-voltage summer courses like ours. It was a slap in the face for a person of his academic accomplishments and a shame for the regular university students, since he was such a brilliant teacher. It was also of course a punishment for his support of the Nazi cause through his enthusiasm for German culture and the sort of culture-based pseudo-religion with which Hitler's government had tried to replace Christianity. Dr. Munch was a kind of object-lesson for me on how easily an otherwise excellent person could be sucked up into a vortex of evil and also how difficult it might be to tell former Nazis from apolitical or anti-Nazi Germans.

During the weeks between the end of Vacation School and the beginning of the Fall Semester at the "Uni," Douglas and I decided to take a trip. The 2nd-class coaches on German trains were comfortable and, for us with our dollars, ultra-cheap. As a matter of fact, we were able to stay at decent pensions and take all our meals out without having to worry about money. Later I learned that my German father-in-law-to-be, at the time an elementary-school principal in a Munich suburb, was earning exactly as much as I was receiving per month to support his family of five. Today I am convinced that in that year of 1958-59 at ages 18 and 19, I had more discretionary income than at any other time in my life.

Our itinerary took us first to Liechtenstein; then the German-speaking part of Switzerland, primarily Zurich and Basel; Vienna, Innsbruck, and Salzburg, Austria; Regensburg, home of the scholastic theologian Albertus Magnus; and finally the Bavarian capital, Munich, before returning by express train to Heidelberg to begin our first of two university terms. The most important thing happened, however, during our outing to the Munich suburb of Dachau. The day was dark, foggy, windy, and rainy. Although the temperature was no lower than 10 degrees Celsius, it felt colder. Dachau was known as an artists' colony. In the larger world of course the name was synonymous with the Nazis' campaign to rid the world of Jews and other "undesirables." It was the site of perhaps the most infamous concentration camp, second only to Auschwitz, in Poland.

Getting to the village proved easy. You simply took the *Bummelzug*, or slow regional train, from the Munich Central Station. Despite the many stops, the whole trip took 45 minutes or less. Once there, things got more complicated. Neither Douglas nor I felt comfortable going up to a local and asking, "Excuse me, *mein Herr*. Could you please tell us where your concentration camp is?" Consequently, we wandered around for half an hour until we chanced upon a U.S. Army guard post. The concentration camp, the sentry told us, was on the base grounds. Once inside the military compound, we quickly found what we were looking for. Maybe because it was a weekday or the weather was so poor, the two of us had the place entirely to ourselves. Talk about a weird feeling! At the time, the camp had not yet been fixed up as a museum. There were no guides, no exhibits, nothing. Just some of the original buildings, a few signs, and us.

At one point, Douglas wandered off, leaving me by myself. Clearly, lots of other visitors had been there. The walls of the *shower room*, where inmates had been gassed, were covered with graffiti. (The sign *Brausebad*—Shower—still hung over the entrance to the chamber.) Among them were people's names and the dates of their visit, lots of the World-War-II-era saying "Kilroy was here" (Whatever that meant!), and comments like "All German men should be castrated" or "They should have finished the job!" There were even Valentine-type hearts sketched on the walls. Most of the graffiti were in English, presumably contributed by our fellow countrymen.

Soon I had wandered all alone into the crematorium. No signs this time. Only two ovens had been left in place, though there were still traces of where the others had stood. The surviving units, built of red brick, resembled pizza ovens, except that the iron doors were higher and wider. Without thinking I put my right index finger onto the grate to make the finger rusty. Who knows but that a little residue of ash might have been mixed in? I thought. Then I drew the capital letter *J* on the back of my left hand. A few minutes later Douglas showed up. It was getting late, and we had no idea when the military post would close. So, we quickly walked back through the guard station to the little train depot and soon returned to Munich.

Usually I tell everything I have recently experienced to those I am with. This time for some reason, although I shared my general impressions with Douglas, I failed to mention my little writing session at the oven. Seemingly I had forgotten it. The next day we boarded the express back to Heidelberg. The trip was not long, only a few hours. One of the stops, still in Bavaria, was Ulm, the hometown of Albert Einstein. Ours was one of the old-fashioned trains with compartments for six people. Thus far we had had the place to ourselves. At Ulm, however, two middle-aged men joined us. They wore belted tan leather coats with matching shoes. In their Bavarian accents, not dissimilar to Hitler's Austrian one, they started asking us about ourselves. In those days, all Germans had to do was take one look at our shoes and they would know we were *Amis*, the German slang for *Americans*, akin to the British *Yanks*.

"You are from America?" One of them asked. We responded that we were. "Why are you visiting Germany? This is not the tourist season." We explained in our German that we were university exchange students in Heidelberg. "*Ach so*," they continued. "And are you here for long?" "Two semesters," we answered. "And how do you like our country so far"? "*Es ist sehr schön*"—It is very beautiful.

I guess the time had arrived for them to ask us our names. To this question Douglas responded that he was called *Wagner*. "*Ach, Herr Wagner*, that is a very German name. Are your ancestors from Germany?" "My ancestors on my father's side came from Magdeburg," Douglas responded in his American-accented *deutsch*. "*Und Sie*—And you?!" They both turned to me.

At this point, to understand what happened next, you have to know that throughout the prior three months I had been in Germany, I had not told a soul I was Jewish. I was afraid. When asked about my religion, I would mumble something about being *katholisch*—Catholic. And, truth to be told, I would occasionally find myself at Mass or at least a concert in one of Heidelberg's Catholic churches.

After a brief pause, I answered that my name was *Feldman*. I was called *Stefan Feldman*, in English "Steve Feldman."

"*Feldmann*? (They gave it the correct German pronunciation, "Feltmahn.")—but that is also a German name!" (Quite true. It means *farmer*, *peasant*, literally *man of the field*.)

"Yes," I responded in German. "The name might be German, but I am Jewish as were all my ancestors."

The two of them started speaking at the same time. They were saying how they had been too young to have had anything to do with the Holocaust or the camps. But I wasn't interested in what they were saying. I was wondering who had given my mouth permission to say what it had just blurted out. Above all, to these two—individuals who looked and sounded like the actors who played Gestapo agents in the Steve McQueen war film, *The Great Escape*.

Then I remembered the experience with my index finger and "the ashes" from the day before. The thought went through me that those people who had died there had somehow given me the courage to overcome my fear. For now I had told the truth I had concealed not only in Germany but also to some extent before—even to myself. *I was Jewish*. Whether I attended synagogue or not. Whether I participated in my religion or not. Had I been born when I was born a few thousand miles to the east of New York City, I would have died with these martyrs no matter what I said or didn't say. No matter what I thought. But now they had died for me. From that moment until the present, I would never again conceal my Jewish ancestry. Not in Germany. Not in a Muslim or Arabic country. The Jews who had been gassed and incinerated at Dachau had not died totally in vain. They had died for me and in so doing would prove the final solution to *my* Jewish problem.

Among my friends that year was Hans Engels. His father, Anton Engels, was a Dutch-born egg wholesaler in Essen; his mother, Äne Engels, a former Miss Ruhr. As it turned out, Hans had a very attractive younger sister, Ulrike, who was still in high school. Hans himself was attending the Interpreters' Institute in Heidelberg, where he was preparing to become a German interpreter for English and Spanish. Hans spoke excellent American English and very good Castilian Spanish. Besides that, he knew his father's language, Dutch, from having spent summers in the latter's hometown, Zeist, Holland. Besides his obvious linguistic abilities, Hans was a friendly person who complemented his good looks with a broad smile and generous nature. People of all ages enjoyed being around him. Douglas and I became part of his circle, and I had the good fortune to spend two vacations with him and his family in the Essen suburb of Heidhausen.

The Engels were among the pillars of local Essen society. They generously invited me out to restaurants, plays, even the gala New Years Eve Ball at the Essen City Hall. Here I had an experience that has stayed with me. Exactly at midnight, 1958/59, hundreds of people in ball gowns and tuxedos or dark suits stood up and sang the rousing strains of the German national anthem. The Federal Republic of Germany had kept the melody. To separate the good, new Germany from the old, bad one, they had selected an alternate verse, beginning "*Einigkeit und Recht und Freiheit.* . . ." "Unity and justice and freedom. . . ." Yet when we stood to sing, the forbidden original text was used. Here was the *crème* of Essen society, citizens of the city that had given the world Krupps artillery and other instruments of war, greeting the new year with a heart-felt rendition of

"Deutschland, Deutschland über alles,/Über alles in der Welt. . . ."
"Germany, Germany above all else, /Above all else in the world. . . ."
How new, really, was the Federal Republic of Germany? I asked myself.

Midway through winter semester I started thinking about what to do when the school year ended in early April. I certainly wasn't planning to go home till July so that I could benefit from being in Europe as long as possible. I settled on two possibilities: Italy or Greece. My stomach, which had bothered me earlier during a trip I had taken in January with my friend Hans to Spain, was now working well again. Plus Italy struck me as the sort of place one traveled to with one's family later in life. Greece, the cradle of Western Civilization, was the better choice for a fancy-free 19-year-old student, I concluded—riskier for one's stomach, perhaps, but also more appealing.

Through the International Student Center, that treasure-trove of information, I found a three-week student-oriented trip to Greece that left Munich April 12, returning on May 1. In between, the bus would visit Austria, Yugoslavia, and Greece as far as Sparta in the Peloponnese. Transportation, shared hotel rooms, breakfast and dinner, as well as an experienced tour guide would cost only DM 400, about $95. We would be responsible for lunches, snacks, incidentals and gifts. It didn't take me long to mail in my deposit and registration form.

A Heidelberg medical student from Mexico City and I joined 28 others in Munich to start the trip. Her nickname in the bus soon became "Mexiko," although her real name was Eugenia. I enjoyed getting to know her and on one occasion dancing to Latin music with her in Athens. The bulk of us were in fact students. At 19, I was probably the youngest. Some were close to 30. About a half dozen, though, were non-students who signed up for the trip at a more expensive but still reasonable rate. Given the intellectual caliber of the lectures we received, we considered them honorary students. Our tour guide, Werner Kubsch, turned out to be the owner of the Munich-based travel agency, called "Studiosus." A well-educated refugee from Silesia, Herr Kubsch knew the geography, history, art, architecture, and literature of all the places we saw. He was even an amateur archeologist. His bus-board talks, moreover, helped while away the long hours on the road while enriching our visits to the main sites.

The very first sight I took in, though, as we were making the short drive from Munich to Salzburg, Mozart's birthplace, was that of two blond German women sitting side by side a few seats ahead of me. By the time we arrived at Salzburg for lunch, I learned they were both secretaries at the Wacker Chemie chemical company, part of the old I.G. Farben conglomerate that had been broken up after the War by the Allies. The taller one who spoke with a Bavarian accent was called Hilde Geyer; the shorter one, whom I found very attractive, Lolly Zimmermann. Her real first name, she explained, was "Hannelore," but when she had been an au pair in England in the early 50s, the child she was looking after couldn't pronounce it. Instead, he called her *Lolly*. By the time she returned to Germany after a year, the name had stuck, and she had been Lolly ever since.

Lolly spoke accent-free *Hochdeutsch*, High German. In fact, she sounded like the female radio announcers I often heard on the Grundig AM-FM-short-wave radio I had bought myself in Heidelberg. It turned out she and her family were refugees from East Prussia, a part of pre-War Germany that had been split between the Russians and the Poles in 1945. Moreover, she had wanted to become an actress, she told me, and had taken diction lessons, in part to overcome a lisp, before the economic realities of post-War Germany had forced her to give up her dreams and become a multi-lingual secretary.

When we arrived in Salzburg, we had our first bit of sightseeing before lunch: Salzburg's Roman Catholic Cathedral. A High Mass had just been celebrated, so the place was still misty from the sweet-smelling incense. Lolly felt sick to her stomach. I suggested a nearby restaurant I remembered from my fall trip to Salzburg. "They have good soups," I told her in German. "Maybe you'll feel better after a soup and perhaps an *Underberg* [the German brandy-and-herb curative for an upset stomach]." She wasn't so sure but came along anyway. After lunch, I offered Hilde my "excellent" window seat and moved into the aisle seat next to Lolly that Hilde had been occupying. (It took Hilde years to forgive me for that move.) That was the beginning of a bus-board romance that turned into a four-year exchange of letters culminating in my proposal in April 1963 and our marriage in New Haven seven months later on November 30.

Austria was charming, just as everyone had said. But I had been there before. As we crossed the border into Yugoslavia, where Marshall Tito still headed the government, I noticed how, the closer we got to Greece, the more the sights, sounds, and cultures changed from Western European to a kind of Middle-Easternized Slavic. It was also clear that, as in Spain, we were now in a military dictatorship. Men in drab green uniforms were everywhere. But the uniforms looked wrinkled, and the men's mustaches drooped sadly. At night, especially in Belgrade, we ate the tasty food, drank Slivovitz, the local plum liquor, and danced. Not only did we dance with each other, but the locals were hospitable and joined in too. Music truly is the universal language, so without knowing more than a few words in common, we were soon smiling and laughing, holding the ends of white handkerchiefs with each other, and hissing every once in a while like snakes as we wound our way around the floor to the Turkish-sounding music. Back at the table, I would lift my glass to our local dancing partners and proudly say my one sentence in Serbo-Croatian, "*Slivowitz dobro*!" "Slivovitz is good!" To be sure, I also learned that the word "*zenshka*" on bathroom doors meant "Women" and that I should enter the bathroom with the other word on it.

One of the dancing couples took a shine to Lolly and me, perhaps because we were dancing more than the rest of our company, and somehow communicated that they wanted to invite us to lunch at their home the next day. We met them back at the hotel midmorning, after our city bus tour, and had a splendid lunch. We all showed family pictures and managed to get along fine with a few common words in German and English. Mainly, though, we mimed and acted to get our ideas across. Lolly and I were really challenged, though, as it got closer and closer to 1 p.m., the time our bus would be departing for Skopje. Finally, our hosts understood what we wanted and walked us back to our hotel, where we were forced to pay a small fine for keeping the bus from departing on time. We were only too happy to pay up, since we had feared our tour guide and company had already left without us.

That day before a rest stop mid-afternoon, Herr Kubsch mentioned that the town where we would be stopping, a mountain village actually, was a place where the Yugoslav partisans had made a surprise attack on the German occupying forces. To retaliate, the SS had taken one male at random from every house in the village, lined them up along the town wall, and shot them all to death. We should therefore speak softly in an effort to conceal that we were a German tour group. Almost all the local women we saw, many of them older, were still dressed in black fourteen years after the War. At Lolly's suggestion, the two of us decided to speak English during that hour-long rest stop.

Our first visit in Greece was the Meteora Cloister, built on top of a low mountain and accessible only by a large basket hauled up by monks working a winch. This was a Greek Orthodox monastery reminiscent of the Essene communities of Jesus' day. The dark rooms were lit by torches and flashes of gold from the ubiquitous icons. The full-bearded monks kept their talking to a minimum, but whether that was from their practice of silence or the lack of a common language, I do not know.

Despite the white-washed Orthodox Christian churches dotting the hills, there was a strong feeling of Islam in Greece, maybe because of the Near-Eastern-style radio music with which Robert, our driver, often filled the 30-person Mercedes bus. Then there were the gypsies with their mules who shared the narrow, winding road with us and all the other vehicles. In fact, the whole scene except the urban areas reminded me of a set from a Biblical film like *The Ten Commandments*. In 1959, the Grecian countryside had little to indicate that one was living in the mid-Twentieth Century.

Something else that struck me was the quality of the light. Everything seemed brighter—the blue of the sky, the white of the clouds, the green of the trees, the tan of the earth. Although it was only mid-April, we were suddenly plunged into summer. Everything was in bloom. Coats were no longer necessary. The change was invigorating and slightly narcotic. When we reached the hot springs of Thermopylae, it was women to the left, men to the right, putting on bathing suits and jumping into the naturally heated water. Herr Kubsch told us we would get used to the egg-like smell of sulfur once we realized it was the traditional source of healing at that spa.

Three other experiences stood out for me. The first took place in the bus as Robert was negotiating the windy mountain roads of Greek Macedonia. He was what Germans call a "sporty driver." That is, he seemed to consider the bus a kind of oversized sports car. Sometimes, if I happened to be sitting in the window seat on the cliff side, I preferred not to look out the window. His turns struck me as dangerously sharp. One time, when I was sitting on the aisle still next to Lolly, Robert took an especially sharp turn. Although the bus held the road just fine, my Olivetti in its case fell out of the overhead rack and missed my head by inches. I thanked my stars for sparing me, since a blow at that speed could have been fatal. Fortunately, the case did its job, and the typewriter still functioned well enough even though the manual return stick was slightly bent. From then on I kept the typewriter, which I had brought along to do my daily journal entries, under the seat in front of me, airplane style. I had had a close call. Now 19, I was forced to remember that life was precious and death never far.

The other two experiences were less frightening. In Athens we had the rare opportunity to visit the Acropolis by full moonlight. The hilltop temple complex is impressive enough by day. We'd first visited it in the late afternoon, had a long dinner with dancing in a nearby restaurant, then returned at 10:30 and stayed for around two hours. As usual, I was with my new friend Lolly. The place was absolutely mystical. It was a time when even a Yale intellectual like me could believe in the gods, or at least in how human beings several thousand years ago might have done so. Lolly and I found ourselves talking about reincarnation, which she believed in and I didn't. Suddenly for some reason, I became conservative and used the Bible to back up my view that we lived only once, and then for only 70 or 80 years. Still, the atmosphere of the place was simply too strong for my brain, and we both fell silent. We found ourselves alone in the altar area of the Parthenon, which had been a Greek Orthodox church after its original role as a temple to Athena Parthanos, the goddess protector of the city in classical times. Indeed, the long horizontal stone which could have been the altar might have also served as the pedestal for the floor-to-ceiling statue of Athena which once dominated the temple.

With moonlight finding its way between the remaining columns, I once again did something spontaneous as at Dachau, or rather my hand did. I took one of my cards, where one could read "Stephen Feldman, Stud. Phil." for Student of Philosophy, as I officially was at Heidelberg. Then I asked Lolly to sign one end after which I signed the other. Next I struck a paper match—I was still smoking cigarettes and cigarillos back then—split it in half vertically, and asked her to ignite the side of the card where I had signed while I ignited the side with her name. Then, without another word, we dropped the burning card onto the "altar" stone and when the paper was fully consumed, left in silence to rejoin our group.

We didn't talk about the experience again for some years. Later, though, I wondered if this impromptu ceremony had anything to do with the fact that 4½ years later we married and managed to stay together for the next 43 years, until Lolly, or Simone as she would become, died. Who knows? Maybe it even had something to do with other lives where we had known each other. Of course, it would be a while before I even admitted the possibility of other lives.

The final experience in Greece I want to share took place at Delphi, home of the Pythia, the oracle Socrates consulted, the sign over whose temple read "Know thyself." At Delphi there is a large amphitheater with incredible acoustics. It was here that Greek comedies and tragedies, still religious rituals back then, had been performed. To test just how good the acoustics were, Herr Kubsch had several of us perform short numbers, while the rest sat in the last rows. There were of course no microphones, and anyway, we were outdoors. For my part, after a brief introduction in German, I recited the first 18 lines of the General Prologue of Chaucer's *Canterbury Tales* in Middle English. Other than being surprised that what I was speaking was in fact some kind of English, the listeners heard everything perfectly even though I was speaking normally. The same was true for the words spoken or sung in German offered by my fellow performers.

After, those of us who wished were given the opportunity to drink from the Castilian Springs, the legendary source of the Pythia's prophetic powers. Lolly and I were among the dozen or so from our group who took up the offer. Herr Kubsch instructed us in the proper protocol without following which one could not receive the promised powers. As I recall, one had to bend over backwards and drink the waters that didn't splash on one's back over one's right shoulder. Lolly and I both followed the instructions to a tee, though it took some hours before our clothes dried. What is interesting about this interlude in retrospect is that in later life we both found we had the ability to remember dreams that foretold future happenings or to know, for example, who was telephoning, even if it was someone we had not heard from in a long time. After our marriage, we established the practice of telling each other our vivid dreams, especially if they seemed to be predicting something, so that later we would have a witness to verify the accuracy of our predictions. Of course, as my father would have said, with that and a dollar you could ride the bus. Still, whether or not our low-level prophetic powers came from drinking from the Pythia's springs, it is interesting to me that we both had them, and in my case, they only started manifesting after this particular experience in Delphi.

We arrived back in Munich on May 1, Europe's traditional Labor Day. After staying there overnight, Eugenia and I boarded the train to Heidelberg. There a surprise, and not a pleasant one, awaited me. Inspired by I don't know what, I decided not to go straight home but to stop by my friend Douglas's place first. When he saw me, he said, "Stephen, what happened? Did anyone tell you to come here before you went home?" Then he told me the following story. My landlady and her husband had read through my journal in my absence. It had been in my dresser which had not been locked. In its pages they found my description of our American landlady, married to a much older retired Swiss scientist of some kind. From my perspective, Mrs. R. was an alcoholic who roamed the halls of their mansion—formerly the home of a wealthy Jewish dentist in pre-War days—in skimpy, revealing nightgowns. (When my months at Frau Laupp's place were up, I found a wonderful top-floor room with a view not far from Heidelberg Castle for a mere DM 100 per month, one-eighth of my monthly stipend.) Since I had been steeping myself that year in the works of Sigmund Freud, you can imagine what my analysis of her problems were. Moreover, she reminded me of a Walt Disney character, Petunia Pig, so I renamed her Petunia in my writings. Apparently, the husband had tracked down Douglas, whom they knew to be my friend, and asked when I would be returning. Herr R. was livid.

After strategizing, Douglas and I concluded I would go to the house as if I knew nothing of what had transpired. When I arrived, the housekeeper took me to the study and called Mrs. R. who in turn summoned her husband. Flushed with anger, she waved a handful of my journal pages in my face. They were richly underlined in red. When her husband arrived, he walked straight up to me—he was a slight, bald, mustached man in his 70s—and punched me in the face. He accompanied this action with words to the effect, "You dirty Jewish pig! How dare you write all those lies about my wife!" I ran downstairs, out the door, and directly to the office of Professor Dick Stavig, a Norwegian American literature professor from Saint Olaf College in Minnesota. He was spending the year teaching American literature as a Fulbright scholar at Heidelberg. We had become friends in fall, and as I ran down the hill to the University, I felt he would be the best person to turn to.

Through tears of anger, I poured my story out. I was clearly in shock. Professor Stavig listened, then dropped whatever he was doing and walked me over to the International Student Office. After he had explained to the head what had happened, that office sent one of their administrators up to the R. house to negotiate a settlement and help me reclaim my belongings. I spent the night at Douglas's place, and the next morning, accompanied by an International Student Office official, I went to the house to collect my things. Everything was there. Only the underlined pages Mrs. R had shook at me were missing.

Fortunately, the evening before, I had gone to Amerika Haus, where I told my story to Denise Abbey, the middle-aged U.S. Information

Agency officer from Alaska who ran it. She was living in a mansion on Philosophers' Way, on the other side of the Neckar River in Neuenheim. It turned out she was looking for someone to help her with light gardening and personal assistance, including German-English interpreting, and if I was interested—she knew me from my frequent attendance at Amerika Haus programs—I was welcome to live for free in the gardener's cottage and even have occasional meals in the villa with her and other visitors. I jumped at the opportunity and had the taxi drive me and my things to Philosophenweg 5.

All too soon, it was late July and time to fly home to Chicago. What can I say now about my year abroad in Germany? For one thing, I had matured a lot, both from the many positive experiences I had had and the few traumas. I had felt amazingly at home there, something clarified for me a few years later in my Subud opening. Also, I had learned another language and a great deal about another country. I had seen countries other than Germany and had gained a more than theoretical understanding that the world was indeed large and varied. There was much more to the planet than the United States of America. As a matter of fact, some of the material culture and a lot of the lifestyle I found in Europe, even in our defeated World War II enemy, impressed me as superior to what I had known back home. For starters, there were traces, architectural and otherwise, that were far older than anything in America. In Europe one lived in the shadow of history on every side; while in America only the new seemed valued. Then there was the café culture, and the concept of friendship as a lifelong endeavor which included mutual obligations and consistent feelings of regard. One had a few lifelong friends rather than the easy-come-easy-go friendships in mobile America, where everyone and no one were considered *friends*. Then there was the easy access to museums, classical music, and opera. In fact, every town of 50,000 or more seemed to have its own opera company, Heidelberg included. Very important, of course, was the gift of coming to accept my Jewishness, something that has lasted down to the present. What I mainly learned from that wonderful year, though, was that every country is comprised of human beings, some better, some worse, some more loving, some less. I now knew without a doubt that all people regardless of nation, race, religion, ethnicity, or any other difference belonged to a single human race and that by working on ourselves individually, we could collectively raise the over-all quality of that race and perhaps even "win" it. This work, regardless of my various job descriptions, would become my lifelong mission.

6
Graduate School, Marriage, and Early Subud Experiences

I BECAME a graduate student in English at Yale in September 1961, three-and-a-half months after my opening in Subud. One of the Chicago Subud helpers, Stuart, had accompanied me from Chicago to New Haven. He also taught me the basics of what in Subud is called *testing*, since he thought the technique might come in handy for me as an isolated Subud member in southern Connecticut. (The next closest Subud groups were in Stamford, Connecticut, about thirty minutes south of New Haven by train, or the larger group in Manhattan, a good hour-and-a-half away if you threw in time on the subway.)

Testing is a form of discernment in which one states a question difficult to decide in the usual way and then does the *latihan* for a few minutes while attempting to dismiss the question from one's mind. Stuart and I were staying in my shared New Haven apartment. My roommates hadn't yet arrived, so we had the place to ourselves. First Stuart asked that we each be shown through our *latihan* how we received YES, or a positive answer. In my case, I went up on my toes and walked a few steps forward. When the question he posed was how we received NO, or a negative response, I did the opposite, staying on my flat feet and walking a few paces backwards. This technique proved invaluable not only in grad school but up to the present. Over time, as I had more experience of the *latihan* and the inner life in general, my testing became more sophisticated, including seeing images, verbalizing spontaneously, and feeling heavy or light in various gradations, the former being negative and the latter positive. Also, my ability to interpret what I had experienced—Bapak's initial Indonesian word for testing was *tinjauan*, "observation"—became sharper and more accurate.

Stuart made sure to tell me that testing on one's own was a tricky business, since it was always easy for one's wishes to creep in so that testing could become, as one New York Subud member liked to put it, "voting with one's eyes closed." Therefore, whenever possible, Stuart advised I should contact several helpers to test the question(s) along with me—even if they needed to do so at a distance. Since they would likely have no interest in the outcome, their responses would tend to be less influenced by personal desire. Nevertheless, in an emergency I could test questions on my own, and if, after having lived with the answers for a day or two, they still felt persuasive, I could follow them. I should be prepared to make mistakes, though, and to suffer the consequences. It was like learning a sport, he said. You developed your skills through trial and error. So it was better not to test really important questions on my own, at least not for a while.

Through my Hungarian undergraduate friend Steve Scher, I had been invited to join two other graduate students, both in Philosophy, to share a professor's apartment while he was on leave. It was an excellent opportunity, since the flat, on the third floor of an English-style apartment building, was only a short walk from the Hall of Graduate Studies, where my classes were held. As I remember, the price was also right, and my roommates, Bob and Chip, proved pleasant, interesting, and easy to live with. Not only that, but all of us had been Yale undergraduates in the Class of '60, so we had that in common as well.

Yale College, though challenging, had been a positive, engaging experience. I had been caught up in a kind of Frank-Merryweather-at-Yale adventure. Plus I'd had that wonderful junior year abroad to refresh myself before returning for a five-star senior year. But that is where the trouble began. As an undergraduate in Yale College, I had been a superstar. The professors expected great things of me and were prepared to reward me richly with high grades and sterling recommendations if I seemed like I was delivering. I had even aced an honors freshman course in atomic physics! Yale Graduate School, albeit in the same department with the same faculty, was a professional school. Love of subject and decent writing were no longer enough. The Modern Language Association (MLA) Handbook became a kind of Bible. Everything turned on the number of relevant articles we cited in our papers and the excellent bibliographies we produced, the dry bones of scholarship versus the living spirit of literature. As my first-year-graduate-school girlfriend Jane Parry (later Tompkins) put it in her powerful autobiography, *A Life in School,* the romance of literary study was gone. The bloom was off the rose. This was now the *business* of literature, the preparation for an academic career. Our peer group consisted of the top English students from the best universities around the country and abroad. The clever footnote and in-class putdown became our stock-in-trade. Intellectual competitiveness and aggressive articulateness were now standard operating procedure for us all.

I remember attending a lecture that first year by the then Sterling Professor of Comparative Literature, Dr. René Wellek, a scholar from Prague. The talk happened to take place on my 22nd birthday, November 6, 1961. If I am not mistaken, it began at three and lasted an hour, after which there were snacks and genteel conversation. Although I have long since forgotten the topic let alone the contents of what the famous professor said, I do remember he quoted in excellent accents, so far as I could judge, his German, Russian, French, and Italian sources in the original, translating for the rest of us. He made excellent connections and reached well-founded conclusions. It was a bravura performance. As I stood up to leave, a voice inside my head—different from the comforting voice I have referred to earlier—told me in no uncertain terms that no matter how hard I worked, no matter how much I learned, I would never be as successful or famous as Dr. Wellek.

It was a dark, rainy fall afternoon in New Haven. Rather than elated by Dr. Wellek's talk, I was depressed. I wasn't doing so well in the early going in some of my courses. The work was intense and not all that interesting. One of my professors who had known me from before told me that during my year away from New Haven I seemed to have lost my flair for literature. In retrospect he was right. Literature had been displaced by Subud as my primary spiritual commitment. By the time I got back to the apartment at 22 High Street, I felt like ending it all. My roommates weren't around. I went into my room, opened the window three floors above the concrete sidewalk, and got as far as putting one leg outside. Once again I heard a voice, but this time it was the other one. "You have your whole life ahead of you," it said. "Please don't end it now. Things will get better for you, and you will find your own way, just as Professor Wellek has found his. Please come inside." Still depressed but comforted, I followed the Voice's invitation. It was a long slog, graduate school, but, as the Voice said, things did get better, as did my grades, and in December 1966, I received my Ph.D.

<figure>✺</figure>

During my first year of graduate school I continued writing long, infrequent letters to Simone and received similar ones from her. In the second year a shift occurred, and I no longer thought of her as simply my German pen pal from 1959. She soon became something more, but exactly what wasn't at first clear. Even before my opening in May, 1961, I had sent her an enthusiastic letter in German about Subud. She was skeptical at first, in part because her Aunt Hanna, after whom she had been named Hannelore, had been involved by an unscrupulous Protestant minister in spiritistic practices. Apparently Aunt Hanna was very intuitive, so this minister, her landlord, began using her without her knowledge or consent as a kind of sleeping medium. The family story goes that, as a result, Hanna became mentally unbalanced. Simone was concerned that I might have gotten myself mixed up in some kind of cult that would disserve me in a similar way.

To make sure, she met with the local Subud contacts, a certain Baron and Baroness von R-L, who lived in the Munich suburb of Neu-Grünwald, only a few kilometers from her parents' apartment in Grünwald. This meeting took place on a historic evening, August 13, 1961, the night in which the East German State unveiled the Berlin Wall, *die Mauer*. After a series of follow-up meetings, Simone felt satisfied that Subud was not a cult and that it might well offer a practical path to spiritual and personal growth. Consequently, on November 27, 1961, just six months after me, Simone and her friend Ingeborg were opened in the Munich group. Now, in addition to all the other things we had in common—Mozart and Rilke, our ability to dance well together, our interest in reading a wide variety of books, our delight in travel, and our culturally diverse circles of friends—we could share experiences as we followed our individual spiritual paths through Subud: something we did as our trans-Atlantic correspondence continued.

In spring, 1963, I did something unusual even for me. I sent Simone a brief letter in English. Typically, she and I wrote each other long letters in German. But that wasn't the strangest part. My one-pager, written in a fit of automatic writing—the first time I had experienced such a thing, though I had heard of it—contained a proposal of marriage.

I remember my feeling upon depositing that letter in the local mail box. "Oh my God!" I thought. "What have I done? What happens if I have just made a mistake—the biggest of my life?" These concerns were logical enough. Besides the spontaneity of my action, she was nearly nine years my senior, we had known each other only three-and-a-half weeks, we hadn't seen each other for nearly four years nor even spoken on the phone, she was Protestant (Lutheran) while I was—officially, at least—Jewish, we didn't know each other's families, we had never lived together, and she was a secretary with a high-school education while I was on track to get my Ph.D. and teach college. You didn't need to be a trained psychologist to figure out that this was a rather unusual route to marriage!

At the beginning of my second year of graduate study, I received a message from Subud North America that a certain Dr. Mizuno, an ophthalmologist from Nagoya, Japan, and a member of the Nagoya Subud group, would be coming to Yale on a post-doctoral research fellowship along with his wife, also a Subud member, and their twelve-year-old daughter, Afumi. Dr. Mizuno and I were doing *latihan* together a few days after that fateful burst of automatic writing. Still a little freaked out by my audacity, I communicated to him my desire to test a question, namely, "Was my wish to marry Simone correct?" I needed some confirmation *ex post facto*, and—to be frank— I am not sure what I would have done had the answer come back a no. So we did a little *latihan* to clear our heads, especially mine, and then I asked the question. Since I had my eyes closed, I don't know what sorts of motions if any Dr. Mizuno received. As for me, I went up on my toes and walked smartly forward. Ah, thank God! A yes! "Dr. Mizuno," I said. "What answer did you get?" "Yesso!" He replied without a pause. "Yesso?" I responded. "But how?" "I see letter Y." Then it struck me. Of course! He's an eye researcher, someone who spends a good part of the day looking for telltale signs through his microscope. His faculty of seeing must be very acute, even in terms of his spiritual exercise. Seeing—observing—must be one of his primary talents.

So by now, dear reader, you must be dying to know how the then Hannelore, whom I find it difficult to call anything other than Simone, responded to my impetuous proposal. Well, two or three weeks went by. Then one day when I wasn't especially thinking about the mail—isn't it always that way?—I heard a knock on my door. It was Mrs. Marchione, the upstairs neighbor. "You have a letter from Germany. I bet it's from your German pen pal," she said with a smile as she handed me the square-shaped envelope. It contained a single sheet. Simone wrote she had been both stunned and flattered by my proposal. After discussing the situation with the Baroness, her helper, she had decided to go off to the Austrian Alps for a week, climb the mountain paths above Thiersee, and see if some credible response might emerge in her. Until then, she asked me to be patient. After 32 years of being on her own, she needed some time to sort things out.

Naturally, I did not breathe a word of this story to my parents or even my friends. If Simone said no, then no one needed to know. Dr. Mizuno would never say anything. And if she said yes, well, we'd cross that bridge when we came to it. God, I was convinced, would provide the right solution. In any case, since that testing session with Dr. Mizuno, I had begun feeling I might not have been so crazy after all. Plus we were talking here about a good human being who also happened to be a beautiful woman with whom I had forged a solid relationship by means of the only thing I had some kind of expertise in: words. So maybe things would work out after all.

Approximately six weeks after my impromptu proposal, Simone wrote me a long letter. Now back from the Alps, she had come to the conclusion, verified by testing with the Baroness, that—despite all our differences—she felt sure of her feelings and indeed wished to marry me. So her answer was yes. I was very pleased. My response however was muted. This was a new type of reaction that had emerged in my life after coming to Subud. If something turned out well, I didn't jump up and down as I once would have done. Or if something happened that seemed bad, I didn't fall into despair. My feelings were just slightly on one side or the other of neutral. Later I read in the Hindu Vedas that this sort of equanimity was the ideal. If the pendulum didn't swing too far in one direction, it wouldn't swing too far in the other. Apparently the Law of Karma applied here too: Much joy would be paid for with much sadness, while moderate joy would cost only moderate sadness. Also, at some point I read where Bapak had said essentially the same thing.

But at that time I hadn't yet read either of these sources. As in so many aspects of my Subud life, these new reactions came by themselves, apparently caused by my spiritual training.

Of course, another factor may have been at play as well. For, as when I was selected a Yale-Heidelberg Exchange Scholar, I knew that now would come the hard part of getting my father to approve—and pay for the year. So here, I was clear that, in more senses than one, we had only just begun. Now there was—again—the issue of my parents. Not that they could prevent my marriage as they did my summer job as a golf caddy when I was still in high school. This time I was of age—23—plus I was more or less self-sufficient financially. Still, I preferred to marry with their blessing rather than otherwise. Then there was the issue of how to pay for Simone's trip to the States. I had early established the practice of living at the edge of my resources, so then as now there was little by way of savings to fall back on. Last but not least, there was the high hurdle of Simone's immigration status. Getting her a Green Card, which was still actually green in 1963, would be a major challenge, even for a sophisticated Yalie like me.

The problem that proved easiest to resolve was paying Simone's way over. Her parents offered, as soon as she had told them and they had adjusted to the idea, not only to buy her ticket, a train to Bremerhaven, then a ship to New York City, but also to send her new Scandinavian furniture at their expense to New Haven. As it happened, my future mother-in-law, who was very intuitive, had observed the letters coming from America over the years and, especially since Simone hadn't said much about it, had a feeling something might be developing. At the same time, she and her husband had begun to give up on Simone's ever getting married—after all, she was 32, a strong candidate back then to remain single. They were thus able to reconcile themselves to the strangeness of our relationship. At least both their children would be married.

My parents had more difficulty. I wouldn't turn 24 till November. I was a few years from finishing my doctoral degree and being able to get a college teaching job. From their perspective, I hardly knew the woman—she was significantly older, only a high-school graduate, a Gentile, a working girl (a secretary) with no assets, and we had known each other less than a month and hadn't seen each other or even talked on the phone for nearly four years. The real deal breaker for them, though, was she was German. Added to all this was my mother's default position on any of my relationships. It was always, "You can do better!" My father was apparently more willing to accept some of the blame for the situation. After all, they had let me spend my junior year in Germany. I was young, impetuous, a product of all-boys education from age twelve. They should have said no back then. Now, he reasoned, it was too late. Plus I was of age and paying my own way. There was really nothing they could do to stop me. Or maybe there was.

Dad's work for international companies gave him some insight into the workings of the U.S. Immigration and Naturalization Service. He knew from Louis Dreyfus employees who wanted to move to the States that there were three qualifications for obtaining permanent residency. The candidate had to be independently wealthy, own significant property in this country, or have a living-wage job awaiting him or her in America. My father was certain that neither I nor my fiancée had any money, certainly not enough to satisfy the INS, that Simone owned no property at all in America, and that it would be virtually impossible for her to get a full-time job sight-unseen from abroad. The remaining possibility would be if someone of financial substance in America were willing to vouch for her. The only individual likely to consider that was him. So he assured my mother not to worry. "All we need to do is sit tight and not sign any sponsorship papers," he told her. Then the whole thing, he felt, would blow over.

He came close to being right. Actually, I tried to find a full-time job for Simone as a native speaker in Yale's German Department. I knew some of the top professors and tried to impress on them that she had performed in the theater as an amateur and had taken elocution lessons. As a result, she spoke "stage German" (*Bühnendeutsch*) and would be an excellent model for Yale's beginning-German students. Yes, the professors replied, but she is merely a high-school graduate, and from a trade school, not even an academic *Gymnasium*. As it was, they informed me, the Department preferred to hire German graduate students already in New Haven whom they could pay with tuition scholarships. Okay, but what about Frau Faust? I remonstrated. She was not a grad student. Well, she was an exception who had taught for the Department for many years. Still, I continued, she was not a student, and she had been, in my experience, their best native speaker. The real issue seemed to be that the Department would not consider anyone sight unseen. Maybe after she got here I could bring her around for an interview, was their suggestion. That's the point, I argued. She needed a job in order to get her Green Card so she could not only get but also stay and work here.

My persistence wasn't without its effect. Professor Peter D., the then chair of German, said he would be in Munich for a few weeks during the summer, and if he could find the time, he would be willing to meet with Simone. Maybe just maybe, I thought, things would work out. For reasons I no longer remember, Professor D. and Simone never got together, so in the end all my attempts to find her a job in the States came to naught. It looked like my father's scenario would come true.

Meantime, another problem cropped up. Simone hadn't heard anything in response to her visa application of some weeks before. She had put it in as soon as she decided to come over. Finally, her father, an elementary-school principal in the Munich suburb of Grünwald, called the U.S. Consulate to find out the cause for the long delay. As it turned out, the staff had filed her application under the Polish quota, since the part of Germany where Simone had been born, southern East Prussia, had become Polish territory after World War II. This was of course a mistake, since Simone was and had always been a German citizen. Given the much smaller annual immigration quota from Poland versus West Germany back then, it was a good thing Herr Zimmermann had had the idea to check.

Yet despite all these initial setbacks, fate had something else in store. I had asked my two favorite professors, Drs. Witherspoon and Sewall, to send character references for me to the U.S. Consulate in Munich. When Simone finally came in for her visa interview, everything was in order except that she had no property in America, insufficient personal assets, no job there, and no American citizen to vouch for her. The U.S. Government, she was told, didn't want to issue permanent visas to individuals who might become wards of the State. Things were looking grim, and Simone started to cry. At that point, the interviewing officer, a sister-in-law of then Vice President Lyndon Johnson, pulled a letter out of Simone's folder. "Do you know what that is?" She asked. "It's a letter from Professor Richard Sewall, one of your fiancé's graduate-school professors. He speaks very highly of Mr. Feldman. Now as it happens, I studied English at Yale Graduate School myself, and Dr. Sewall was my favorite professor. His words carry a lot of weight with me. So, if your chest x-ray is negative, I am prepared to waive the usual requirements and approve your application for permanent residency in the United States."

Now Simone's tears came from happiness, not disappointment. What were the probabilities of such a thing? We asked ourselves later, when she was safely in New Haven. Very small indeed! From our perspective, nothing less than the Hand of God had been at work.

We did have one small disappointment, though. The Second Subud World Congress was to be held that summer of 1963 at Briarcliff College, just north of New York City in Westchester County. Simone and I had been planning to go, but by the time her Green Card was approved, it was too late. That summer I was working as a clerk at the Yale Art Gallery. Summer jobs in university towns are always in demand, so I had been lucky to get mine and needed for financial reasons not to lose it. My boss, an older single woman, was a good supervisor but not known for flexibility. Had I tried to take a week or ten days off to go to the World Congress, she would have given my position to one of the other people on her list. What to do? I really wanted to go, but then, I also needed to keep my job. So I did what most Subud members would have done in a similar situation. I tested. "Dear God, please show me through my *latihan*, separate from my heart, mind, and desires, whether it is appropriate for me to go to the World Congress regardless of my job situation." After a few seconds, I practically ran backwards. The answer was clear. Absolutely not!

I remember calling one of my peers from the New York Group while he was at the Congress. "How was it?" I wanted to know. "Fantastic," Wallace answered. "I've never experienced anything like this before." That was the last thing I wanted to hear. Then he added, "I know it's a bummer, Steve, that you have to work and can't be here. But there is good news. Bapak has asked the New York group if he could visit there next Saturday evening, after the Congress is over, especially to be with all the Subud members who were unable to attend the Congress. Maybe you can arrange to get to that."

When I got off the phone, I immediately called my co-worker, a young woman who lived in a nearby community with her family. "Rachel, would you mind switching next weekend for this one, when you're scheduled? My guru is going to be in the City that Saturday night only, so it's my one chance to meet him, and I've been dying to do so for two years." "That's fine, Steve. I was going to go out on a picnic with my boyfriend that Saturday afternoon, but I'm sure he'd be happy to move our date up to this weekend." "That's great!" I said. "Thank you so much."

As usual, whenever I went to the City, as everyone within 100 miles of New York calls Manhattan, I would stay with my Aunt Eva, who lived in a rent-controlled apartment on 104th Street and Broadway. This time was no exception. After dropping off my suitcase, I took the subway downtown. When I entered the old loft building on East 21st Street in the Gramercy Park District, hundreds of people had already taken their places on the uncomfortable wooden folding chairs that had been lined up auditorium style. I managed to find one about halfway to the front. Before long, we all stood up as Bapak and party made their way to their places. Bapak, wearing the typical black Indonesian fez (called a *peci*, pronounced "petchy") and his hatless interpreter, Muhammad Usman, took their seats on the dais. The rest of the party, consisting of Bapak's wife, Siti Sumari, and Bapak's eldest daughter by his first marriage (His first wife had died.), Siti Rahayu, took their places in the front row.

As all this was taking place, a voice inside my head said, "Your prayer has been answered." "What prayer?" I thought. As far as I knew, I was totally blank. I hadn't been praying at all. Then it struck me. Back at Peddie, I remembered how disappointed I had been to be living in a world filled with technological wonders but seemingly devoid of people like Jesus. I remember thinking that if I had been given the chance back then, I would have surely followed him and not doubted. What a shame that there was no chance now! But maybe there was after all. Maybe my prayer *had* been answered.

That evening Bapak did the three things he usually did, as I later learned, when he visited Subud centers around the world. He gave a talk. He did some public testing with groups of women and men. And he did *latihan* with the men, while his wife and daughter joined in the women's *latihan*. During the talk he explained the fundamentals of the *latihan* and clarified how, if we practiced it regularly—two or three times a week for a half hour—our souls would eventually be purified and our instruments, the heart and the mind, would become willing to accept the leadership of the soul, itself surrendered to God, rather than doing things of their own devising. As a result, our lives would become harmonious, we would find work that accorded with our true talents, and we would be able to live in a way that conformed to God's will for us. Moreover, when we died, we would be prepared for living in the world of the Great Life Force.

Bapak tested about fifteen minutes each with perhaps three groups of five men and five women. Bapak's tests with us were to check how far our *latihans* had progressed, not to answer questions, as in personal testing. They were also to be illustrative for the other members looking on. He made sure to ask—all his Indonesian words being translated by Mr. Usman—that only those who had not gone to the World Congress should come up for testing. As I recall, I was among the second group of men. He would ask questions like, "Where are your hands?" At that moment, we were not supposed to "do" anything but let our hands, as it were, speak for themselves. In other words, we were supposed to go into a *latihan* state of surrender and give space for our bodies to answer if they were able. My hands went up and displayed themselves to Bapak, whom the five of us, eyes closed, were facing. "Now show what your hands can do," came the next question. Mine started mimicking long-hand writing, then typing. "What else?" Usman asked in English after Bapak's Indonesian. I forget now what else they could do, but there were a few more things. "Can you cry?" All of us started sobbing in various tenor, base, and baritone versions. "What about laughing?" A few of us could laugh from the *latihan*, but not me. There was nothing funny. I simply couldn't laugh. In fact, it took years of spiritual training before I could laugh either in *latihan* or a testing session. "You all can cry," Bapak commented, "but only a few of you can laugh. But don't worry, if you practice your *latihans* diligently, one day you will all be able to laugh, and this laughing from the inner will serve you well. Especially in the face of adversity it is important to be able to laugh, for laughter is something that can penetrate the clouds of emotion that often weigh human beings down and keep them from living satisfying lives." Finally, he asked, "Can you sing?" To a man, all five of us, eyes still closed, sang "hoo" to our own individual note. We sounded like the Mills Brothers at the beginning of one of their songs. Bapak commented that he was not asking if we could make the sound of a ship, but could we sing? The audience laughed. "*Lagi*!" Came his basso command. "Again!" Usman interpreted. This time we each produced some kind of rough melody that seemed to form a collective piece of modern music. "Enough!" Bapak said in English. Then he explained. "Right now your purification has not proceeded far enough for you to be able to sing something beautiful and original from your souls. That will come later. It is important to be able to sing from inside. In olden times, not only could mothers quiet their babies as today, but people in general, who were still closer back then to their true selves, could sing in such a way as to cheer themselves up when they were sad or gain courage when they were afraid. This is truly something that human beings could use again today when the world is so much more complicated and dangerous. So it is important for you never to forget this gift of the *latihan*, which little by little can make something fine out of something coarse. All right. That's enough. Finish now and return to your seats. Thank you."*

The next evening, on the bus back to New Haven, I was still in a special state. My feelings were wide and at rest. As far as my thinking was concerned, it was almost as if my mind had taken a sabbatical. Everything was fine. Everything would get done in due course. There was nothing to think or worry about. I was totally relaxed and content. To be sure, this special state lasted only another day. Once back to graduate life, there was plenty of thinking to do plus the usual patches of worry about whether I would get all my work done well enough and on time. Also, when I did my next *latihan*, alone in my living room, I felt a sense of sadness and even envy for my friends who had had the opportunity to spend not one evening with Bapak but the entire ten days at the Briarcliff Congress. If I had gotten so much from a mere three or four hours, just imagine how much they must have gotten from nearly two weeks! At that moment the quality of light in the room shifted, and although I could not see him, I was aware that Bapak was now with me. "Why are you sad?" He asked. "Don't you know that in the case of your friends, Bapak poured slowly? But in your case, Bapak poured fast. All of you got as much as you were able to receive." Then I began to

---

*The above is an approximation of what Bapak said, both in his talk and to our testing group, based on my memory of something that took place 45 years ago. It should not be construed as an exact rendering of what he actually said.

cry. I was so abashed at my spiritual greed and ignorance. Yet I also felt the love streaming from this man who had made sure all his spiritual children received the full measure of what they needed and could digest from his visit. This was a big lesson for me.*

Simone arrived in New York City with the *S.S. Maasdam*, a Holland-American ship, on October 26, 1963. She had written my parents a careful letter in English—having spent a year in England as an au pair in the early 50s, her English was good—so perhaps because of that letter, perhaps out of curiosity, my parents chose to join me on Pier 86 to meet my fiancée.

Simone was wearing a jaunty brown-and-white-checked riding hat and looked very dashing as she searched for her trunk inside the closed-off customs portion of the pier. My parents were standing behind me as I waved and shouted. I overheard my father say to my mother, "She reminds of Natalie [my older sister], Dear." To which my mother responded huffily, "Jack, how can you say that!" Trying to console her, my father replied, "Well, knowing Stephen, it could have been a *shvartze* [a black woman]!" In time my parents would come to like, respect, and even love Simone, but that transformation would take some years, getting a jump-start when our first child, Marianne Michèle, was born in September 1966.

Our wedding took place in Dwight Chapel on the Old Campus of Yale on November 30, 1963. Our landlady, a retired high-school English teacher named Dorothy Berry, owned two side-by-side houses on Lynwood Place in New Haven. From the old school, she didn't want Simone staying in my apartment—my roommate Phillip had since graduated and was back in Hong Kong—until after the marriage. So Miss Berry kindly invited Simone to sleep in a room in her house next door until the knot had been officially tied. That would be her wedding present to us.

During Simone's first week in America, we visited several rabbis and Protestant ministers to arrange for the service. The rabbis would not agree to marry us without Simone's promise to convert, something she felt she could not do. Fortunately, Pastor Richard Olson, the

---

*Bapak followed the older practice among Javanese of using his relational title, *Bapak*, literally "father," in lieu of "I." A servant I knew in Jakarta, Ibu Rus, likewise from Central Java, also spoke in the third person. "Ibu Rus just make brownie. Would Pak Reynold like to eat one?" (Translated from Indonesian).

Lutheran Campus Chaplain, was not only willing to officiate but promised to take out as many references to Jesus as he legitimately could in the event that my parents showed up, which to their credit they did. He also added a reading from the Book of Ruth, which demonstrated how human relations could flourish across religious differences when Ruth, a Gentile Moabite, famously decided to stay with her Jewish mother-in-law, Naomi, after Ruth's husband had died. Everyone remembers the famous lines, "Whither thou goest, I will go, etc."

Since we didn't have much money even with the few monetary wedding gifts we received, it was a pretty bare-bones ceremony. The chapel, to be sure, was a beautiful Yale building which we got to use for free, and gold rings back then, even engraved with our initials, cost a mere $25 each. If memory serves, I believe that is how much we gave the pastor for his services too. My and later our Asian Indian painter friend, Tutu, served as a kind of major-domo; our Subud sister the late Baroness Irina von Tucher of New Rochelle was the maid of honor; Tutu's friend Carolyn Huggins played the organ; little Afumi Mizuno, the Japanese Subud ophthalmologist's daughter, was the flower girl; my Subud brother Wallace Klein was my best man; and the Subud jokester from Hamburg, the venerable Francis [Franz] von Kahler, gave away the bride.

Francis, a half-Jewish Austrian baron who grew up in Hamburg, where his father was the long-time commercial consul from Vienna, was without doubt one of the funniest human beings I have ever met. Brother of the famous Princeton political scientist Erich Kahler, Francis was a successful insurance broker who had the time and money to run around with the fast crowd in New York City. Salvador Dali was apparently one of his buddies. Francis was among the first cohort of Subud members when the New York group started in 1959, having come to New York in the 30's to escape the Nuremburg Laws under which he would have been considered Jewish. He liked to tell how honored he felt when he would listen to President Roosevelt's fireside chats on the radio. "Vhy, the President vould alvays greet me personally vhen he begahn: 'Dear Franz [Friends]!'" Francis did have some trouble at first eating in America. "My English vas not zo goot like now. So vhen I vent to the café, the man vould ahsk, 'Hamburger?' Belief me, I vas delighted he knew vhere I vahs from. So I alvays said 'Ja!' As a result, I ate nothing but beef patties for my first month in the United States!"

You can imagine that this sort of deadpan humor found its way into our wedding ceremony too. At the reception in the very room where the Jewish students at Yale had their Sabbath services and *oneg Shabat* [post-service refreshments] and where Reb Zalman Schachter-Shalomi had once had us sophisticated Yalies dancing in the aisles, Francis, appropriately dressed in a black suit with a gray vest, read the telegrams and cards of well-wishers out loud to the 50 or so people on hand. He added his commentary whenever he saw an opening for a wisecrack. But best of all, after reading and translating all the German cards into English, he mechanically began translating the English ones into German. Before he left, Professor Sewall came up to me and asked, "Where did you hire that guy? He's terrific!"

A few months later, during a trip to Germany, Francis took it upon himself to visit my new in-laws and report on the wedding ceremony. They were most interested in hearing about their new son-in-law, "Shteef," whom they had never met. "*Ach*!" Francis, a bachelor, told them in German, "Giving that beautiful daughter of yours away to that young whippersnapper was one of the biggest mistakes of my life [dramatic pause, while my in-laws frowned with concern]. I should have kept her for myself!"

To round out this portrait of my rotund friend and mentor, I can't resist sharing three Subud stories. One took place in maybe 1965 at Subud House in New York City. An isolated male member in Connecticut called one Sunday afternoon just after *latihan*. He was in a panic. Whoever picked up the phone requested a male helper to handle the call. Francis, who was closest, took the receiver: "Von Kahler!" He said in the European fashion. The next thing we heard is, "You did vaht?! . . . But my good man, daht iz very zerious!" As we heard the story later, the man, who had been latihaning on his own, suddenly became aware that he was doing his spiritual exercises in the same room where he had a pet turtle living in an aquarium. Bapak had said at one point that it was better for both us and the animals not to do *latihan* in the same room with our pets. He was referring to larger pets like dogs and cats. Anyway, the man was freaking out on the phone. As usual, Francis came up with just the right thing: "Tell me, my good man, vahs it a male or a female turtle?" (As you'll remember, the Subud exercise is done by men and women separately.) Those of us listening practically exploded with laughter.

Then in summer, 1967, at the World Subud Congress in Tokyo, Francis was being tested by Bapak in front of the plenary session to see if he had the capacity for serving as the treasurer of the newly established international Subud organization. Although I didn't witness this event myself, the story spread rapidly around the Subud world, including Honolulu, where Simone, Marianne, and I had just moved. Apparently, Francis's gyrations in response to the question were so vigorous that his pants fell down, leaving him standing there with his belly out and his boxer shorts on. Two thousand delegates, including Bapak on the dais, laughed until they cried. When he finally contained himself, Bapak suggested that the first thing Francis should do after the session was go out and buy a pair of suspenders. The best Francis story, however, came from the Subud World Congress in Jakarta in 1971. My friend had wanted to get an additional three months on his visa so he could spend more time with Bapak in Wisma Subud, his compound in Indonesia. After asking around, he was sent to a certain building, where visa matters were being handled. Once there, he lined up with a bunch of others, all of whom seemed to be young men. Francis, in his 70s at the time, didn't know that these men, impressed by the Islam they had witnessed in Indonesia, had decided to become Muslims and had come for the obligatory *sunat*, or circumcision. The person just ahead of Francis, who was of course well-known in the Association, turned to him and said, "Francis, this is incredible—I can't believe you are going to be circumcised at your age." "Vaht do you mean, circumcised?" Francis replied, not missing a beat. "I have come for an *extension*!"

Actually, given the tension with my parents, it was just right to have Francis there. He helped keep things light. After the service, my father invited 14 of us, effectively the bridal party, to dinner at a Hungarian restaurant in town. Against all odds, Simone and I were now married and managed to stay that way for the next 43 years, until Simone's death from pancreatic cancer in September 2006.

Before ending this chapter, I want to share several early Subud experiences that happened outside of *latihan*. According to William James in his *Varieties of Religious Experience*, many of the most interesting mystical happenings don't occur during "official" religious experiences but between one such experience and another—i.e., when the individual is not expecting anything. Actually, after the dramatic occurrences of my opening, I was expecting each subsequent *latihan* to be just as exciting. Consequently, as it seemed in retrospect, during the next several months of *latihan*, nothing appeared to happen. I just stood there or walked around a little. But two interesting things did occur outside *latihan*.

Once I was spending time with a fellow new Subud member named Trudy. She was petite, a dancer, and a few years older than me. (At the time I was 21.) One evening I fell asleep in her apartment, where I had been hanging out with her. During my sleep I had a vivid dream in which I was the telephone operator at an old-fashioned switchboard, the kind where one had to plug wires in and take them out. I noticed that many were crossed so that I could no longer see which belonged to which calls. Just as I was about to give up in frustration, someone from behind me took my right hand and gently assisted me in pulling out wire after wire and re-plugging each one so that soon all the wires were neatly lined up. In the dream I realized that the switchboard represented my heart and mind where a number of wires had been crossed. Thanks to the *latihan* and the guidance it contained, I (my soul) would be able, little by little, to straighten the rest of me out. After that dream and from that day forward for the next 30 months, I refrained from all physical relations with women— not that I had had that many—until my marriage.

The other experience a few months later occurred on a drive from Chicago to Benton Harbor, Michigan. I was sitting in the front passenger seat. For some reason I had been trying to get something out of the ashtray when my right index finger got caught between the rim of the ashtray and the little metal protuberance where a smoker could tamp out a cigarette. Because of how the mechanism was built, my finger got really stuck. Suddenly I began to panic. Then the Voice began to instruct me: First do this; now do that; now make this other movement. Just one more slow turn to the right, and now your finger will be free. And that's exactly what happened. Bapak states very clearly that we should never look for special experiences. We should live normally and try to do everything in an ordinary, rational way. Still, he assured us that God and his angels were always near and that by doing the *latihan* diligently, we would be guided by agencies higher and more enlightened than ourselves. As a relatively new Subud member, I was blessed to experience some of this help early on.

7
Queens College and Subud New York

SIMONE AND I moved from New Haven to Flushing, New York, in summer 1965. We had been married 20 months. I had completed the coursework, foreign-language test, and oral comprehensive exam for my Ph.D. and was about two-thirds the way through drafting my doctoral dissertation. Rather than staying in New Haven for another year, I had found a full-time job as lecturer in English at Queens College, the City University of New York. My plan was to start teaching while completing my dissertation.

My supervisor at Queens, Professor Sears Jayne, turned out to be a wonderful human being—a mentor more than a boss. He was also an excellent lecturer. I was assigned to him as a section man for his Introduction to Fiction course. Dr. Jayne would address the whole class once a week, while several other lecturers in English and I—low people on the academic totem pole—would meet twice a week with two groups of 20 students to review and discuss the texts. Also, we would assign and grade the students' periodic essays as well as their mid-term and final exams. Besides these sections, I started out teaching two classes of freshman composition as beginning college English instructors have done since time immemorial.

I remember my very first class at Queens. I got to the room 20 minutes early. Fortunately, no course had met there before ours, so I had plenty of time to write my name, the class, the forthcoming assignments, and an outline of the day's activities on the blackboard. One of the students had arrived early too. When he saw me put my briefcase down on the teacher's desk—bear in mind I was 25 at the time, a mere four or five years older than the student—he glanced up at me and with the typical self-assurance of a New Yorker, said, "Hey, kid! I wouldn't sit there if I was you. The teacher wouldn't like it!" "But I'm the teacher," I stammered. "Oh yeah," came the response. "What's your name?" "Feldman," I said, "Stephen Feldman." The student carefully studied the catalogue and then, looking back at me, still skeptical, said, "Let me see your draft card, kid!"

I tell this story because, a few years later, now an assistant professor of English at the University of Hawai'i in Honolulu, I was teaching a graduate seminar on Mark Twain. I don't know if it was the subject matter or the recent strengthening of my wise-guy tendencies from two years in New York City or both, but I was suddenly moved to present a total fabrication to the class: "I'm really happy to be teaching you folks here in Honolulu," I said, "because, well, my mother is Chinese." After class three local students, Hawaiian-born non-Caucasians, came up and asked in their pidgin-tinged accents, "Gee whiz, Dr. Feldman, that's so interesting that your mama is Chinese. What was her maiden name?" The point being that it was always a challenge to get New York students to believe anything, while local students in Hawai'i had so much respect for authority they would accept everything. You had to be really careful.

I don't remember much about those two years at Queens except that at first I tended to over-prepare and have way more material on hand than I could cover in class. Still, by the end of the first term, I decided I liked college teaching, and in general the students seemed to like me based on the anonymous evaluations I got back. In the second semester, moreover, Dr. Jayne was kind enough to lend me his teaching assistant, a graduate student in English, so that I didn't have to correct all the student papers and exams myself. It was his way of helping me have more time to complete my doctoral dissertation, which thanks in part to his generosity I was able to do by Independence Day 1966, just a year after our move and 42 years from the day I am writing these words.

Although we went to the New York Subud Center only once a week for a few hours, our limited time there made a greater impression on me than my work or colleagues at Queens College. For one thing, the people in the group were more memorable. To be honest, they were a rare collection of characters. You've already heard about Francis von Kahler. But he was not the only one. There was Armand Gono, the Central European florist who looked like a professional wrestler—he could without question have stumped the panel on "What's My Line?" to Richard Stecko, the intense window washer from the Ukraine who worked high up on New York City skyscrapers; Reynold Osborn, the 30s actor who later reminded me that he had received his new name from Bapak a full five years before me; Julia Schusterman, who could easily have played Maude on TV's "The Golden Girls"; Virginia Bonner, a proper New England lady from Boston; Raymond and Sonya Owens, University of Wisconsin-trained radio and TV actors and cartoon voices who were the first pious Catholics I had met in Subud; Ed Kerner, a UN official from Sri Lanka, and his wife Alfatah; a postal worker and child survivor of the Holocaust named Walter Siegel; and last not least Ferensz "Fery" Francois Farkas, a Hungarian cinematographer, and Lucienne, his Turkish wife, raised in Cairo, who almost always spoke French with her husband.

One time the debonair Fery was the helper on duty at a special *latihan* for some of us young members who received strongly—i.e., moved around a lot and made loud noises in our free-form spiritual exercises. We were called the O Group, a term imported from Subud England with the "O" standing for "Overactive." Of course in Subud one is supposed to "do" whatever comes during a *latihan*, be it loud or soft, physically active or more reserved. Still, some of the older or quieter members were disturbed by the more shall we say *dynamic latihans* of us younger members, so this special session was set up periodically so we could do our thing without bothering others.

It was a stifling summer day in Manhattan. Our loft building with no AC had only a few large floor fans. So there was Fery Farkas, dressed in his trademark long-sleeved white shirt, impeccably pressed, with French cuffs held closed by gold cufflinks and a pair of neatly creased gray Dak slacks held up by suspenders. He never seemed to break a sweat despite the heat and his mode of dress. Anyway, when he said "Finish!," the *latihan* ended with a mass of exhausted men strewn around the floor. Fery deftly picked his way across the bodies, opened the door, turned back to us, and in his rich Hungarian-accented English said, "Gentlemen, it vahs a pleajour!" Then he closed the door and made his exit.

There was also a famous color photo of Bapak from 1959 or 1960 which Fery had taken. As the story goes, he had asked our Spiritual Guide to pose by saying, "Bapak, please think of God!" It turned out to be a wonderful picture.

Fery's wife, Lucienne, was an original in her own right. One of the first lady helpers appointed by Bapak in New York, she made sure the new helpers were up to snuff. Simone had been appointed a helper by Bapak in Munich before immigrating to the States, and the Subud practice is, once a helper anywhere, the individual is a helper everywhere. So, on our move to the New York area, she immediately became a member of the ladies' helpers group. True to form, Lucienne kept an eye on her. One Sunday after *latihan*, Lucienne raced up to Simone and me. She was obviously excited. "Do you know Turkish, my dear?" She asked Simone, who answered in the negative. "But then you have just had a Subud experience, for you were saying '*Bahallu!*' in your *latihan*. In Turkish that means 'servant of God.'" From then on, Simone was okay in Lucienne's book. A German woman who could receive in Turkish was obviously well prepared, from Lucienne's standpoint, to serve in the New York ladies' helpers group.

In spring 1967, Bapak paid his first visit to New York since the 1963 World Congress. The latter was the time, you'll recall, when—after the Congress proper, at the New York Subud House—four other men and I responded by hooting like a boat in response to his test question "Can you sing?" Anyway, this time the group asked me to coordinate the visit, so Simone and I were often at the East Side apartment the Group had rented for Bapak, his wife Ibu, and their party. One day Lucienne, who had not signed up for any particular task but who had known Bapak and Ibu from previous visits, swept into the apartment and with a dramatic gesture stated, "I am *en charge* of the soaps and the *parfums*!" And with that, holding a bag from an expensive store in clear sight above her head, she entered Bapak and Ibu's living room. That was Subud New York.

Prior to Marianne's birth on September 1, 1966, Simone and I had written to Bapak for possible Subud names for our baby. Incidentally, we had also asked what religion the child should be raised in and added this P.S.: "Neither Stephen nor Hannelore has felt moved to change their name. However, if Bapak considers it appropriate, what names would he give Stephen and Hannelore?"

Let me now explain a little about the practice of changing names in Subud. According to Bapak, names are very important for the proper development of human beings. Ideally, each person should have a name that encourages the growth of their true talents and selfhood. An incorrectly chosen name could have negative consequences for the individual. You may remember from the first chapter that when Bapak was born in 1901, his parents had called him *Soekarno*. As the story goes, the child was so sickly, the family feared for its life. Then one day a wandering holy man, an Arab not a Malay Indonesian, passed through their village. Somehow he ended up at Bapak's parents' house where he told them that unless they changed the baby's name, it would surely die. Then he suggested its proper name was *Muhammad Subuh*, the second element being Indonesian for the first of the five daily prayers in Islam. After the man left, the parents took his advice, and little Subuh immediately started gaining weight and growing strong.

Simone and I, like the Pharisee in the Biblical tale, were proud that we were not like the others—the Subud members who, the day after their opening and sometimes even during their three-month waiting period before getting opened, would write to Bapak in Jakarta for their correct name. We had held off for a full five years. Still, we added our P.S. just in case. Some weeks later the answer came back: "Dear Stephen and Hannelore, Bapak has read your request and says that the child to be born, if a boy, should be named Leonard and if a girl, Marianne. As to religion, Bapak would like to explain that Subud and religion are not the same. While Subud is a direct receiving from God, religion is a matter of personal belief and depends also on one's family. Therefore Bapak leaves it up to you to decide which religion your child should be raised in. Sincerely yours for the Secretariat, Sudarto Martohudojo. P.S. Bapak says that if Stephen and Hannelore would like to change their names, then they should each send a list of ten names starting with R for Stephen and S for Hannelore so that Bapak can select names for them."

The same day we received that letter, we starting looking around for ten new first names we could live with. I listed Richard, Robert, Raymond, Russell, Reginald, Reynold, and a few others. From some experienced members I had heard that if one asked, Bapak would also tell what the name he received for us meant. To make things go faster—patience wasn't yet a very active virtue for me—I drafted my letter in Indonesian and got it off in the next few days. My feeling was that if I wrote Bapak in Indonesian, which I had begun learning in graduate school, it would not get slowed down in the Secretariat in Jakarta by having to wait for translation.

Anyway, about three weeks later I had a vivid dream early one morning, just before awaking. In the dream I was walking along an urban street when a public telephone in a nearby phone booth rang. As in the then-popular TV show and later movie series *Mission Impossible*, I entered the booth and picked up the receiver. A radio-quality baritone voice (the Voice) asked me in authoritative-sounding American English how I liked the name *Reynold*. My response was, "It's okay, I guess." Then I awoke, and, as was our practice, I told Simone my experience so that way, if the dream came true, there would be a witness. Sure enough, that afternoon around three I received a call in my office from Simone. "Guess what! A letter came today from Indonesia." "Did Bapak give me the name Reynold?" I asked. "Yes," she said. "And for you it means 'one whose feelings are firm.'"

Over time I came to discover that these Subud names serve several functions. First, they are like the ball in American football that the quarterback throws downfield, not to where the intended receiver is at the time the ball is released, but where he is supposed to be by the time it gets there. So our Subud names are intended to be out in front of us, pointing us in the direction we are supposed to go. In my case, my feelings were sometimes weak and vacillating, but clearly Bapak felt I should develop more firmness of character, with corresponding feelings. Secondly, Subud names could be prayers for us to become the persons God had meant us to be. So, every time these names were said, they would in effect be a personal mantra or prayer to help us in our spiritual development.

Another experience confirmed this last point for me. In 1987, when I was dean of Program Development at Northeastern Illinois University, Chicago, a new president came to the institution who was old-school in the sense of not really favoring the sort of innovative programs my area fostered and in some cases managed. So out of a sense of self-protection I did the common thing in academia and started looking for a new job. By September I was one of three finalists for the position of vice president for academic affairs at Metropolitan State University in Minneapolis-Saint Paul, Minnesota. Each of us finalists had been required as part of the three-day interview process to give a public lecture on two recent books on higher education. I knew the books, agreed with much of what they said, and had fun preparing my talk.

On day one of the interviews, I was waiting in the then Hilton Hotel in Saint Paul for 2:45 p.m., the time when I would be met in the lobby by the University's Human Resources director, who would take me to the lecture venue. As I was standing in my hotel room and getting quiet, Bapak and my father, both dead at that point, appeared at the far end near the window. The former spoke through me in Indonesian. He said, "You will get this job because I need you to be my helper in this group. Of course, you have to support yourself and your family. Consequently you will get this job so you can move to this place and work here for Subud. During your interview including this lecture, don't say anything from yourself. We will take care of everything." He must have noticed my puzzlement about my father, who didn't say anything during the entire encounter, since Bapak continued, "Your father is here since he is on your committee and is in charge of your worldly life." Then both disappeared, and, looking at my watch, I saw that it was time to go downstairs and meet Jan Anderson, the Human Resources director.

The two of us had a nice chat as we walked the five skyways to Metropolitan State University's facilities. (Skyways, I should mention, are inter-building indoor pedestrian bridges, one story above the street, that are signature features of both Minneapolis and Saint Paul. They can be mighty handy during Minnesota's long, cold winters. At present each city has between 40 and 50.) Anyway, when we arrived in front of the lecture hall where I would be speaking, I heard someone calling "Reynold! Reynold!" Now I was convinced that except for a few of the Twin Cities' Subud members, I didn't know a soul there, certainly not anyone who would be attending my lecture. At this point, a handsome middle-aged man who looked like Robert Redford came up and extended his hand. "Remember me? I'm Tom Jones, a History professor here at Metro State. You and I were both at the Shakertown Conversation on General Education some years ago in Kentucky." "Oh, yes," I stammered, a bit embarrassed because I hadn't actually remembered him. Then he took me aside, gave me his card with his home number written on it, and said, "You're my candidate. I'm on sabbatical this term, but I made a point of coming to your lecture to support you. Call me at home tonight, and I'll give you the lowdown on the University and the state of the search."

Then Jan Anderson, my hostess, ushered me into the lecture hall. What happened next was one of those amazing experiences with which I have occasionally been blessed. As I said, I had prepared a solid enough presentation. However, after I got up to the front and was introduced, I was unable to do more than place my notes on the podium. I simply could not look at them. Instead, "I" just started talking. The interesting thing was that although my voice was producing words and my mouth was speaking them, the normal me had nothing to do with their creation. I was listening to them myself as they came out and watching as the audience made notes, smiled and laughed. It was without question the best lecture I have ever given, before or since—sound, interesting, and funny. Unfortunately for my ego, I couldn't take any credit for it. The Committee upstairs was in charge, playing Edgar Bergen to my Charlie McCarthy. The next two days of interviews followed in kind. I was astounded by some of the things I was able to say or ask. For instance, when I had my interview with the president, who had been at the school ten years, I wondered if she intended to stay there much longer. She was taken aback. In fact, six months later she would announce her intention to resign.

The point I want to emphasize, though, is that when Tom Jones, the history professor, called my name and I was so sure I knew no one there, I felt it as a confirmation of everything Bapak had just said. In one sense, then, when the lecture took place, I wasn't so surprised at what occurred. After all, it seemed to flow from the original experience with Bapak and my father back in the hotel room and was part of the same unusual sequence of events.

To get back to Bapak's letter in the summer of 1966, a month or so before Marianne was born, we were at first disappointed, not with the names he gave but with his response to our request about a religion for the child. The names, *Leonard* and *Marianne*, were actually fine, because they existed in English and German and were spelled the same way in both. Only the pronunciation differed. As for the child's religion, another young couple in Subud New York had just had a baby. They too had asked Bapak about what religion to raise it in. Like us, one of them was Protestant (the husband) while the other was Jewish. In their case, however, Bapak had said that the baby should be raised Protestant. No fair! We thought. He had told them but not us.

The very next Sunday when we arrived at Subud House, the first person we ran into was Francis von Kahler. When he saw us, he acted embarrassed, the last thing you would expect from him. "Vel, you zee, I haf brought you a gift from za Holy Land," he said. But if you do not vant it, just trow it avay!" At this juncture he produced a vial of what looked like water. The simple black-and-white label said in Hebrew, English, Arabic, and French that this was water from the place in the Jordan River traditionally considered the site of Jesus' baptism by John. Simone and I looked at each other. Later, we described having had the same experience of feeling our chests widen while understanding that this was Bapak's *other* answer: The child to be born would be baptized a Christian.

Fast-forwarding to spring 1967 and Bapak's visit to New York, I remember that Simone and I joined some 500 other people at Kennedy Airport to greet him and his party on arrival. Through Ed Kerner's connections as a UN diplomat, he, his wife, and I (as the head of the local committee) were able to meet the party just after Immigration and help them through Customs. After, I walked ten feet behind Bapak as we proceeded down the long corridor to the exit. Above on either side behind glass partitions, Subud members waved and smiled. I felt as if I were following in the wake of a great ship. I also felt as if I were enclosed in a kind of glass bubble, protected from all worries and concerns. I had never experienced such a feeling of absolute freedom and detachment since my opening, when I had gotten an inkling of how blissful it would be to be dead.

During the weekend Simone and I were able to bring Marianne, then nine months old, to Bapak and Ibu's apartment. Tuti, Ibu's 21-year-old granddaughter whom Bapak had adopted and invited along on this trip to assist him and Ibu, took Marianne from us and disappeared with her into Bapak and Ibu's sitting room. Apparently all the Indonesians, including Bapak, took turns holding and playing with the baby. Later Tuti explained that it was much easier for them to be with children, especially Subud children, than adults, since children didn't think so much and never placed demands on Bapak and party.

I had one other noteworthy experience during that visit. I was doing men's *latihan* with Bapak at the church we had rented for that purpose on Central Park West. My eyes were closed as is normal during *latihan* to keep other exercisers from feeling they are being watched. Every once in a while I felt forced down from standing into the Muslim prayer position on the carpet. Then my eyes opened by themselves, and there, close to my face, I saw Bapak's brightly polished brown alligator shoes. This happened not once but three or four times. Although Bapak claimed consistently that he was just an ordinary man whom God had chosen to disseminate the Subud spiritual exercise, my own experience led me to a different conclusion. For if he were ordinary, then, as Varindra Vittachi, our long-time international Subud chair, used to say, he was the most extraordinary ordinary person imaginable.

I'd like to report one final thing from that visit. Unlike me, Simone had been patient about asking for her Subud name. By the time she was ready to write, the news came that Bapak was planning to visit New York on the trip I have been writing about. So she sensibly decided to wait until he arrived to ask for her name. In her case, of all the ten "S" names on the list, the two she liked best were *Sonya* and *Simone*. Just before the party was to leave for its next destination, Tuti came out of Bapak's room with our original sheet of paper. The name circled was *Simone*. Actually, I had always thought of my wife as a kind of Rococo lady from the French court, a companion to Marie Antoinette perhaps. She would even dress up in this style for costume parties and always looked like a million dollars. So she was delighted with the name as was I. We hadn't thought this time to ask Bapak for a meaning; however, Simone didn't mind. She didn't seem to need or want anything besides the name, not even a meaning. She was completely satisfied.

8
University of Hawai'i and Subud Honolulu

IN AUGUST 1967 Simone, Marianne, and I left Flushing for my new job as assistant professor of English at the University of Hawai'i. Despite all the research we had done, we were not prepared for the sights, sounds, and smells of Honolulu. Airports are generally built in industrial neighborhoods, and Honolulu's was no exception. Still, on leaving the plane, we all received fragrant plumeria flower garlands (*leis*) and the first of many friendly smiles that would continue to characterize Hawai'i during all our years living there. Apparently, the Aloha Spirit—the spirit of love—was more than tourist hype. Then, there was the air, like velvet stroking your skin. And in those days, with the Dole cannery only a few miles from the Airport, the redolence of pineapple greeted you on arrival. And oh, if you looked inland, there were the emerald hills and mountains ascending dramatically to 3,000+ feet. Then, looking toward the sea, you saw Diamond Head, Waikiki's famous landmark, giving way to the endless blue Pacific. It was an experience a person would not quickly forget, especially the first time.

The students at the University were attentive, hard-working, and, like everyone else in the Islands, smiling. Unlike New Yorkers, though, they were harder to engage in class discussion. The old Japanese proverb was often cited in the faculty lounge: The nail that sticks out gets hammered in. No one wanted to lose face by saying something dumb. This situation led to what could be called "the first mid-term phenomenon." You'd be grading your first set of mid-term exams and get outstanding papers from students whose names you had not yet memorized nor connected with faces. When you handed the graded exam books back, *you* would be smiling this time as you congratulated some heretofore silent students on their excellent work. Indeed, a main topic of discussion among *haole* or "white" faculty—still most of us at that time—was, "How do you get them to talk in class?" I had a few of my own ideas, so I tried with some success to put them into four-person discussion groups. They seemed much more comfortable talking with one another. Once the pump was primed, most class members seemed more willing to speak up in front of the other 25 – 40.

Before leaving the Mainland for our new assignment in the Fiftieth State, I checked with the national Subud office for other Subud members in Honolulu. It turned out there was only one—a Chinese-Hawaiian-Portuguese man, a Korean War veteran named Donald (later Langfred, then David) Vierra. While recuperating from a procedure at the Veterans Hospital in Los Angeles, he had happened upon one of the early books about Subud, John Bennett's *Concerning Subud*. On return to Honolulu, he wrote Mr. Bennett in England, who answered that there was currently no Subud group in Hawai'i and that the next closest was a large one in L.A. Fortunately, Donald had a brother living there, so the former hopped a plane and was opened in Los Angeles perhaps a month before Simone and I arrived in Honolulu.

When we met him, he was our first real Hawaiian, although as we soon learned, pure-blooded Hawaiians formed less than 1% of the population. "Our ancestors were too friendly back then," Donald told us, "so now almost all of us are *part*-Hawaiian." I still have a photo from our first Christmas party with Donald holding up a pack of Kool cigarettes. With his gentle Island voice, Pidgin accent, and easy-going manner, he was one of the coolest people I had ever met. Later, when he became my driving teacher and risked life, limb, and his classic '57 Chevy instructing me, he would say something like, "Hey Reyno—he could never say *Reynold*—maybe you better stay right. That big truck is heading right for us." If the roles had been reversed, I would have grabbed the wheel.

Before long, other Subud members started moving to Hawai'i, mostly to our island. (Oahu, though only third largest of the major Hawaiian Islands, is the most crowded, with 850,000 of the State's current 1.3 million inhabitants. It is also the governmental and business center, with Honolulu the capital.) Among them were Dr. Pieter and Lynn van Royen. Pieter, a Dutch botanist who had recently completed the research for a two-volume study of the flora of New Guinea, had landed the job of chief botanist at Honolulu's renowned Bishop Museum. He and his British wife Lynn, now both deceased, had been members of Mr. Bennett's Gurdjieff group in Coombe Springs, Kingston-on-Thames, England, for ten years before Subud had arrived there in 1957. They had been among the first people opened and were thus, by the time they came to Honolulu, in Subud for ten years, a long time by American standards, where the oldest members had been in eight years and Simone and me a mere six. A Catholic family, they had brought their seven small children with them, with an eighth on the way. Moreover, like Simone, both Pieter and Lynn were helpers, authorized by Bapak to give explanations about Subud to interested people and to open new members.

Two more helpers soon arrived as well: Rayner (now Rozak) von Hohenstein from Chicago, one of the helpers who had opened me (He was Lee then.), and Lola Stone, a Barbara Walters look-a-like and sound-alike from the Huntington, Long Island group. Leonard Keigher came from Chicago with Rayner, and there was also a young hippie couple, Parker and Leonore Mead from L.A. and their daughter, Royce, who must have been eight. Then two young men from the Columbus, Ohio group showed up: Robert Jones and Hamilton Manley. In addition to all these, three or four people were soon opened, including Donald Vierra's mother, Grandma Rose (later Rosalind) Vierra, and his wife Phyllis (later Melissa). So, despite the influx of *haoles* from East and West, there was at least an Island flavor to our rapidly growing group. To top it all off, by the end of 1967, the Baron Ludwig von Royk-Lewinski and his wife, the Baroness Michèle, the Munich helper who had opened Simone, arrived on the Big Island to develop a new sub-division near Hilo called Eden Roc Estates. A number of Subud members had bought one or more one-acre plots there. Simone and I invested in two acres ourselves, which we paid off over several years. So, within eight months of our move to Hawai'i, our new group hosted Bapak's first visit to the Islands. In fact, he, Ibu, and party would end up staying in our three-bedroom apartment in the Kaimuki District of Honolulu.

☼

To be precise, Bapak and his traveling group stopped twice in Hawai'i in 1968—first at the Honolulu airport for three or four hours on April First on their way from Indonesia and then for three or four days on Mother's Day weekend that year on their way home. It was during the second, longer stop that we cleared out of our apartment, fixed it up with the help of the group, and stayed with the Vierras so that Bapak and party could have free run of the place during their visit.

Even the brief rest-stop in the airport's VIP Lounge proved memorable. All our members, including the kids, crowded into the room to be close to their spiritual guide and his Indonesian helpers. Both our new local members wanted to get Subud names, so I asked Muhammad Usman, Bapak's interpreter, if Bapak could take care of the matter on the spot. I asked loudly enough in Indonesian that Bapak overheard and said "*Boleh!*" "Certainly!" So I showed him the two women, explained they were our two newest members and stated they brought up our local non-white contingency to three. Then I handed Bapak the two lists of ten names the ladies had selected for themselves.

At this point, the activities of the horde of little kids, the van Royens' seven plus our Marianne, made the lounge seem like a perpetual-motion machine. Bapak and the Indonesians, far from being annoyed, seemed to take pleasure in this young, innocent life. But when Bapak got quiet and received for a few moments about Grandma Rose's name, an invisible force seemed to pervade the space, and even the kids stopped what they were doing and made no noise. The effect was so dramatic that I was reminded of the classic sci-fi film *The Day the Earth Stood Still.* For no one had shushed the children or anyone else. "*Nomor tujuh,*" "Number seven", Bapak said. With that, Rose's name became Rosalind. The kids and all the rest of us, freed for the moment, went back to what we had been doing before. Then Bapak received again, this time for Donald's wife, Phyllis. Again the same thing happened. Total stillness—no movement and no noise, not even from the little kids. It was incredible. "*Nomor empat,*" "Number four", Bapak announced in his rich bass. So Phyllis became Melissa. I thanked Bapak, and as before, the adults went back to visiting while the kids resumed their play.

It may strike you as you read the above paragraph that the name *Rosalind* is not so different from *Rose*. You may even ask yourself whether Bapak ever told people that their names were already right for them. In fact, he did. I remember one occasion. It concerned the erstwhile taxi driver, Raymond, from whom I had learned about Subud back in Chicago in 1961. His mother, Renee, a strongly built German beautician who lived to be nearly 100, proudly told me one day that when her son had asked Bapak for a Subud name, the latter responded that he had the right name already. "So I told my husband, 'You see, Willy, remember how I dreamed when I was pregnant that our child would be a boy and we should call it *Raimund* [German for *Raymond*]. And now Bapak has confirmed it!'"

As soon as Bapak moved into our apartment seven weeks later, it was transformed. Although six people versus Simone, little Marianne, and I were staying there—Bapak in the master bedroom, Ibu in the second bedroom off the kitchen, Muhammad and Aminah Usman— the party's interpreter and cook, respectively—in the third bedroom, and two lady helpers from New York City (Laura Labby and Paula Mason), who assisted as needed, on mattresses in the livingroom, the apartment somehow felt bigger. Also, the atmosphere when we visited it was deeply quiet, like in a cathedral or deep in a virgin forest.

When he was not on duty, Bapak liked to watch TV. It was just mindless enough to be relaxing for him. The second day of the visit, Simone and I showed up with Marianne, then 1½, to see if the party needed anything. As we were talking with Aminah, Marianne slipped past the temporary curtain we had hung in the little corridor between the living room and the kitchen. As Simone was about to run after her to keep her from disturbing Bapak, who was watching TV, Aminah told her not to worry. Bapak would be happy to visit with her. When Simone peaked in, Marianne was carefully lifting the glass lid to a little bowl of macadamia nuts. Bapak pretended not to see. Then, he suddenly pointed at her and gave her his big Bapak grin as if to say, "Gotcha!" Marianne burst out laughing. Then, when Simone peaked again a few minutes later, Marianne, standing in front of the TV set, said, "Bakak, look!" (It took her a few years until she could say "Bapak.") Then she began to do a pretty impressive hula for an 18-month-old toddler. "Pappa," Simone said to me afterwards, "I think our daughter was doing *latihan* for Bapak." Who knows? I thought. Maybe she had been opened during the months Simone was doing *latihan* while pregnant with her.

Another story I remember from this period has to do with the Baron and the Baroness, who by this time had just started living on the Eden Roc land along with the Meads from California. Now there was an odd pairing if ever there was one: older European bluebloods together with young American hippies! Michèle, the Baroness, had flown to Honolulu to attend to Ibu's needs. They had known each other for nearly ten years, since Michèle had been Ibu's companion during the former's first trip to Germany. The Baroness, a descendant of one of the former Governors-General of the then Netherlands East Indies, could even speak Dutch with Ibu, who was old enough to remember the language from the colonial days in Nederlands Ostindie.

The plan was that Michèle would fly back with Bapak and Usman to help her husband, the Baron, present several acres of Eden Roc land—four, I believe—to Bapak. She would prepare a light lunch while Ludwig was taking Bapak and his traveling companions to see the land and have tea in a little gazebo he had constructed in the midst of his property. But as so often in Subud, something else happened instead. As Bapak's granddaughter Tuti liked to say, if you want to make the Almighty laugh, tell God your plans. In the event, Ibu decided that she wanted Michèle to stay with her. The airlines were not so particular in the late-60s, and it was possible to fly on someone else's ticket. So in her broken English, Ibu told Simone, "You go with Bapak to see land and help Ludwig. Michèle stay with Ibu. Simone can be baroness for one day!"

The traveling party included Bapak, Usman, Varindra Vittachi (about whom more in a moment), Sharif Harris from San Diego, another Subud Reynold called Reynold Weissinger from the Bay Area, Simone, and me. We got to the airport in time for the brief early-morning flight. It was canceled, however, so Bapak invited us all to be his guests at the airport restaurant for breakfast. Since I knew that Bapak always traveled with his own cook in order to have the Indonesian food he was familiar with, I wondered what he would eat. Once he took his place at the head of a long table, he ordered a typical American breakfast and, as I recall, cleaned his plate. The whole thing seemed to be a big adventure for him, and as he sat there with this selection of his international children around him, the big smile on his face showed that he was enjoying the outing.

When we got to the land, about a half hour's drive from Lyman Field, Hilo's still pretty primitive airport, Simone told Bapak through Usman that one of the reasons she liked Hawai'i so much was that, tropical paradise though it was, there were no snakes. Using his hands, Bapak demonstrated the circumference of one of Indonesia's infamous pythons (*ular sawah*). Then he went on to say that Indonesia had hundreds of varieties of snakes. After translating, Usman added, "And the most poisonous are the two-legged ones."

※

At this point I'd like to tell a little about Varindra Tarzie Vittachi, who at the first Subud World Congress in England in 1959 had been appointed by Bapak as our organization's international chair—a position he held till shortly before his death in 1993. Varindra was already well-known outside Subud by the time of his opening in 1958. A Singhalese Buddhist nicknamed *Tarzie* because of his Tarzan-like agility as a youth in his native Sri Lanka, Varindra had studied journalism in London's Fleet Street and by the time Ceylon attained its freedom from England, had become the first native-born editor of the *Times* of Colombo, Sri Lanka's (Ceylon's new name) newspaper of record.

As a crusading editor who had gotten his start in journalism as a pamphleteer for the Trotskyite Communists in his country, he had a sharp, critical pen which he began to use against his fellow ruling Singhalese Buddhists, the country's majority, because of their discriminatory treatment of the minority Hindu Tamils. Given his large following, this stance did not go over well with the Sinhalese government at the time, which tended to overlook human-rights abuses toward Tamils. At one point Varindra received a call from one of Bapak's secretaries. He and family should leave the country immediately. Later, Varindra learned that a contract had been put out on him and a hired assassin had been arrested shortly after Varindra's departure while staking out his house. Varindra asked Bapak at the next occasion why the latter had saved his life. Bapak replied, per Varindra's recounting, that there is a right time to die and a wrong time to die and that that would have been the wrong time for him. He still had a great deal to accomplish in the world, and it was God's desire for him to live on for some years in order to do so.

In this period, Varindra wrote and the English publisher André Deutsch published Varindra's *Emergency '58*, his critical account of the Sri Lankan race riots of that year—a book for which he received the Ramon Magsaysay Award, known as the Asian Nobel Prize. Subsequently he brought out the first of his three Subud books and still one of my favorites, Subud or not—*A Reporter in Subud*. I had briefly seen Varindra at Subud House in New York during my visit just after the Briarcliff World Congress. We had even ridden up in the elevator together for *latihan*. But now in Hawai'i was my first time to get to know him personally.

As it happened, his return flight via Philippine Airlines to Manila, where he was directing the Press Foundation of Asia, had been canceled because of mechanical difficulties, so he ended up staying in Honolulu for five days after Bapak, Ibu and party had journeyed on. Consequently, Paula Mason, Laura Labby, Simone, little Marianne, Varindra, and I all enjoyed an idyllic time in Bapak's "former apartment," where Varindra, one of the world's great raconteurs, regaled us with stories of his other meetings with Bapak and of how things were in the earliest days of Subud in the West, the three or four years before any of us had been opened. This interlude reprised my experience of walking behind Bapak at Kennedy Airport: a feeling of unalloyed happiness, freedom from worry, and a sense of being in love. All of us were like a harmonious extended family where every minute together felt meaningful and rich.

From then on, whenever Varindra would pass through the Islands, whether going East or West, he would stay with us, visit the group, and tell us his latest stories of Bapak and Subud. Over the years I became one of perhaps a dozen young men in Subud whom Varindra mentored. Fortunately, I would one day be in a position to get him paying gigs as a guest speaker at the various universities where I worked, and he returned the favor on several occasions by inviting me to participate in conferences organized by Dr. Jonas Salk, the discoverer of the first polio vaccine and founder of the Epoch B Foundation. Varindra would also tell us that of the various world leaders he had interviewed—later he would work together with Mikhail Gorbachev and the astronomer Carl Sagan—and of all the great people he had ever met, including even Gandhi, none had impressed him more than our own Muhammad Subuh, a person of whom very few in the world were as yet aware.

※

I spent the 1969-70 academic year on staff at the Center for Cultural and Technical Interchange Between East and West, familiarly the East-West Center. A federal institution at the time, it was housed on the UH campus. Fall 1969 was also my first experience of the Muslim fast of Ramadan. With plenty of Muslims at the Center, many were fasting for Ramadan. By that point I already had gained a lot of book knowledge about Islam but had never done the fast, during which one does not eat, drink, or smoke during the daylight hours for the 30 days of a lunar month. In addition, one is not supposed to become angry, criticize, or look at anything disturbing to one's inner calm—from violent movies and potentially upsetting newspaper articles or newscasts to (in the case of men) sexually attractive women. Bapak had suggested that although Subud members "could not go faster than God" in their spiritual development, one thing they could do to supplement the *latihan* was the annual Ramadan fast. When asked, he mentioned that fasts from other religious traditions would be helpful too, but as a Muslim, he knew the Ramadan fast best. The EWC students meanwhile teased me by saying that if I knew so much about Islam, I should put my money where my mouth was and give the fast a try. I did, and boy, was it hard! I remember the headaches I got during the first week, and for most of the month I could not stop looking at my watch in mid-afternoon to see when I could eat. Still, by the last ten days I had found my groove, and the whole thing became easier as I became quieter inside. Since then I have done the fast 35 more times. It has actually become an annual practice for me and one of the best things I do. Maybe if after 9/11 President Bush had fasted with the World's Muslim population. . . . Oh well, to judge by world history, doing so might have gotten him shot—by some of his erstwhile supporters.

※

One of the most unforgettable characters in my life or that of my family showed up during my year at the East-West Center. One day a late-middle-aged Southeast Asian woman knocked on our house door. From her dress I thought she might be a Filipina or even a gipsy. As it turned out, she was an Indonesian with the unlikely name of Farida Snoekievit, which Simone always insisted was pronounced "Snoikowitz." It turned out that her last husband had been a Finn. Anyway, the Indonesian language professor, Dr. Soenyono, had sent her to us. Farida had been touring the world in search of spiritual adepts of all kinds. In Hawai'i she badly wanted to meet *kahunas*, traditional healers and magicians. As a Javanese, Professor Soenyono couldn't bring himself to say that he didn't actually know any. So he said that although he didn't have contacts with any Hawaiian *kahunas*, he did know an American one, Dr. Feldman, who was a Subud *kahuna*. "Subud!" Farida replied, excited. "*Saya Subud!*" "I'm (in) Subud!"

As she later told us, she had worked at the Indonesian Embassies in first Holland, then Germany. While serving as a secretary at the Embassy in Bonn, she was diagnosed with a uterine tumor, which the German doctors insisted be taken out. At this point she was checked into the hospital and was awaiting her operation the next day. Then someone delivered a German tabloid newspaper to her room. On the front page was a large picture of Bapak together with Eva Bartok, the Hungarian film star who had been married to the German actor Curd Jürgens. The headlines read, "Indonesian Wonderworker Heals Starlet of Tumor." Excited, Farida read the article through. Then she became angry. First, she didn't want any German male doctors looking at her private parts, something they would have had to do during surgery. Second, she felt that if Bapak could cure a European starlet, then what about her, his fellow countryman? By way of background, I should report that Farida had been a famous palmist in Indonesia. She had even been President Soekarno's private palmist until she told him something he didn't want to hear.

In any case, looking intensely at Bapak's picture in the paper, she said in Indonesian, "Pak Subuh, if you can cure that Hungarian woman's tumor, you can cure mine too. After all, I'm an Indonesian, someone from your own country!" She repeated this statement over and over until tired out by the effort, she fell asleep. The next morning, as she was being prepped for surgery, the surgeon had some final x-rays taken. When they were developed, he compared them with the earlier ones he had. They were of the same person, for sure, only this time there was no sign of a tumor. So Farida got her wish and was dismissed from the hospital by the puzzled medical team. On returning to the Embassy, she told her story. As it turned out, Bapak and party were in Munich at the time opening new Subud members. Farida's colleagues urged her to take sick leave to visit him and tell him her experience.

When she arrived at the Four Seasons Hotel in Munich, she was able to go straight to Bapak's room. Dressed as an Indonesian, she was taken by the local Subud members as part of his party, so she walked right in. The first person she saw was Ibu Siti Sumari, Bapak's wife. "Ibu!" Farida said. "It's you!" As it turned out, she and Ibu had known each other before the latter had become Bapak's second wife. Farida had no idea of her old acquaintance's new role. Anyway, still filled with her miraculous cure, she told Ibu what had happened. Ibu in turn sent her to Bapak's room with instructions to tell him the story. She did and, while there, read his palm. "Why Bapak," she said, "your hand has similar lines to those attributed to the Prophet Muhammad." Bapak smiled and told her he had been born on the same day and in the same Muslim month as well as at the same hour as legend had it the Prophet had been born and his name too, like the Prophet's, was Muhammad. At this point, he sent Farida back to Ibu to be opened. After, Farida took additional vacation and traveled with the party to Switzerland, where the then Indonesian Ambassador, whom Farida knew, was also opened.

From that first meeting on, we would see Farida from time to time. She would suddenly show up or call from the airport. "Reinhold, it's me, Farida. Can you pick me up, and can I stay with you, Simone, and the family for a while"? We almost always could, and she would repay our hospitality with tales of her most recent exploits. She told us, for example, how while she was in Germany, she had steered Adam Malik, then Indonesia's foreign minister, to a Subud naturopath in Munich, who had been able to keep the former's son from going blind. Because of this happy outcome from her referral, Farida was protected, furthered, and financed for the rest of her life by the well-to-do Malik family. In fact, she was able to travel the world in search of spiritual practitioners thanks to their generosity. Subud benefited, too. In 1971, when the Fourth Subud World Congress was held in Jakarta, Adam Malik made it possible for members of the large South African group to attend even though at the time Indonesia had no political relations with the country because of Apartheid.

Farida was happy to read our palms, and I was always impressed with how much she knew and was able to say from the lines in our hands. At one point she warned me about an important mistake I was about to make at work. I steered clear of that decision and was happy with the outcome while I was brought up short by what could have happened. Thank goodness I had listened to her.

Although I transferred back to the UH English Department from the East-West Center September 1, 1970, I didn't stay there long. During the spring that year, I had been approached by a History professor, Dick Rapson, who had just completed a year-long interdisciplinary course in which a group of honor students and he designed an experimental cluster college. As "New College—the Experimental School for the Humanities," it had received faculty and UH presidential approval for a three-year trial run. Some of Rapson's students had studied with me or were in the Liberal Studies Program I coordinated. They suggested he recruit me as New College's assistant director. After he told me about the program, in which students would take eight common interdisciplinary courses in freshman and sophomore years and then do a self-designed project during their upper-division years and that the College would be run democratically by the students and faculty, I was sold. Specifically, because of my administrative experience with Liberal Studies, he wanted me to take responsibility for the Upper Division component—the students' independent projects. It took me about ten seconds to reach a positive decision. I wanted in. An added benefit was that the College would be housed in the Admiral Spitzer house, a white Victorian mansion right across Hunnewell Street from our humble white cottage. It seemed a deal made in heaven.

When I told my Department chair about the need for another leave, he was willing to accede to my wishes but was cautionary. These were the very years I was supposed to be teaching in my field while publishing juried academic articles and even a book. Receiving tenure was getting harder at UH as the University struggled to enhance its reputation. Spending time in innovative education projects, regardless of how heady, wouldn't persuade my colleagues to recommend me for tenure a few years down the pike.

As soon became typical of my professional life, I took the road less traveled even if it disadvantaged me in my scholarly career. What really interested me was the idea of participating in a democratically run educational community. So, damning the torpedoes, on Marianne's fourth birthday, September 1, 1970, I became assistant director of what would soon become known locally as UH's "hippie college."

During this period, 1970-72, which turned out to be the last of our initial five-year stint in Honolulu, Bapak came back to town several more times. The first new visit in fact took place in 1969, just over a year after his initial one. This time we housed him and party, again the Usmans, at the Hawaiiana Hotel in Waikiki. We no longer had our apartment in Kaimuki, and our present quarters in Lower Manoa were too small and in other ways unsuitable. Since the Hawaiiana was made up of studios and one-bedroom suits, we rented two of the latter. The first night the group planned to have *latihan*, group testing, and a talk in the conference hall at the Bishop Museum, where Pieter van Royen was still working. But once Bapak, Ibu and party were installed at the Hawaiiana, Bapak decided to hold the evening's activities at the hotel instead. I should mention that the Hawaiiana was a low-rise complex of two clusters of buildings, one adjacent to the other. Both were built atrium style with a pool in the middle of the second. Our guests were located in the section to the rear. Because the living rooms of the apartments were small, fitting in all our members would be a challenge, even if we managed to remove all the movable furniture. Plus how in the world could we do that, and where would we store it?

Usman suggested we carry the furniture into his and Aminah's apartment until the evening's activities were over. Then we could move it back. The only problem was, we'd have to walk everything across the open atrium and around the lighted pool to get them to Usman's room. Oh well, I thought, don't panic! If that's what Bapak wants, we'll just do it. Should a guest or hotel employee blow the whistle, we'd simply explain as best we could. I didn't dare ask the management, since I was convinced they would say no. Meantime, I tried to suppress the idea of our being carted off to jail by thinking, should that happen, it would be for a higher cause.

Then a minor miracle occurred—twice. We managed to make perhaps a half dozen furniture-moving trips between where Bapak wanted to speak with us and Usman's room and then, later that night, another half dozen to move the furniture back, without any outsider taking notice. In fact, busy though the hotel was, during those times absolutely nobody except Subud people seemed to be around. I couldn't believe it.

The effort proved worth it too. I'm sure there have been few other occasions where such a small group of Bapak's spiritual family was huddled together in such cozy proximity to their spiritual guide. It reminded me of our trip with him to Hilo the year before, when he had taken the group of us out to breakfast and then, on the way back, he bought us ice-cream sundaes at the Hilo Airport when our flight had again been canceled. (A diabetic, Bapak had played the naughty boy that afternoon and had had a sundae with the rest of us. I remember few people enjoying their treat the way Bapak seemed to, eating every last bit of that forbidden dessert.)

The next evening proved special for me and Simone, though for different reasons. That night we *did* have *latihans*, group testing, and a talk at the Bishop Museum. During the talk, which like his others Bapak gave in Indonesian with interspersed translations into English, he pointed to me and said, "Bapak has received that our brother there will someday be famous. People all over the world will know his name. Bapak does not say it will happen, but it may. If it does, our brother should remember that it did not happen because of his own cleverness but only because of the Greatness of Almighty God." For the next year I was in crisis. I would be driving around town by myself, and the refrain would keep running through my head, "I'm going to be famous! I'm going to be famous!" Of course, after a while when nothing at all happened—indeed, I got into difficulties at New College for being too permissive with my students—the crisis disappeared, and I was back to my ordinary self. If fame were to come, I for one would not be standing on the corner waiting for it.

When the time for testing arrived, Bapak called Simone forward. He asked her to demonstrate through her *latihan* the state of her soul when she was ten, 25, then 35 years old. In each case, she got something different, with her motions becoming more beautiful and harmonious with each test. When Bapak asked her to test age 35, the local Subud members started snickering. Bapak looked around, puzzled. I explained in Indonesian that although Simone was in fact 38, because she was nearly nine years my senior, she had kept her age to herself. Therefore, most of the brothers and sisters thought she was my age, 29. Bapak joined in the laughter. But from then on, the secret was out. For my part, although Simone was biologically older than me, I had been opened in Subud a half a year before her and had always told her that in our spiritual fellowship at least, I was her senior. Of course, she was blessed with youthfulness and beauty, inside and out, that lasted until her death at age 75. Most people apparently thought we were the same age or even that I was older.

I also had the opportunity to take Bapak shopping at the Liberty House department store in Ala Moana Shopping Center. He needed to buy a few items for himself. As it happened, one of our helpers, Robert Jones, was working in the men's department of the store, so I called ahead to arrange for Robert to take care of Bapak. It was interesting to see how Bapak went about this task. On entering the store, he scanned the horizon as if some kind of inner radar were at work. Then he headed straight down an aisle to where he wanted to be. I was a little apprehensive, since there was not much credit on my credit card at the time, and I didn't know what I would do if Bapak chose to make some expensive purchases. The thought never crossed my mind to ask Bapak to pay for his own things. Anyway, all he wanted was some suspenders and three pairs of socks—a modest purchase well within my capacity. Then he turned to me and smiled, as if to say, "See. There was no need to worry. All I wanted were these few, inexpensive things."

During that trip I asked Bapak in Indonesian which Western countries in his opinion were the most advanced spiritually. He responded that England was first, followed by Germany. Then he said, "Bapak plans to visit his children in England next summer. Maybe you and your wife can come see Bapak there." Simone was already planning to take Marianne that summer to be with the family in Germany, so it would be only a short trip for her to England. To my delight, I found inexpensive charter flights from L.A. to Frankfurt for the two of them and a single flight from L.A. to London for me that landed a few days before Bapak arrived in England. In short, we spent two weeks with Bapak at the British National Subud Congress and could even do a little sightseeing in London, where Simone had lived as an au pair in the early 1950s. Then, unexpectedly, she sold a number of expensive Indonesian batiks back in Munich that enabled us to travel with my mother-in-law, also a Subud member, Marianne, and a lady friend of Oma's to look after our daughter, to spend time with Bapak in Vienna.

Back in Leicester, England, I remember a huge men's *latihan*. There were hundreds of men all doing the spiritual exercise with Bapak in a large meeting hall downtown. The women, meanwhile, were with his wife, Ibu, in another large hall in the same complex. In our *latihan* I found myself going around the huge space in figure eights. Although my eyes were closed, they opened by themselves on several occasions. I noticed that Bapak was doing the very same thing in the opposite direction. At one point, in fact, when my eyes opened, there he came, pointing at me and laughing, as if commenting, "Ah, so you are doing the same thing as Bapak. Look at that!" After, while I was waiting in the corridor for Simone, Ibu was brought out past me in her wheel chair. I managed to ask her how she was in something like High Javanese. Unbeknown to me, Bapak was standing just behind me, where Ibu could see him but I couldn't. She commented to Bapak in Indonesian, "This one is clever in Indonesian," to which Bapak responded with a smile: "Oh yah, him!"

A few weeks later, when Simone, Grandma, and I entered Subud Haus in Vienna, we unwittingly walked into the room where Bapak, Ibu, and party were resting prior to beginning the evening's activities. Bapak again pointed to me, smiled, and said in English, "You again!"

Other than the time spent at Subud Haus, our fivesome had fun walking through the streets of old Vienna. Thanks to a record we had at home, Simone and I knew the melodies and texts of a half dozen traditional Viennese songs. With merely a glass of wine under our belts, we trod the cobblestones while singing our repertoire. The locals looked at us. They must have been thinking, "Those crazy Germans. There they go singing our songs!" But we didn't care. We were having a great time.

Up until now, from September 1, 1965, until June 30, 1972—nearly seven years—I had always had a full-time salaried job. Not only that but the salary had gotten progressively better, and every year I had made additional money by teaching summer school. A traditional family, even by the standards of the time, only I worked outside the house, while Simone stayed home to take care of our two daughters. We had enough money, even in expensive Hawai'i, to pay the bills, help support our Subud group, and do the occasional trip to visit family in Germany or on the U.S. Mainland. What we didn't seem able to do was save anything or start a money-making portfolio. The lone exception was our investing in those two acres in Eden Roc Estates on the Big Island.

Several years before our move from Hawai'i, Bapak began promoting the idea that Subud members should do enterprises to become independent of non-Subud bosses and at the same time make money to subsidize Subud social enterprises like homes for the elderly, special schools, hospitals, and the like. The idea was that these institutions would be owned, managed, and staffed by Subud professionals who, in addition to education and experience in their fields, would bring to their work the guidance and inner training of the *latihan*. Since Simone and I occasionally played hosts to international Subud leaders like Varindra Vittachi and Mas Prio Hartono, an experienced Javanese helper whom Bapak had sent to the States as his ambassador, we heard a lot about "enterprise." It was Prio who first suggested that we start a batik-importing business, which he thought Simone could run from home while still caring for the kids. The idea wasn't an impossible one, since she had an eye for fashion. Mutti, her mother, moreover, was living with us and could manage the household and take care of Marianne. So in 1969, with a $500 loan from my father, Simone started Alohalani Batiks. She shared the little office with several other small Subud enterprisers. The rent was $55 a month, paid in part by the Subud group, which used the space twice a week for *latihan*.

In those years she sold *kain*, batik pieces, both traditional and modern, nearly two meters long by a meter wide. Indonesian women wrapped them around their lower bodies as sarongs. They provided just enough material for a clever seamstress to create a dress or muumuu up to size 12 or 14. With East-West Center students modeling, we took color photos which Simone showed to potential clients. We even put on a few fashion shows including one at the East-West Center. As time went on, Simone sold more and more pieces. The overhead was primarily her labor and the inventory. Soon Indonesian students started selling us their stock of batik *kain* at reasonable prices. Of course, the money that came in, with the notable exception of that windfall in Munich the summer of 1970 when we went to see Bapak in Vienna, got recycled into the business. So our household income didn't increase at all.

Sometime in 1970 Simone received a call from a Chinese-Hawaiian businessman, a Mormon named Kenneth Fong. He and his wife Eileen, a former Chinese-American beauty queen in Hawai'i, had come into a king's ransom of batiks. Having been to one of our shows, they wanted us to take a look at their stock and advise them on whether the batiks and bolts of printed batik materials were salable. In fact, after we spent several hours going through their considerable stock, they took us out to a Chinese meal to discuss what we thought. So, before we knew it, we went into business with the Fongs. They would supply the inventory and funds to cover running expenses, while Simone would supply the expertise and would market the wares. As it happened, the Fongs were part owners of a hotel in Waikiki, where there was a spot in the lobby for what came to be known as the Batik Boutique. They also hired our Indonesian seamstress, Zarah Wirawan, the wife of a Balinese Ph.D. candidate in Botany, who worked part-time in the boutique as salesperson and the rest at home sewing special-order dresses.

To market the goods, we created and put on more ambitious fashion shows, now including professional models as well as Indonesian students from the East-West Center performing on traditional instruments or doing traditional dances. Several shows at major hotels had more than 500 attendees. At one, clothed in batik and adorned with an Indonesian *peci* (pronounced "petchee"), a black fez not unlike the kind Bapak wore, I served as master of ceremonies and scriptwriter for our biggest show.

One of the unanticipated effects of this new joint venture, now no longer a Subud enterprise, was that the Fongs began proselytizing us for their Mormon religion. Actually, it was not a hard sell, but still, it was useful to see how people would feel if we took a similar approach to others with Subud. Now I understood better why Bapak had advised us not to make propaganda about Subud but to let people come to the *latihan* naturally. If they saw positive changes in us, he said, some people might ask what we had been doing, and then we could tell them about Subud. Later I read in the Qur'an that there should be no force concerning religion.

By the time we decided to leave for Europe in spring 1972—we actually left July 5—the Fongs had come to the conclusion that the business was growing too slowly and they should get rid of their inventory at a bargain price. Thus in less than two years the Batik Boutique was history. Meantime, we were able to sell the name and inventory of Alohalani Batiks to another Subud member, who also bought my 1970 Toyota Corona. These funds along with the pay-out of my pension deductions made it possible for our family to get to Germany and pay for our upkeep—we were staying for free in Mutti's apartment—until I could begin earning money.

9
The Subud World Congress, Indonesia

ONE OF the most important experiences during our first period in Hawai'i was my attendance at the Fourth Subud World Congress in Jakarta, Indonesia. The first occurred in Coombe Springs, England, in 1959, two years before my opening. The second was much closer to home, at Briarcliff College, just north of New York City in Westchester County, in the summer of 1963. By this time I was already a Subud veteran of two years and only an hour away in New Haven, Connecticut. As you may remember, with my student job at the Yale Art Gallery, I was unable to attend and had to content myself with seeing Bapak for the first time that summer at Subud House New York. You may also remember that that experience, though brief, had had a powerful effect on me. For now, as the Voice had informed me, I had met someone like Jesus in the 20th Century, and as Bapak himself subsequently said when he appeared to me in New Haven, I had received as much from him as if I'd attended the entire Congress.

The Third World Congress took place in Yomiuri Land, Tokyo, while I was teaching my final summer session at Queens College in 1967 just prior to our move to Honolulu. Hence it was out of the question. The Fourth World Congress, though, was possible for at least me to attend, since we were now living in Honolulu. Simone had just given birth to Christine, our second daughter and final child, on July 26, 1971, and the Congress was to begin August 1 in the Subud international spiritual center, Wisma Subud, Bapak's home compound in the southern Jakarta suburb called Cilandak (pronounced *chee-LON-dock*). I had put aside my summer-session salary to pay for the trip. This time, in fact, I was a trustee of Subud North America, so I could deduct everything except personal gifts from my income taxes. Simone's mother was on hand in Honolulu to help with Marianne and the baby. So my attending a Subud world congress, an every-four-year event where organizational matters were discussed and leadership for the next four year was selected, was possible. Along with a half dozen members from Hawai'i, I would spend two weeks in Jakarta with 1,500 brothers and sisters from all over the world. In addition, we would get to be with Bapak in his home country and perhaps gain some insight into his culture. Most importantly, he would give us talks to deepen our understanding of Subud, and who knows but we might also receive something of value, an experience perhaps, that would change our lives in one way or another. In all the above I was not to be disappointed.

Although Honolulu, located midway between the Continental U.S. and Japan, is closer to Indonesia in the Southwestern Pacific than, say, New York, London, or Paris, the air flight via Sydney, Australia, seemed to last forever. Fortunately, by busying myself with memorizing Indonesian vocabulary, I made the hours fly. Before I knew it, our Pan Am jet touched down at Jakarta's (now old) Kemayoran Airport. The other members of our group had left a few days ahead of me—I wanted to stay in Honolulu as long as possible to be sure Simone and Baby Christine were okay—so I flew to the Congress alone. On arrival, I and other Subud members arriving from around the world were greeted by representatives of Subud-Indonesia, who loaded us onto a bus for the hour-long trip to Wisma Subud. It was already dark, but the streetlights revealed plenty of the Third World urban squalor one saw on television or read about in newspapers and books. Hordes of poorly dressed people thronged the streets. Here and there makeshift shelters of tin or cardboard housing families sped by. The bus, as I recall, was not air-conditioned. When we turned into the front gates of Wisma Subud, however, everything seemed to cool down. Although tired from our travels, we were all wide awake from excitement. We were finally at Bapak's home. The World Congress would soon begin.

Wisma Subud comprised eight to ten acres back then—it was later expanded—with several larger buildings and a number of small one- and two-family houses. The principal large buildings were a guest house, Bapak's home (known as "The Big House"), and in the center of everything the brand-new Latihan Hall, a huge white-domed structure capable of seating 1,500 auditorium style and accommodating perhaps half that number doing *latihan*. In addition, Ramzi Winkler, a German architect and Subud member from Munich, on Bapak's orders had designed a number of temporary wooden longhouses in the Minangkabau style of Sumatra, where all the participants from overseas would be lodged. I for example stayed in *Arjuna*, a longhouse named for one of the heroes of the Hindu epics Indonesians loved from their adaptations into shadow-puppet or other forms of *Wayang* plays. The other longhouses were similarly named. Although personal spaces were small, they were adequate, and sleeping on the wooden floor on the Japanese folding mattresses we had brought proved surprisingly comfortable.

The Congress began with the Opening Session the next afternoon. Since Ibu Siti Sumari, Bapak's long-time wife, had died the year before, he was accompanied by both his eldest daughter, Mbakyu Rahayu, as she was then called, and his new wife, my friend from Subud New York, Ibu Mastuti, whom Bapak had recently married. Lots of government officials were present, since the Congress was to be formally opened with a speech by Indonesia's president, General Suharto. As a result, when Bapak addressed the assembly, he read a prepared statement that sounded stiff and formal in contrast to his usual way of "receiving" when he spoke to us Subud members about spiritual matters. In any case, I could understand most of what both opening speakers said. Later I learned that our Congress was the largest international assembly in Indonesia since its founding in 1947, bigger even than President Sukarno's Bandung Conference of Non-Aligned Nations in the early 50s. No wonder President Suharto came and spoke so long. This Congress was a big deal not only for us but apparently for Indonesia itself.

On the spiritual side, several things surprised me. First, Bapak did not schedule any *latihans* for nearly a week. And second, when we finally did do *latihan*, the usual difference between how one felt in everyday life and in the *latihan* was totally absent. Then I realized that during our first week at Wisma Subud, we had been in the *latihan* state the entire time. So, when we finally did do our spiritual exercise, there was no feeling of difference. Others had similar experiences. Presumably, Bapak wanted to give us a taste of what "living the *latihan*" versus merely doing it might be like.

Another experience sticks in my mind. The nations in attendance were each to present reports on the state of Subud in their country. As a trustee representing America, I was called on in due course and gave a brief, factual accounting. Since by this time Bapak had heard a number of sometimes long, rambling, spiritually oriented reports, he took a moment after mine to comment that this was how a report should be: short, factual, and to the point. He was more concerned, he said, with facts and figures than the spiritual state of affairs which in any case he could intuit for himself.

Any elderly gentleman, a naturopath from Western Canada, was walking across the stage to give the Canadian report. Suddenly to the shock of the 1,500 attendees, he fell down and lay on the floor. Bapak got up, very deliberately it seemed to me, walked over to the supine body; stood over it for a few seconds; then returned to his chair. Meanwhile, some Indonesians helped the man sit up and take a few sips of water. Bapak explained: Our brother had fainted. Apparently he had been intimidated to give his report in front of Bapak as well as the large audience. By this point the Canadian representative had been helped out. His report would be presented later. Bapak continued that he, Bapak, had only a seventh-grade education and some night-school training in bookkeeping. Yet he knew that many in the audience were doctors, lawyers, professors, engineers, and the like. But he never felt intimidated, he said, because to him it was as though we were all one. So when he addressed us, it was as if one part of him were talking to another part. (In this context I thought of the fact that it is impossible to tickle oneself.) It was a lesson I would carry with me to the present. As a result, I have never been frightened to address any group, regardless of size or importance. I simply feel at one with them from the moment I begin.

Another experience is a case in point. Dr. Fuad Hassan, at the time professor of Philosophy and Psychology at the University of Indonesia, Jakarta, had invited me to speak to one of his classes. The topic was to be the East-West Center's Indonesian Humanities Program, whose advisory committee I was chairing. Since any off-compound presentation by Congress participants had to be cleared through Bapak personally, I was invited to meet with him and Usman, his secretary/interpreter. Once again, I was able to speak with Bapak directly in Indonesian. When I explained that I was going to discuss the East-West Center's program to develop curricula for *ilmu perikemanusiaan*, literally, the "science of being truly human," he and Usman nearly bent over with laughter. Then Bapak asked me in Indonesian, with his big Bapak smile, "What? *You* are going to teach Indonesians how to become true human beings! Okay, *boleh*! You have Bapak's permission. Only don't talk about Subud unless someone asks you a question. *Terima kasih*. Thank you. And good luck!"

A few days later I found myself in a waiting room at U.I., the acronym for Indonesia's Harvard. As I tried to jot down a few key terms for my talk, which would be in Indonesian, my pen simply refused to meet my yellow legal pad. I must have tried two or three more times with the same result. Then I gave up. I'd have to go with what I already knew. At that moment a young woman invited me to follow her. There, in a long rectangular classroom with 40 to 50 students, Professor Hassan introduced me as Dr. Reynold Feldman, an East-West Center official from Honolulu who was currently in Jakarta as one of the North-American representatives at the Subud World Congress in Cilandak.

By way of background, Fuad and I had sat up most of a night

discussing Islam back in Honolulu. He was apparently impressed that I, a Jewish-Christian American, should know as much as I did about Islam and would even be willing to participate in the Ramadan Fast, something that as a non-Muslim I was under no obligation to do. When I dropped him off at his dorm—he was at the time a Senior Scholar at the East-West Center—he asked me to wait a minute, since he wanted to give me a little something in memory of our meeting. A few minutes later he returned with a rolled object which proved to be his spare prayer rug, one, he said, that had the dirt of Mecca on it. Fuad was also a Hadji, who had made the requisite Muslim pilgrimage there.

My talk went smoothly. I was able to describe the program clearly. Indeed, my Indonesian seemed to flow by itself with no help from me. Meantime, I was able to observe the students and had a sense of what they were thinking and feeling. When the talk was over, Dr. Hassan asked for questions. Unsurprisingly, given his introduction, every single one was about Subud. After, two students, a young man and woman, offered to drive me back to Wisma Subud. On the way, the young woman told me she was a classmate of Tuti's, Bapak's granddaughter, and that the latter had never told her anything about her grandfather's spiritual program. After driving me into the compound, they met with one of the Indonesian helpers, Usman's wife Aminah, to learn more about Subud.

One experience in Indonesia has doubtless had a major impact, at least health-wise, on my life: I quit smoking. Or more accurately, smoking quit me. Here's how it happened. After the Congress proper, I took three trips: One to Jogyakarta, one of Java's two cultural capitals, to buy batiks for Simone's enterprise; one to Bali as Varindra Vittachi's assistant at an international reporters' conference; and one to Bandung, where I also addressed a college assembly on the Indonesian Humanities Program, this time at the IKIP-Bandung, or Bandung Teacher Training Institute. Concerning the third activity, I was again not permitted to prepare but this time was not so nonplussed. Again I was able to watch the faces as I spoke, while my Indonesian seemed once again to flow by itself.

It was on the way back from Bandung that the habit of smoking left me. At the time I was mainly smoking cigarettes and the occasional cigarillo. As for cigarettes, I used the clove-spiced Indonesian kreteks almost exclusively. As our train pulled into the station just before the one where I was planning to get off, a boy was hawking cigarettes, including kreteks, just outside my window. I bargained with him in Indonesian for a pack of the latter and managed to get them so cheap

I later felt guilty for depriving the boy of a few more cents. Still, these proved to be the worst and the best cigarettes I ever bought. As the worst, they were dry as straw. Wrapped as they were in only a paper pack, they no doubt were old as the hills and had lost all their moisture and most of their taste. They were the best because the more I tried to smoke them, the less I was able to. Puffing on these once-fragrant sticks was like inhaling burning straw. My throat pained with each draw. I just could not continue. By the time I reached the fourth or fifth cigarette, I had to throw the entire pack away and with it my fifteen-year career as a smoker. After, I always thought of this experience as a kind of farewell gift from Indonesia, since a few days later I returned to Hawai'i. In the intervening 37 years I have never smoked again.

Finally, as our train pulled into the suburban Jakarta station I had chosen because people at Wisma Subud had told me it was closer to the compound, two Indonesians raced through the train car yelling "Taksi!" Seeing me, one of them went to grab my bag. Quickly recalling everything I'd read or heard about innocent Westerners being accosted, even kidnapped, by rogue taxi drivers in Third World countries, I grabbed my bag even tighter and ran toward the door. Finally locating the station police, I explained my plight and asked the officer to find me an honest cabbie to take me to Wisma Subud. So you can imagine my embarrassment when the man led me straight to the taxi of the very two Indonesians who had been "accosting" me for my business. They were honest cabbies after all, simply marketing their service Jakarta-style! And in case you're wondering, I got back to Wisma Subud without having lost anything except my face.

10
The University of Maryland (Europe) and Subud Germany

I ENJOYED my time at New College, being a participant as much as an official. The year was 1971, and a female colleague from the English Department wanted my job as assistant director. Although I managed to retain it for the second year, trouble was brewing. Also, our Indonesian psychic friend, Farida, warned that something might happen soon with my mother-in-law's health. Word from the English Department indicated my chances for receiving tenure were getting slimmer each day. Fortunately, Bapak came in spring 1972. So I asked him whether it would be advisable, all things considered, for our family to move to Germany. At the time a number of Subud members were teaching at a gymnasium (academic high school) in Wolfsburg, where there was also a very strong Subud group. Bapak approved the move but advised me to teach at the university level. Shortly thereafter, my colleague Loren Ekroth told me about the possibility of working for the University of Maryland on military bases in Germany. He had done so early in his career and even offered to write the director for Germany, whose office was located in my old student city, Heidelberg. So, I gave notice to New College, the English Department, and the Arts and Sciences' dean's office; we had a monster garage sale; and on July 5, 1972, my father's sixty-seventh birthday, we flew to L.A. After stop-offs there with Subud friends in Santa Monica, my parents in Chicago, and a Subud family in Greenwich Village, New York, we boarded the *S.S. France*, at the time the longest passenger ship in the world, for the trip to Bremerhaven and an unknown future.

A joke back then went that the two best French restaurants in the world were the first- and second-class dining rooms on the *France*. Whatever the case, we had a good trip to Europe, beginning with our on-board send-off in New York City with our Subud friends Victor Margolin, the incomparable Francis von Kahler, and the Owens family. Just before arriving in South Hampton, however, Christine, not quite a year old, came down with the flu. Fortunately, she was treated by the ship's doctor and was able to travel by the time we got to Bremerhaven a few days later. More concerning was the news we received just before our arrival: A telegram came from our brother-in-law, Wolfgang, in Munich. "Mother unable to meet you in Bremerhaven. Seriously ill." When I phoned, Simone's older sister, Gerda, told me Mutti had had a stroke while visiting her best friend near Bonn, she was in a local hospital, and her prognosis was uncertain. The long train trip from Bremerhaven to Munich filled us with doubts. All we could do was pray. On arrival we got more details. Mutti had been washing dishes at Tante Greta's house in the countryside near Bonn. The two of them had just had their afternoon coffee. Suddenly, Mutti became unwell. Greta called the emergency number and an ambulance took Mutti to the nearest hospital. At this point, she was resting comfortably but appeared to be paralyzed on her left side. It was not yet clear what brain damage she had sustained.

Our family now installed in Mutti's apartment in suburban Gruenwald near Munich, I decided to start my Eurail Pass by traveling to Tante Greta's and checking up on Mutti in the hospital. Meantime, I learned from Bob Speckhard, the director of the University of Maryland in Europe's English program, that while I had been accepted to teach courses for them, he would not know till a week before the next eight-week session, to start in a few weeks, whether there would be enough students for me to teach two (the maximum number of) courses or even one. So, as we drew down our savings and had no idea what would happen with Mutti, let alone whether or not I would get enough work to sustain our little family, there was nothing to do but put our trust in God and be patient.

For the first seven years of my professional life, I had had a job, a title, and a regular income. Now suddenly, we were living off rapidly dwindling savings—Germany was less and less the bargain for Americans it had been for me as an exchange student in the late 50s—and I had no clue whether the University of Maryland's programs on U.S. military bases in Germany would have enough, or any, work for me. Actually, this was my first real experience as a Subud member of eleven years that God would in fact provide. First, we had our apartment free. After a month, when Mutti was well enough to come home, Simone found herself caring for her mother as well as our two kids. Fortunately, I was able to get a full load of courses every session. By the end of the first eight weeks, I had built a following—this despite the fact that the University compelled me to grade on a curve, with the number of higher grades "balanced" by a similar number of lower ones. Still, the students seemed to enjoy my classes and kept coming back for more. By the Grace of God, I always managed to get just enough students for the courses to make, as we say in the academic world. Had even one of them not done so, Family Feldman would have been hard pressed to pay its bills. Of course, the downside of this good fortune was that for the first three eight-week sessions I was eight hours away from where the family was. Living on U.S. military bases, I was unable to help Simone who had her hands full caring for her mother as well as our two kids, then six and one.

In March 1973, right around Simone's birthday, we were able to move to an affordable three-bedroom rural apartment 80 miles away from my work in Odenwald (Odin's Woods), beautiful hilly countryside a half-hour north of Heidelberg. This good fortune was thanks to a Subud member who wished to relocate his family to Hamburg, in northern Germany, but needed to sublet his apartment first. We had other luck too. Over Christmas break another Subud member, an actor in the Munich-Planegg group, had helped me buy a used VW four-door sedan for DM 3,000, approximately US$1,000 at the time. With a loan from my godfather, the Baron von Royk-Lewinski in Hawai'i, we could close the deal, and with cheap gas available to me on U.S. military bases, we once again had the convenience of a car.

After the family was installed in the new apartment, Simone helped Mutti re-learn walking up and down our 30-foot-long railed balcony. It was heartening to watch Christine, nearly two, practice walking along with her invalid grandma as they looked out on the rolling farmland just beyond our backyard. My schedule at the military bases in Zweibruecken was such that I could drive off Monday afternoon for my Monday evening class. (Each class lasted three hours.) I would stay at the Bachelor Officers Quarters and teach each subsequent evening. Then I'd make the 90-minute Autobahn drive to our place in Zotzenbach after my last class ended at 9 p.m. Thursday. Often I would take the laundry with me and correct student papers while sitting in the post laundromat. Generally, I was the only male among a dozen or so Army or Air Force wives. I learned from them the fine points of sorting and folding. Sometimes I would take a week's worth of garbage to the base, since we had only one tiny garbage can in Zotzenbach, far too little for what a standard American family managed to accumulate in a week.

Teaching on military installations—I was at an Army post and an Air Force base in Zweibruecken, near the Luxembourg border—was an eye-opener for me. As an intellectual and young professor, I had a snobbishly negative attitude towards all things military. Like most of my fellow academics, I was left of center politically and saw our armed forces as the ready tool of war-hungry Republicans. (Never mind that President Johnson, an established Democrat, had been hounded from office by anti-Vietnam youth and others only a few years before.) To me the concept of *military intelligence* was an oxymoron. By the end of my year at the University of Maryland, however, I learned that members of the U.S. military were human beings like everyone else. Many hailed from small Southern and Western towns where there were few job opportunities, and the peacetime military, with its promise of world travel and free education, was an appealing way up and out of a limited life.

During that year I also met and became lifelong friends with Jimmy and Joanne (later Halinah Rizzo-) Busack. A West Point graduate, he was at the time an Army first lieutenant and finance officer at Kreuzberg Kaserne in Zweibruecken. She was a recent graduate of a Catholic high school in Staten Island, New York, and was working part-time as a teller at the American Express bank on post. I was her first college teacher. In fact, our first class together back in September 1972 took place on her twentieth birthday. She and Jimmy more or less adopted me, taking me to their officers' apartment for ice-cream sundaes, Scrabble games, and occasional dinners. After they met Simone and the kids in Munich, where they drove me—they were going to the Oktober Fest that year—we all became friends. Joanne was the one, I am sure, who rallied the other students to keep taking my courses. She knew that without a certain number of enrollees, my courses wouldn't make, and I'd be out of luck. Later, when the family moved to Zotzenbach, she would sometimes drive the 80 miles to babysit our kids. Imagine! I returned the favor in a sense by bringing both Jimmy and Joanne to Subud. They were opened on Bastille Day, 1973. I remember marching around and singing the Star-Spangled Banner in *latihan* during Jimmy's opening. Years later, Halinah told Simone before she died not to worry. She would look after the kids—including Reynold. She also spoke the eulogy at Simone's funeral Mass and later gave me an envelope with a small pack of hundred-dollar bills so I could spend Christmas with Christine, a Fulbright scholar, in Hamburg. It wouldn't be good for her to be without family that first Christmas after her mom's death, Halinah said.

Now let me share some final words about our experiences in Germany and as members of Subud-Deutschland. During the year I experimented with the possibility of not returning to the States. Simone after all was a German citizen, I spoke good German, and an extended time would do wonders for the kids' understanding of their mother's language and culture. To stay on, however, would mean finding a job to support the family and getting an *Arbeitserlaubnis*, a working visa. My inquiries at various German colleges and universities didn't yield much. One opportunity did emerge from Dr. Hans-A. Fischer-Barnicoll, the director of the Institute for Intercultural Research in Heidelberg. Simone and I had met him a year or so before at the East-West Philosophers Conference in Honolulu. His institute was looking for an assistant director, and except for a deeper background in philosophy and theology, I seemed to fit the qualifications. In fact, after a series of interviews, he selected me for the job. It was a matter of waiting for a large grant expected from Japan. By this point we had been in Zotzenbach, near Heidelberg, for several months. I even had an interview in the south of France with one of the Institute's most famous and influential Board members, the French Christian existentialist philosopher Gabriel Marcel. I remember discussing the issue of UFOs with him in French. (Parts of the interviews were also in German and English.)

Meantime, I had saved enough money to purchase a large, new American clothes washer at the Post Exchange in Heidelberg. My job teaching on U.S. military bases provided me with so-called uniform privileges, like grocery shopping at post commissaries, other kinds of shopping at post exchanges, and the purchase of dirt-cheap gasoline at American installations throughout Europe. Given the Spartan payment for my teaching, these privileges supplemented our buying power by perhaps 40% and were a godsend.

I remember the sunny day when the spanking new machine arrived. The PX even supplied free delivery and installation. Shortly after the technician, a local German, had wheeled the unit into our cellar, he came to me and told me in the *Badenser* dialect that there was a problem. Apparently, the place where the machine would go had only a cold-water line, because German washers heated the water whereas American ones, like the one I had purchased, took in both hot and cold water from a house's supply. So, if I wanted to use my American machine, a plumber at considerable cost would have to install new piping clear across the cellar to reach it. So much for our wonderful new purchase! I tipped the man, who reloaded the machine and returned it to the PX. In due course I received the full purchase price back, but the unhappy event seemed like an omen.

That evening my father called from Chicago. Dr. Jerome Sachs, the president of Northeastern Illinois University in Chicago, had phoned him to say that he, Dr. Sachs, had placed my résumé in the search for director of the University's innovative Center for Program Development and that I was now a finalist for the position. If I was interested, I should contact the search committee's chair as soon as possible. My father then gave me the latter's number. He also said how nice it would be, with my sister, brother-in-law, and their kids in Argentina, if Simone, our girls, and I were to move back to Chicago and be closer to them. Could this be another sign? I asked myself.

I should explain that, like Dr. Fischer-Barnicoll, I had also met Dr. Sachs in Honolulu, where he was attending an international conference at the East-West Center on innovation in higher education. At the time I was still working at the Center, so I had access to the conference sessions, where I heard him deliver a paper on Northeastern Illinois' commitment to new forms of education and, in particular, its innovative administrative arm, the Center for Program Development. While he and his wife were in town, Simone and I drove them around a bit, and before they left, he noted my parents' phone number in Chicago and promised to give them a call, which he did. Dr. Sachs and I had had good chemistry during that visit, and I think he even mentioned he would love to have someone like me helping him make the university even more cutting-edge but that currently there were no positions available. Then, on our way through Chicago to Germany in July 1972, Simone suggested I call Dr. Sachs "just to say hello." By that point in our marriage, nearly nine years, I had learned from experience that following Simone's suggestions generally yielded beneficial results, whereas disregarding them had the opposite effect. Fortunately, this time I listened, and the outcome was my father's phone call and what came next.

A few weeks later—this must have been May 1973—I was flying to Chicago from Luxembourg on an Icelandic flight. Though the flight was inexpensive by then-current standards, it was more than I could afford even if Northeastern would reimburse me the New York/Chicago portion. My father was only too happy to pay the difference, and fortunately it was between terms at the University of Maryland – Europe. So I could spend a few days with my parents after the all-day-Friday interview.

I was still hoping for the *international* position in Heidelberg. As a result, I was able to respond to all the Chicago interview questions without appearing too hungry for the job. At the time I really didn't want work that was limited to at most a national context. To top it off, when the academic vice president, Dr. Goldberg, asked me what annual salary I was expecting, I named a figure I thought high: $20,000. At the time that was considered an executive salary in the academic world, plus it was $5,000 more than my highest salary in expensive Hawai'i had been. Although I wasn't that interested in the job, the people I met were all sympathetic, plus the possibilities of fostering new, innovative programs seemed great. I still loved Chicago—home of WFMT, the wonderful classical-music station of my youth, Studs Terkel, and the Subud group where I had been opened. And it would be nice for the kids to be near their grandparents.

Soon after my return to Germany, I received a call from Dr. Fischer-Barnicoll. The long-awaited Japanese money had finally arrived. If I was still interested in the job, it was mine. Now what? The family and I had previously scheduled a long-weekend trip to Wolfsburg, in central West Germany. Besides being home to the Volkswagen Works, the city housed a renowned Subud group, led by a well-known painter Richard "Haro" Engels. On returning to Wolfsburg from a prisoner-of-war camp in Russia after the end of the World War, Richard fulfilled a vow and started a youth group dedicated to internationalism, intercultural understanding, and world peace. While in the camp, he had learned Russian from a guard in exchange for drawing lessons. For people at the camp, prisoners and guards alike, boredom was an overwhelming problem. So both Richard and his guard were happy to have something to do to while away the time.

When Bapak first came to England in 1957, Richard, who had been a follower of the Gurdjieff work as taught by John Bennett, took a number of his older youth—individuals had to be at least 18 back then to be opened—to meet him. Most or all of the young people, along with Richard, became Subud members. Meanwhile, back in Wolfsburg, these youth were among the first members of Subud in Germany, along with Ruth Gruson and Michele and Ludwig von Royk-Lewinski in Munich.

Richard, a wonderful storyteller, had a charismatic personality. He also had an artist's taste for beautiful objects and stories from faraway lands. Consequently, the Wolfsburg group leased and years later bought a centuries-old forester's house with a large barn and several acres of wooded property adjoining a forest. In the barn, under Richard's direction, the group had created a Russian village. When guests came— there were always many—Richard would propose they take "a nice valk in da voods." The Wolfsburgers had also designed and sewn Russian folk costumes and had learned matching dances. Later the group, after appropriate study, visited the Holy City of Isfahan in Iran and on another occasion a Sufi group in the Sahara Desert of North Africa. As a result, a *caravanserai*, or caravan stop (with appropriate home-made costumes), was also created. The weekend we were there, the group would in fact be performing an English play, *Hassan—The Golden Road to Samarkand*, in English with accompanying program music by Frederick Delius.

Meanwhile, concerning my career, I had left Vice President Goldberg at Northeastern Illinois University the number of the Wolfsburg Subud Center in case he needed to call me while the family and I were there. And that is exactly what happened. President Sachs wanted to offer me the job as director of their Center for Program Development at a starting salary just over $20,000 per year. I asked Dr. Goldberg for a day or two to think the offer over. Then I went to Richard, who arranged for testing the two jobs that night after *latihan*. Seven of us, including several helpers from the nearby Wendhausen group, were on hand. Most of them were hoping the answer would be the job in Heidelberg, since they were enjoying having Simone, the girls, and me as part of Subud-Deutschland. The unanimous result, however, showed that whereas there were negative factors involved in the German position, the directorship in Chicago would be excellent for me both inwardly and outwardly and that the move there would be good for the family. As I later learned, in the Heidelberg job I would have been a kind of stay-at-home executive secretary while my boss would be doing the international traveling. In any case, I called Dr. Goldberg the next day and accepted the offer.

During our year in Germany, we belonged to two Subud groups: one in suburban Munich and the other in a town (Nieder-Walluf) not far from Wiesbaden. We also participated in such events as the German National Congress, several visits to Wolfsburg (there were lovely guestrooms in the forester's house), and the summer camp in Rambach, central West Germany, just a few kilometers from the patrolled East German border. While the family was still living outside Munich and I visited every eight weeks for a week, we would attend *latihan* and activities at the Munich-Planegg Group. As with every Subud group, there was a selection of interesting people, generally including several characters. The Planeggers had Ruth Gruson, the elderly co-founder of Subud in Germany, along with Samuel Guenther, a classical as well as dialect actor on the Bavarian stage, and our Bavarian friend from New York, where she had been an au pair while we were there, Pauline Mueller. Samuel was the one who had helped me get our car. Pauline, before we had a car, would generously lend us hers so that we could go shopping or take Oma to a doctor's appointment.

At the Wiesbaden group, which had mainly older people as members, there was the nice tradition of having sweets and herbal tea after *latihan*, while one of the helpers would read part of a Bapak talk in German translation. After, we would share experiences related to points he had made. For us, the Autobahn drive at 80 MPH between our apartment in Zotzenbach and the Subud house took an hour and a half. Still, we happily made the trip weekly, for *latihan* with a group is almost always stronger than when one exercises on one's own.

Undoubtedly the crowning Subud experience was our week-long visit with Halinah and Jimmy Busack to the summer camp at Rambach. Since we had already booked our travel back to the States, this was to be our last Subud hurrah in Germany, at least for that year. Talk about something out of a fairy tale! Under Richard's genial direction, a large team of young people had gone to the land where the camp would be held ten days beforehand to set things up. Working long days, they had created showers, latrines, a cooking area, split-log sidewalks—the land was a bit swampy—large tents, and small raised wooden tent-covered spaces where individuals and families would sleep. Lamps were strung from the tent tops with earthy-red flowerpots as lampshades. There was even an adjoining medieval-style camp for the kids, where Subud youth served as counselors. The largest tent, used for *latihan*, musical performances, and all-camp gatherings, including a performance of *Hassan*, was called the Caravanserai. It contained several layers of large, expensive-looking Turkish carpets. In the middle of the camp grounds was a watch tower where people would take turns "standing guard." Nearby was an impressive campfire site, where a "sacred fire" burned like an eternal light day and night.

Speaking of *Hassan*, it was announced that on a particular night each of us would need to come to the Caravanserai in costume for a performance. We would be more than an ordinary audience. We would be distinguished guests from far and wide. I happened to have brought along some Javanese clothes, so on entry I was announced as the ambassador of the Sultan's court at Jogyakarta. Simone came as Zulayka, a Turkish princess. I don't remember if the children were present or not and, if so, what their costumes were. In any case, midway through the play, a group of desert marauders in full costume broke into the tent, caused a few minutes of make-believe mayhem, then left, to be followed by appropriately clad houris who served Near Eastern snacks—baklava and North African mint tea. That was the intermission.

It struck me as incredible that anyone would develop something so elaborate for the enjoyment of 100 or so adults and children for just a few weeks. But that was Richard and Subud Wolfsburg. Bapak had said that Subud groups tended to represent the cultural patterns—both the positive and the negative—of the places where they were located. In the case of Germany, the Wolfsburg group in particular seemed to bear him out. For all the fantasy and hard work, members who lived there would sometimes comment one on one that they had no life of their own. Everything centered on the group, and the group took its lead from the ever-creative but sometimes undemocratic Richard. The German sense of what was and was not to be done was frequently in evidence. Once at the camp, for example, Simone, who was still smoking at the time, unconsciously tossed her cigarette butt into the campfire. One of the Wolfsburg helpers happened to notice and took her aside for a good ten minutes to lecture her on how inappropriate it had been to desecrate the sacred fire. In 1975 at the World Congress in Wolfsburg, Bapak made it clear that Subud was a social democracy and that no individual person, not even Bapak, was in charge. That job was reserved for God. In the years following, "the cult of Wolfsburg" and the idea of "Richard's group," gratefully went the way of all flesh. Wolfsburg became simply another Subud center, not a full-time communitarian experience—stimulating for people like me who were just visiting but oppressive for the full-time residents. Yet, all that notwithstanding, I have to say that that week at the Rambach camp was a magical experience for us all, a temporary coming together of Subud with A Thousand and One Nights. As in all fairytales the end would come and did. But the experience would stay with me for a lifetime. It was the perfect way to end a hard but educational year in Germany, an intermezzo between my early career in New York and Hawai'i and the longer stints in Chicago and Saint Paul that were to come. The latter are the subject of the next chapters.

11
Northeastern Illinois University and Subud Chicago

THE LONGEST part of my career, some 23 years, took place in just two cities: Chicago and Saint Paul. I spent the first and longer stretch at Northeastern Illinois University, from September 1, 1973, until September 15, 1987. Initially, I was director of the Center for Program Development (CPD). Because of the work I did in developing programs, I was promoted to dean of the Center in the late 70s. By the time I left for Minnesota and the academic vice presidency of Metropolitan State University, Saint Paul, CPD contained three alternative bachelors programs, a Program for Interdisciplinary Studies, Women's Studies, Service Learning, Continuing Education, a Hispanic field center, and an initially Kellogg Foundation-funded faculty-development program. Much of the success was doubtless due to student-faculty advisory committees working together with a diverse staff, around 14 full-timers at the high point. Through the Kellogg (faculty-development) Program, a newsletter ("The Innovator") sent to all University faculty and staff six times a year, and CPD's involvement in general-education reform, we managed to have an impact on the institution as a whole and not be just a ghetto for cutting-edge ideas and programs. Over time, CPD staffers and I became known nationally for various aspects of curriculum reform, including general, urban, interdisciplinary, and adult education as well as faculty development. Our area was also a model of staff diversity in terms of gender, race, ethnicity, sexual orientation, and age.

During my years at Northeastern, I was able to start an international association of innovators in postsecondary education. Called *Interversitas*, it went on for three or four years, during which time we put out picture directories. But we were never able to get the Union for Experimenting Colleges and Universities to take the association over, fund and manage it. That had been our goal. It was to have been the individual component for "experimenting college and university" teachers and administrators. Also, with three decades of hindsight, I see now that a professional-networking project like this would have been much more feasible nowadays with the capacity of the Internet and its related networking technologies. Still, the experience brought me into contact with lots of interesting people, and we were even able to persuade Carl Rogers, the noted American psychotherapist and major founder of Humanistic Psychology, to become a member.

From the Subud perspective, I was now in a leadership position where I could put my ideas of "human enterprise" into practice. At our weekly staff meetings, we had free and open discussions, and often the ideas that prevailed did not come from me or even one of the program coordinators. Within a hierarchical organization, we managed to create an oasis of egalitarianism, where creativity, not position, was the primary criterion. I was also fortunate, thanks to the Kellogg grant, to gain a full-time administrative assistant, a position I managed to have "institutionalized," i.e., funded by the University once the grant funds were used up. The three persons who staffed this job over a decade were all exceptionally bright, hard-working, and—unlike me—detail-oriented. So, thanks to Jill Bohlin, Paula Wolf, and Aline Faloona, CPD and I looked a lot better than we would have otherwise, turning out masses of required and well-received paperwork and meeting all our deadlines.

One surprise I had on arrival from Germany was that Dr. Sachs had announced his retirement as Northeastern's president effective the day before I started. This was a disappointment, since I had hoped to work with and for him. He had been the charismatic founding president and after ten years of trying to preserve and strengthen UNI, the University's acronym then, had had enough of Illinois academic politics and bureaucracy. The next president, Dr. James Mullen, didn't have the same commitment to innovative education but was pleasant enough and didn't do anything negative to our area. When he left for health reasons after three years, we got the institution's first African American president, Dr. Ronald Williams. By contrast, he *was* interested in our area and actually saw it as one of Northeastern's distinctive features. He also brought on board a provost (chief academic officer), Dr. John Cownie, who was young, bright, and fair. Under the Williams-Cownie administration, CPD prospered. It didn't hurt, moreover, that two of my program heads eventually became associate provosts. After President Williams died in the mid-80s and Provost Cownie a year or so later, however, things started going south for us with the advent of a new president from Texas. He was a traditional top-down administrator. Word had it that he had been selected by the Board to clean up some of Northeastern's "flakiness," part of which he or they seemed to associate with CPD. This was the point when I began to look around for new jobs and finally got the vice presidency at Metro State.

In retrospect, Subud during these years became more humdrum and less dramatic for me. Actually, I felt less of a separation between Subud and life. It was perhaps the difference between taking French lessons and living in France. This was the effect many of us had first felt at the 1971 Subud World Congress in Indonesia. So I can't think of as many special spiritual experiences as in prior chapters. I do remember that during my initial *latihans* in Chicago, the exercise by group members seemed somehow less disciplined and sloppier than those in Germany. This may have been yet another manifestation of how culture can influence the character of Subud groups. After a short time, however, this feeling went away, and everything seemed natural and unexceptional once again.

During the year in Germany I had begun a long poem, *The Song of the New Human Race*, which I completed during my earlier years at Northeastern. An excerpt was printed in a now-defunct Subud publication, after which Subud Publications International wrote me of their interest in publishing the whole thing. Francis von Kahler even remarked on hearing me read from it that it was, in his opinion, "really Subud." I still like parts of it, but the poem was never published. Maybe one day.

One interesting thing happened at Northeastern that almost got me fired. I was able to hire two Subud members to serve as secretaries in one of CPD's programs. For a while, moreover, my long-time Subud friend Victor Margolin ran a city-wide higher-education consortium from an office in CPD. Then, almost like an incoming tide, a half dozen or more Subud members found their way to the University as students. Frequently, a bunch of us would go out for lunch, and when we got together in the CPD area, spirits were usually high. I had visions of our becoming like the *Gymnasium* in Wolfsburg, Germany, where a number of Subud members were teachers while a portion of the student body were Subud kids. On a particular day, however, one of the non-Subud CPD secretaries met with me. She told me she was about to file a union grievance against me for favoring employees who belonged to my "meditation group." Since I had always been good to her, she wanted to tell me first, to give me a chance to change my behavior. This news hit me totally unawares. I hadn't realized my actions could have been taken as prejudicial to the interests of the non-Subud workers in my unit. I assured her I was sorry, that I hadn't realized what I was doing and hadn't done it intentionally, and that I would change my behavior forthwith. She thanked me, said she was happy to give me a chance, and told me she would postpone filing her grievance.

On reflection, I knew I had two choices: either to stop being friendly to the Subud workers and students or to become equally friendly with everyone, Subud and non-Subud alike. Knowing myself, I really had only one choice, the latter. Fortunately, the grievance was never filed, and things went along smoothly after that. Within six months, most of the Subud members had gone elsewhere, with only a single secretary left. But I had learned a lesson that reached beyond labor-management relations at Northeastern. It was crucial not to re-create a Jews/Gentiles dichotomy in our feelings and actions between Subud on the one hand and non-Subud on the other. From that time on, I began to treat everyone as my brothers and sisters.

Early in our fourteen years in Chicago, I was named a Subud helper, in 1977 or 1978. Now I was authorized to explain about Subud to interested persons, open individuals who wanted to join, test with members about issues that concerned them, time the *latihans* (that is, say "Begin!" and, 30 minutes later, "Finish!"), and work with the local helpers group to discuss, *latihan*, and test about matters concerning Subud-Chicago as a whole. We were also called on to give moral support to the local committee.

During the Chicago period, I was fortunate to have been sent to Brazil for two weeks as a representative of Subud in North America. The occasion was a meeting of the so-called Compact Council, an assembly of Subud representatives from the eight international zones. Since Bapak and party would be in attendance, about 500 other Subud members from North and especially South America arrived in São Paulo as well. Since I already knew Spanish, French, and some Italian, I took advantage of the opportunity to study Portuguese during the four months preceding the trip. As it happened, our Pan Am jet arrived in São Paulo on May 22, 1981, my twentieth Subud birthday. What a present! I remember thinking.

Some important Subud experiences occurred during this trip. Up till then I had received many experiences in *latihan*; however, "seeing things" was not one. During a group *latihan* in the convent we were using, I suddenly became aware of a large emerald-green cross hanging in mid-air before my closed eyes. It just emerged in my mind's eye, stayed for a few seconds, then disappeared. I remember feeling very happy that I could now could *see*.

During the same visit, I was in a group of men Bapak was testing. He said that, if God willed it we might be able to receive indications about our true talent. When he said "Relax!" and "Begin!," I started spontaneously to make the motions of leading a symphony orchestra. I would signal one invisible section to play more quietly while, turning to another, I would gesture vigorously for them to increase the volume and gusto of their playing. In my mind I understood this miming to be a metaphor. It didn't indicate that I had the talent to be a symphony conductor. Instead, it suggested that my true talent was leadership—the ability to blend the efforts of many into a harmonious whole. The test pleased me, because as a dean I was responsible for leading the efforts of a number of colleagues and making best use of state funds.

I also discovered another talent during the Brazil visit—fundraising. Someone mentioned to me that a Mexican brother had received in his *latihan* to accompany Bapak on the next leg of the latter's trip to Colombia. The only problem was, our Mexican brother didn't have the $500 (US) to do so. Could I help? Why the individual, another Mexican, came to me, I don't know. I hadn't seen myself as much of a fundraiser up to that point. Anyway, something inside me prompted me to say I would take care of it. Bapak, I knew, was speaking that afternoon, so I explained the situation to his interpreter, Sharif Horthy, and asked if I could make my appeal to the assembly before Bapak left the stage. Sharif checked with Bapak, who initially wanted to know why I couldn't ask for the funds after he had left the room. I pressed Sharif to explain to Bapak that the assembly would likely be more generous if the collection took place in Bapak's presence. Then Bapak agreed. At the appointed time I made my short pitch in English, Spanish, and Portuguese. I had arranged for several people to pass sombreros which Mexican members willingly lent for the purpose. When the money was counted, we had not only enough for the plane ticket but also for the brother's food and other expenses in Colombia.

By far the most significant of my experiences at the Compact Council Meeting came from a mistake I had made—lending credence to the commonplace that mistakes can sometimes lead to good outcomes. Because I was due to arrive in São Paulo as the first of our three-person North American delegation and because I knew Spanish and some Portuguese, I had promised to arrange for my two colleagues, who knew neither language, to be picked up at the airport. In the case of the first, I did so with no problem. But somehow, in the spiritual sea I was swimming in, I totally forgot about the second, a psychotherapist from Frazer Valley, British Columbia. That night as a bunch of us were standing around chatting, there was Mahmud. He came over and asked what had happened. "Oh, my God!" I thought. I had totally forgotten about him. Thank goodness he had somehow made it.

As Mahmud explained, when he arrived in the airport and found no Reynold there to meet him, first he waited for a while. So great was his faith in me that he hadn't taken along a name, a phone number, or even an address for a Brazilian Subud contact. He was sure I'd eventually be there. When more time went by, however, and I still had not shown up, he found a Brazilian Catholic priest who fortunately knew English. After Mahmud told him what had happened, the priest went to a public phone, found a number in the directory for Subud-São Paulo—thank God there was one!—and made the call. The person at the other end was just 30 minutes away, she said; told the priest where Mahmud should stand; and everything worked out fine.

I apologized profusely and promised myself I'd find a way to make it up to Mahmud. My chance came twelve days later, appropriately enough at that same airport. This time Bapak and party (and that Mexican brother) were about to leave for Bogotá. Hundreds of us had gone to the airport to wave them off. Bapak and Sharif were ensconced in the VIP lounge. On either side of the door to the room two big security guards stood to keep the VIPs from being disturbed. Suddenly I saw Mahmud. Without thinking, I grabbed his hand and said, "Come with me!" He was surprised but didn't ask any questions. We headed straight for the VIP-lounge door. In the moment before our approach, the guards each turned away, like two oversized ballet dancers in a carefully choreographed *pas de deux*, to bend over and light their cigarettes. So Mahmud and I slipped in without being noticed.

I greeted Bapak and Sharif in Indonesian, wondering why Bapak, who was much older than Sharif, looked fresh, while Sharif himself seemed wasted. Sharif responded in Indonesian that it was always like that. Bapak simply lit up the room with his smile. This time I didn't forget my friend but introduced him to Bapak and Sharif. I also briefly recounted how I had unintentionally left him stranded at this very airport two weeks before.

Bapak by this point was sitting in an easy chair by a big window overlooking the taxi strips and runways. I went over to offer *sunkum*, the traditional Javanese leave-taking ritual, whereby one kneels and kisses the ring of a respected older person. Known for not looking others directly in the eyes for reasons we all speculated on, Bapak looked straight into mine. It was one of those once-in-a-lifetime moments, where time seems to stand still. I felt he knew everything about me, all the good things and all those that were not so good, and that he was none the less bestowing on me an incredible gift of unconditional love. I also flashed on that evening in the summer of 1963, the first time I had seen Bapak, when I had rushed over to shake his hand, leaving dozens of folded chairs to crash to the floor in a cacophonous chain reaction, and received his dead-fish hand and averted face and eyes, while an undeniable look of disgust played over his lips. What a difference! This time I had expected nothing and had received everything—in God's time, not mine.

Another noteworthy thing in my spiritual life happened during the Chicago years (1973 – 1987). My daughter Christine, then in high school in Skokie, Illinois, and I were supposed to go to Ft. Lauderdale, Florida, for my father's eightieth birthday on July 5, 1985. A week before the big day, my sister phoned to say that Daddy had fallen in the lobby of his apartment building, had broken his hip, and was in Holy Cross Hospital. We'd still have some kind of party but scaled way down and in the hospital. It wasn't until we were actually there that I found out the reason he had fallen was that his bones had been weakened by multiple myeloma, bone-marrow cancer. My sister had failed to tell me that, so I had to learn it from the surgeon who wanted to give him a hip replacement. In the end, my father turned the operation down. Maybe he already suspected or even knew that his cancer was fatal. So why, he figured, should he risk the stress of an operation for a year or two with a new hip.

Precisely a year later I was back in South Florida, this time solo. My sister had called to tell me that Dad was not expected to live much beyond his eighty-first birthday, which fell on a Saturday that year. He was back in Holy Cross Hospital with the shingles, a contagious disease which required him to have a single room—a good thing, the single room, as it turned out. My nephew Robert let me know that Grandpa had had some kind of near-death experience before I arrived. He had told Robert that he felt himself going through a tunnel where he got stuck. Eventually, though, he had managed to reverse direction and get out. That story gave me the idea of giving him a copy of Dr. Raymond Moody's first book on the topic, *Life After Life*. I remember going to the shopping mall in North Miami Beach the morning of his birthday and looking in two or three stores before I finally found it. While waiting to cross Collins Avenue to get a card at the nearby Hallmark Store, the Voice visited me once again. This time it told me the most important birthday present I could give my father was the *latihan* so that he could die in peace. But how? I thought. My father had always been antagonistic toward Subud. At best after many years he was now perhaps neutral. I had visions of his rising from his sickbed, cursing me for inflicting my cult on him, then falling down dead. Oy! "Don't worry," the Voice said. "We'll take care of everything." At this point, the light changed, and I crossed the busy street and bought an appropriate card.

That afternoon, I took the Moody book and the card to Dad's hospital room. He hadn't eaten for several weeks and looked very small and pale, hooked up as he was to IVs, one in each arm. I still didn't know how I would broach the idea of his being opened in Subud but had faith the way would somehow emerge. Mother accompanied me to his hospital room, where I asked her to give us some time alone. She said she would wait for me in the hospital cafeteria.

I told my father I had three birthday presents for him. He didn't say anything. By this point, besides being weak, he had a chronic cough. He was listening, though. First, I told him I'd take care of mother from a distance—my sister Natalie, who lived with her, ended up doing most of the work, since Mother hung on for another 13 years till a few months past her ninety-fifth birthday, most of the last years in dementia. I would also pay off as many of his debts as I could, I said. Then I came to the Moody book. "Remember, Dad, how you experienced getting stuck in that tunnel and having to back out? Well, Dr. Raymond Moody talks about those tunnel experiences right here in this little book. I'd like to read you a short passage." Then I read him something about individuals going through the tunnel to get to "The Other Side."

As I was reading, the solution about how to broach Subud to him suddenly hit me. "Remember those spiritual exercises called Subud I've been doing for 25 years?" I asked. He nodded. "Well, one of the benefits of Subud is that it strengthens the soul and makes it possible for the individual to pass smoothly through that tunnel and not get stuck. If you want, I can give you the Subud exercise—you won't have to do anything, just lie there. It would be your third birthday present."

For a long moment he said nothing. I was half thinking that a curse was imminent. Then, with a little shrug he said quietly, "What could it hurt?" We were on! The Voice had once again been right. As I was preparing to begin, there was a knock on the door and an East Indian nurse, Mrs. Sharma, came in to take Dad's temperature and blood pressure. By this point I felt as if I was on a roll. After Mrs. Sharma had written down his readings and was about to exit, I asked her if she wouldn't mind putting the "Do Not Disturb" sign on the door, since I was about to do *puja* with my Dad. Thanks to my time with the Vivekananda-Vedanta Society in Chicago in the early 60s, I knew that was the Hindu term for prayer. "Oh, Jack," she smiled at my father, "you are very, very lucky to be having a son who is doing *puja* with you." She tiptoed out the door with the Do Not Disturb sign in hand. Before she left, she stuck her head back in the doorway and, with another big smile, repeated, "Very, very lucky indeed!" Then she carefully closed the door.

Even with the sign, I wasn't sure how long we would have before someone knocked. So I got right down to business. Shortening the usual spoken ritual before the Opening, I simply said a short prayer inviting God to give my father the blessing of the *latihan*. Then I said "Begin!" and started my exercise. Although my eyes were closed, I could hear the frequency of his chronic cough decrease. After about 20 minutes I stopped, saying "Finish!" for his benefit. When I asked him if he had felt anything, he said no. Then he asked me, "How is Mr. Bapak?" I remember when I was first opened that he would contemptuously refer to Pak Subuh as "the Hindu Jesus." (In retrospect, that was not such a bad characterization.) In my head, to be sure, I would always think of the phrase "power pack" when thinking of the term *Bapak*. So who was I to criticize? For that matter, mine wasn't such a bad characterization either!

"He's 85 now and pretty frail," I answered. "And what about Madam Farida?" He asked next. Farida, you might remember from an earlier chapter, was a wild Indonesian woman who had been Sukarno's palmist. Although an early Subud member, she mixed in every other possible spiritual and New Age method she came across, so that it was hard to say exactly what Farida was. All her craziness notwithstanding, she was a fantastic palmist. Once when she happened to be visiting us in Chicago, Simone and I took her to my parents' apartment on the Near North Side. Despite their dismissive attitude toward such things, neither one said no when she offered to read their palms. I distinctly recall their eyes getting bigger and bigger as they exchanged glances. Apparently she was telling them things they thought only they knew. So, whatever they thought about Subud, they were definitely blown away by Ibu Farida.

"She passed away last year at her son's place in Canada," I told him. At this point, my mother arrived. She hadn't wanted to wait in the cafeteria any longer. I told her I had just opened Daddy in Subud. She nodded and smiled. I guess she figured it couldn't hurt either. So I took leave of my dad. This would be the last time I saw him alive, for the following Friday, six days later, he died. I was back in Chicago at the time. That night Victor Margolin, the other group helper, and I tested "How is the state of Jack Feldman now?" Victor received that his state was very positive. I was moved to say, "The *latihan* is terrific, Kid! Why didn't you tell me about this before?" (Of course I had many times, but he had always dismissed it out of hand as "a bunch of crap!") He continued in my receiving, "But don't worry, I'm doing it here now."

That weekend I got a call from my sister. Although Dad had told me he wanted his ashes scattered at sea, the family put its foot down. They all insisted on a plaque somewhere where they could go and pay their respects. Even though I had given Dad my word, what could I do? I was outnumbered. Plus they did have a point: The plaque in a Jewish cemetery would be for them—us—not so much for him.

Furthermore, they wanted me to do the service. After all, as my sister put it, I was the educated and religious one in the family. Moreover, since they didn't belong to any Jewish congregation, my sister was embarrassed to call some rabbi out of the blue for fear he would try to shame her into going to his temple. So I was the one. "Only make sure not to put any Christian or Subud stuff into it!" Natalie strongly warned. (As you'll hear in a later chapter, I had become a Christian—a Lutheran like Simone—in March 1967.) "Don't worry," I assured her. "I'll keep it simple and even add a little Jewish flavor." So I put together a short service with quotations from Walt Whitman, Rilke, Kahlil Gibran, and a few others plus a reading of the traditional Jewish mourner's *Kaddish*. I handed out copies of the program with all the texts and asked different family members to each read one. Then, just as we were about to start—it had been sunny a few minutes before—a fierce electrical storm with driving wind and rain broke out. We were all huddled beneath the cantilevers of the outdoor section of the cemetery where the urns where placed in receptacles. There were some loud thunderclaps, and several lightning bolts struck nearby. Given the timing and all, I felt my father's spirit was expressing its displeasure. He did have a bad temper after all. So I went away to a covered spot fifty feet from the others, looked up, and said, "Dad, give us a break. This isn't for you, it's for us." Five minutes later, the storm stopped as quickly as it had started, and the sun came out again. The only signs of the recent pyrotechnics were ubiquitous puddles and a bunch of wet but still legible programs. We quickly went through the 20-minute service without a hitch, and afterwards everyone went back to my parents' and Natalie's apartment for cold cuts, coffee cake, and hot drinks. As we pulled out of the cemetery lot in Natalie's boyfriend's Cadillac, I noticed that a block away the streets were bone dry. "It must have been a localized storm," David offered. "Yes," I thought to myself. "Very localized!"

While I was in Ft. Lauderdale, my nephew Robert told me a few stories about Grandpa's last week. "For one thing, Uncle Reynold, he would be talking with me, clear as a bell, and then he would look up and start speaking some foreign language. When I asked him what he was doing, he said his own grandfather was in the room to tell him all about how things were on the other side. Even crazier was the thing with the beautiful blond woman in white. When he told me about her, I was sure he meant Charlene, the day nurse. 'No, it's not a nurse, Robert.' He said. 'It's the lady who's going to take me to the other side.'" How interesting, I thought, that the Angel of Death would come to my father of all people as a beautiful blond *shiksa,* Yiddish for a Gentile woman! A ladies' man, he would have followed her anywhere, even to his death. And how compassionate on the part of God to send him the perfect person to take him on his final journey to the land from which, as Shakespeare put it, no traveler returns.

A week or two later, back in Chicago, I had a vivid dream. It was as though I was looking down from above through one of those Las Vegas-style ceiling spy cameras. The scene wasn't a casino, though, but the dining room of a cruise ship. There at the captain's table was a finely dressed collection of handsome men and women, all elegantly elongated like figures in an El Greco painting. In the midst of them sat the captain, impeccably clad in a gleaming white uniform with shiny brass buttons, golden epaulets, and a chest full of medals. He had a gun-metal-silver crew cut and penetrating blue eyes, the bluest eyes I had ever seen, like the blue in some of David Hockney's Los Angeles paintings. My father, one of the guests, was arrayed in his white dinner jacket with the maroon bow tie and cummerbund I had inherited. All of a sudden he became aware of my spying on him, raised his eyes in my direction, and said in his New York accent, "As you can see, Kid, I'm having a mahvelous time!" Not surprisingly, when I awoke, I felt fine. I knew Dad was in a good place.

12
Metropolitan State University and Subud Twin Cities

MY FIRST day of work at Metropolitan State University was September 17, 1987. Just as the coordinator of Women's Studies, who reported to me, had been the unsuccessful candidate for the head of CPD, so at Metro State two of the deans, both talented women, had been the internal finalists for academic VP. The president, Reatha Clark King, a black woman, had apparently decided that rather than make the difficult choice between the two, she would go with the male outsider, me. I thus spent a good part of the three months before Christmas interviewing not only the core faculty but also the people who reported to me—to get the lay of the land as well as build positive relations and assuage any hurt feelings. This proved an effective strategy.

Again, I was eager to create a positive, collaborative community. Metro State, after all, was one of the premier innovative universities in America. Initially, there was no campus, only an office above a drugstore in downtown Saint Paul. A small core of resident faculty would be supplemented in their work with adult students by so-called community faculty, practical experts in their fields. Also, there would be no grades, only narrative transcripts in which the respective resident faculty would recount what the students had learned and could now do as a result of each course. Besides a small cluster of offices, Metro made use of leased classroom space in churches, synagogues, union halls, YMCAs, and the like. The model had been sold to the State University System as being cheaper than the old-fashioned campus-based college or university with costly buildings and a large faculty and support staff. These would not be needed for self-motivated adults who would work collaboratively with faculty in transcribing prior college-equivalent learning and mix in individualized educational projects alongside their coursework.

As someone who had become involved early in so-called innovative education, I was delighted to be the chief academic officer—the number-two person—of this cutting-edge institution, now a "university" in name with a nursing and business college as well as the original college of arts and sciences. By this point in Metro State's history, however, outside forces at the State level were pressing the institution to become what some Metro faculty called "Mankato State in the Cities." I should note that at that time there were four distinct post-high-school educational systems in Minnesota: The University of Minnesota System, the state's flagship; our State University System—seven universities with "State" as their second name—of which Metro State was the youngest; the community-college system; and the technical-college system. The "U," as it was called, one of the largest federal land-grant universities in the country with a number of famous programs and departments, and its Big Ten football team, was itself located in both the Twin Cities of Minneapolis and Saint Paul. (As the largest metropolitan area in the Upper Midwest, people in the surrounding states of Wisconsin, the Dakotas, and Iowa, not to mention the four million residents of the State of Minnesota, familiarly referred to it as "The Cities." One would hear someone in Mitchell, South Dakota, for example, say, "I'm going up to the Cities for the weekend.")

Now Mankato State University, located in Southeastern Minnesota, was the largest and one of the oldest of the seven member institutions in our system. Mankato had a range of master's programs and maybe even a few doctoral ones by then plus a traditional campus with a stadium, student union, dorms, the works. Academically, they were traditional too. No narrative transcripts, no Individual Learning Contracts, no community faculty. They were meat and potatoes with an annual budget that dwarfed ours. By contrast, we were sushi. And wonderful state that it was and is, Minnesota with its "bachelor Norwegian farmers" was more meat and potatoes, or at least *lutefisk* and potatoes, than *sushi*. Long story short, I spent a lot of time and energy during my two-and-a-half years as VP trying to maintain Metro's uniqueness in the face of strong forces wanting it to become more traditional. After perhaps nine months, Dr. King left Metro's presidency to become head of the General Mills Foundation in Minneapolis. As interim leader—in part at my suggestion to our System chancellor—we got Dr. Charles Graham, a veteran president who had piloted the other larger institution in our system, Saint Cloud State, followed by seven years as president of Hamline University, a Methodist school in Saint Paul that claimed being the oldest higher-education institution in the state. A handsome silver-fox of a man, just 60 when he joined us, Chuck Graham came from the Illinois town next to the one where President Ronald Reagan had grown up and had that same laid-back style and soothing accent. He always suggested to me a 747 pilot who calmly announced in flight that three of the four engines had cut out but that the fourth one was working fine and that we passengers should sit back and relax since we'd be landing safely in an hour—and we'd believe him.

Chuck was a wonderful leader with a light hand on the tiller. When we VPs would meet with him each Monday morning, he was genuinely interested in what we had to say about any given subject, and while he had ideas of his own—good ideas—he never had a problem putting his aside and taking up ours if he thought they were better. Supportive not intrusive, Chuck encouraged each of us to manage as we thought best. Although a traditionalist, he understood Metro State's claim to fame was its distinctive programs and pedagogy, and he was always willing to seek ways to improve quality without forcing us to become another run-of-the-mill state university. Sticking up for us, moreover, required him to stand his ground with the System chancellor and above all the Vice Chancellor for Academic Affairs, a strong-minded, bright, but controlling woman who was not so sure about the correctness of letting Metro State continue its historic commitment to innovation.

I knew from the outset that Chuck Graham would pilot Metro State for a year at most. About six months into his interim presidency, the System Chancellor began the search process for a new permanent leader. The Committee selected two finalists, an African American man currently head of a community-college system in another Midwestern state, and a Japanese-Filipino expert on artificial intelligence who was at the time the academic vice president at Boise State University in Idaho. The former seemed laid back but not too exciting. I and most of my colleagues favored the latter, who, though from Montana, evoked positive memories in me of Asian American colleagues in Hawai'i. In the event, he became Metro State's next president. Less than seven months later, however, I was requesting the Personnel Office that I be terminated so that I could lay claim to my statutory one-year reassignment while looking for another job. The new president turned out to be a real autocrat. The tipping point for me came when he kept pushing me to fire the dean of Business and Management, whom I had hired a year before and who impressed me as doing a good job. I kept demurring but knew it was only a matter of time before we both got fired.

I still remember the Friday when I stayed up all night in a kind of argument with God. After the family fell asleep—Simone was aware of my dissatisfaction with my new boss but not of the current state of affairs—I snuck down to our family room and did a quiet *latihan*. During this all-night session, I kept trying to receive guidance about what to do. Should I fire the Business dean and save my job? No. Should I hang on, temporize, and ultimately get fired along with that dean? No. What should I do? No answer—at least not at first. Finally, it became clear to me that I would have to request my own firing. First, though, I would check to see if I could be transferred to the State System Office in downtown Saint Paul. My desire was to work again with Chuck Graham for a year, since he had now become the Associate to the Chancellor for International Programs. His main focus in fact was on coordinating the first years of the System's new bi-national community college in Akita, Japan. The idea was that American students in our System could spend up to two years there learning Japanese and becoming familiar with the culture while the Japanese students would learn English and complete their Minnesota general-education requirements. After, the latter would have free access to our System's Minnesota institutions at highly affordable in-state tuition rates. My background both academically and internationally was perfect for such a position. Plus working with Chuck would be healing after a tough seven months with my extremely difficult new boss—a period that had played havoc with my self-esteem.

By three in the morning, I was so tired that my upset about the situation had abated to some extent and my decision about what to do had become clear. Then the Voice commented, "If you knew the role of your boss in your life, you would consider him an angel from God." It took me years before I understood or could accept what that meant. At that time and for some months thereafter, the Devil would have been a better comparison as far as I was concerned. But now, at a distance of 18 years, I can say that interesting work for foundations, the Literature of Wisdom course, my new career as an academic and nonprofit consultant, the founding of the nonprofits Blue Sky Associates and Wisdom Factors International, the move to Hawai'i, the writing of four books, my work as a fundraiser, and the making of wonderful new friends in the Islands and elsewhere—in short, the rest of my life—would not have happened as it did. Moreover, my work with Chuck for the System had the additional benefit of garnering me a free work-related trip to Japan, where I could use my rudimentary Japanese, see a bit of the country, and visit my old East-West Center student, the late Munetsugu Uruno, an English teacher at a high school in Ibaraki-ken. In the end, everything worked out just fine. As usual, the Voice had been right.

As far as my spiritual life goes, two other noteworthy things happened during the Minnesota years (1987 – 1996). They both had to do with

Subud.

Although I usually did *latihan* with our small group of five or six regularly exercising men, once in a while I added a third exercise per week at home. During one of the latter, I had another of my rare visualizations. I remember lying on my stomach on the floor. My eyes were closed, and I was in a half-sleep state—what I came to call a "sleepy-*han*." Suddenly I became aware of seeing Bapak's face, which morphed into the face of a golden Buddha and then back again. This transformation occurred three or four times before the visualization stopped. There were no accompanying words, but I immediately concluded that this was an indication of who Bapak really was, an enlightened soul among us. I had always *thought* that was the case. But here from my inner was a kind of independent confirmation. And although one result of doing *latihan* for so many years has been to relieve me of much of my memory so I could be free to live in the present, this experience has stayed with me for over 15 years.

The next Subud experience concerned helper work. My fellow helper, a retired minister named Carl Peters, was dying. One day I was doing *latihan* with him at home. We were alone, just the two of us; his wife, Donna, was in another room. Carl lay on a couch, while I did my usual active exercise in which I walked around and sang. Suddenly, toward the end of the 30 minutes, I began to sing the *Nunc Dimittis* in English: "Now let thy servant depart in peace. . . ." As a trained Lutheran clergyman, Carl was of course familiar with this Biblical prayer. Afterward, when I was about to go, he thanked me, especially for those words. A few weeks later he passed away peacefully at a nearby hospital.

※

By the time my extended one-year transitional assignment ended on June 30, 1991, I still didn't have a job. I had been fairly confident that with my background and experience, I would have found at least one acceptable position. However, there isn't much room at the top, and each college or university presidency or vice presidency might have 200 candidates, most of them qualified. Fortunately, I was able to get two fairly well-paying longer-term consultancies in higher education that would begin July 1. Also, for the first time in my life, I applied for and received unemployment insurance. Still, when July first came round, I was apprehensive. Ever since my first job had begun in September 1965, I had never been unemployed. There had always been an adequate salary and good benefits. The lone exception had been that year in Germany. Now I was on the high wire without a safety net once again. "Don't worry," my old University of Hawai'i buddy Loren Ekroth counseled. "You're not unemployed—you're *self-employed*." Not wanting to leave anything to chance, I also tested. "Would our family get through this time okay?" I asked tentatively. Then the Voice took the opportunity to answer one question with another: "When was the last time I let you down, Reynold?" "Never," I responded. "Then don't worry. I don't plan to let you down this time either." And as the next seventeen and a half years have proved, "He" didn't.

Bapak in Germany – late 1960s

Husein Rofé, who brought Subud to the West, has tea with us. Kaneʻohe, Oʻahu – late 1990s

English physicist John Bennett, who helped spread Subud in the early years, with Ruth Gruson - Planegg – Bavaria, 1962 or 1963

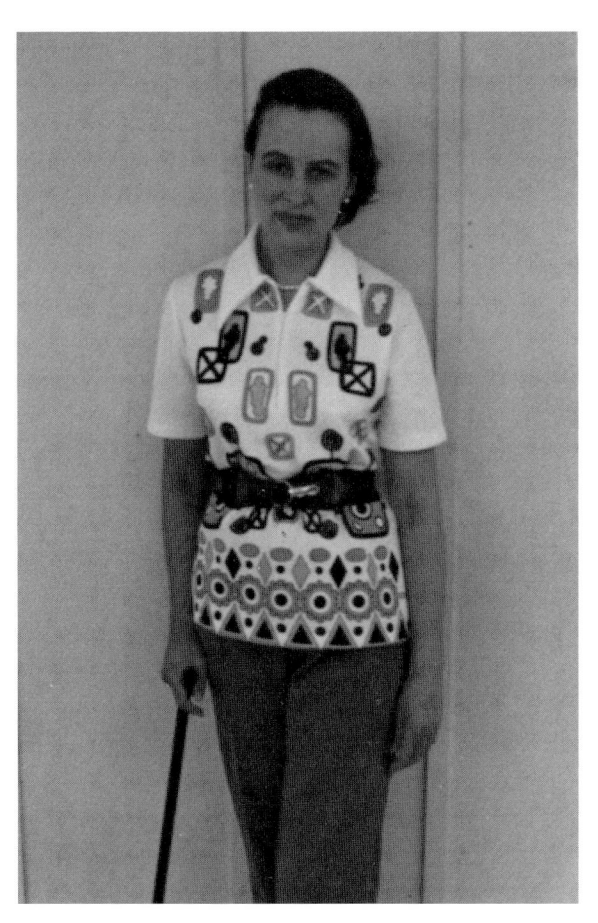

Baroness C. M. "Michèle" von Royk-Lewinski, the helper who opened Simone. Photo taken on the Island of Hawai'i, 1973

The incomparable Francis von Kahler
(l) entertains another Subud member in
Germany – late 1960s.

Sharif Horthy, grandson of the wartime
regent of Hungary and Bapak's long-time
secretary and interpreter, with his wife, Tuti,
Bapak's grand-daughter

Simone (and Marianne) greet Bapak at
Honolulu International Airport –
April 1, 1968.

Bapak makes a comment at Hilo Airport,
Island of Hawai'i, during the May 1968 visit
to his land. Baron Ludwig von Royk -
Lewinski (l) and interpreter Muhammad
Usman (r)

Ibu Farida, the famous Indonesian palmist, visits us in Honolulu – early 1970s.

Bapak, Ibu, and party with the Honolulu Subud Group in the Honolulu International Airport VIP Lounge – April 1, 1968

Members of Subud-Honolulu before *latihan* at Dick's Danish, Kaimuki, with Marianne – ca. 1970

Varindra Vittachi, long-time World Subud Association Chair and my mentor, gives me some advice – Honolulu Airport, ca. 1970.

Florine Tolson Bond, my first spiritual guide, shows Simone and Christine how to work a well pump – Kent County, Maryland; summer 1981.

Grandpa Max and Grandma Sarah Potash(nik) with ten of their eleven children; Mother, back row right next to her twin, Helen – ca. 1915

Dad's younger brother, Murray, marries Aunt Eva; Dad, Grandma Ida, and Grandpa Paul stand beside them (l to r) – early 1940s.

Mother, elegant as ever, at our wedding –
New Haven, Connecticut; November 30, 1963

One of the last photos of the four of us (me, Mother, Natalie, and Dad) – Palm Beach, Florida; May 1981

Grandma Ida Feldman – Liberty, New York; Fall 1963

Mother, looking good at 90, on probably her final cruise

Stevie, age 9 or 10 but trying to look older, during a late-fall trip to Atlantic City, New Jersey

Now fourteen but still trying to look older – Santa Monica beach, California; summer 1954

The Peddie Varsity Swimming Team; I'm first row right – Hightstown, New Jersey; winter 1956

Sailing the E-Class scow, North Star Camp – Hayward, Wisconsin; summer 1956

Dad and me –
Chicago; 1960-1961

John Travis and I cross the Honolulu Marathon finish line together to raise money for the homeless – December 12, 1999.

UNIVERSITÄT HEIDELBERG
STUDENTENAUSWEIS

für stud. phil.
Stephen Michael Feldman
Vor- und Zuname (in Blockschrift ausfüllen)
geboren am 6. 11. 1939
zu New York City
Wohnort der Eltern: Chicago/Ill.
des Ehegatten:
Staatsangehörigkeit: U. S. A.

10. Dez. 1958
(Immatrikulationstag)

DER REKTOR:

Unterschrift des Studierenden

Main page of my student I.D. at Heidelberg University, West Germany – fall 1958

My nice Heidelberg landlady, "student mother" Frau Laupp – Heidelberg, spring 1958

Celebrating New Year's 1959 at the Essen City Hall with Family Engels; my friend Hans is at the right and I am fourth from right.

After years at boys' schools, I learn to date, *auf deutsch* – with Elisabeth; April 1959.

Exploring the ruins of Delphi, Greece; Simone is first with "Mexiko" behind her; I'm fourth from the front – April 1959.

Ticket stub from the National Museum – Athens, Greece; April 1959

Dean Feldman makes a point at
Northeastern Illinois University, Chicago –
ca. 1980.

Making an announcement at Blue Sky's
"Teaching from Within" Conference –
Northfield, Minnesota; July 1996

At a Trinity
Lutheran Church
Choir party –
Northbrook, Illinois;
summer 1987

Celebrating my 50th
birthday with a
morning Flamenco at
home – St. Paul,
Minnesota;
November 6, 1989

As Stanley Tutter, the Christmas elf, in the musical
"The Birthday Party" – Trinity Lutheran Church,
Evanston, Illinois; Advent, mid-1980s

With Yale English professor Richard Sewall, whose
1963 letter made Simone's Green Card possible –
Chicago, mid-1980s

Sharing a joke with Subud brother and friend the late Hamilton Manley – Kilauea Crater, Hawai'i; late-1990s

Louise in Denmark playing "big horsey" with me; I'm the horsey, of course! Winter 2008

Simone as Zulayka for Fasching (Carnival) –
Grünwald, Bavaria; 1954

In the "Hat Parade" on the *Maasdam*, coming to America – October 1963

As a lady of mystery – Honolulu, ca. 2000

Simone chatting with Former West German
Chancellor Willi Brandt – St. Paul, Minnesota;
April 17, 1988

Opposite top: My confirmation as a Lutheran with
Pastor Waldo Johnson – Evanston, Illinois;
early 1980s

Opposite lower: With Pastor Doug Olson at Calvary
Lutheran Church, Honolulu – 1988

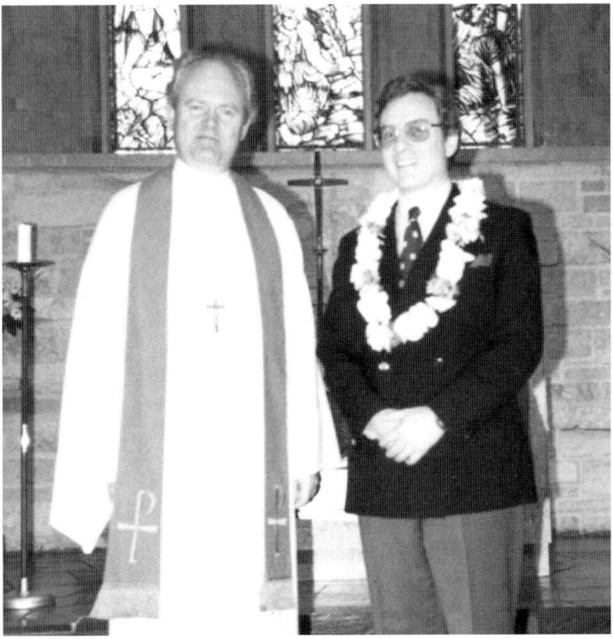

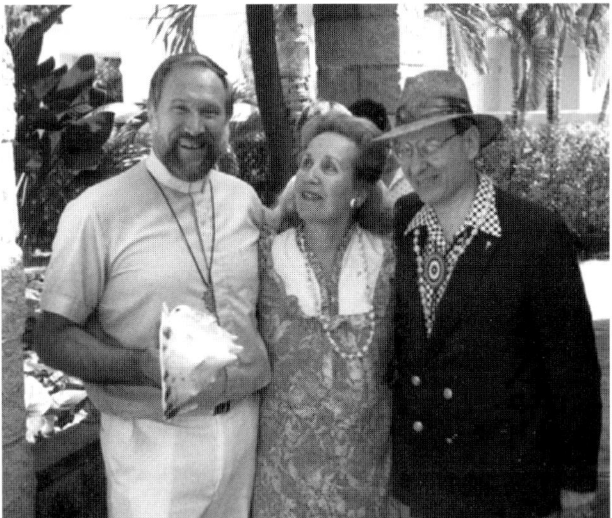

Christine Jacqueline Feldman, our younger
daughter, as bridesmaid at her sister's wedding –
Honolulu, June 1998

Marianne Michèle Feldman (now Levine) – "Marianna" at her Confirmation party – Cavalry Lutheran Church, Honolulu, Spring 1980

Sister Eileen Rice, O.P., at our St. Paul home –
October 1988

With Bishop Larry Silva, head of the
Catholic Diocese of Honolulu – 2006

Dr. Jonas Salk, my wisdom mentor, makes a point at the Salk Institute, La Jolla, California – ca. 1980.

Sister Hèléne Louise Zimmerman, R.S.H.M. – New York City, September 1998

13
Simone

IN TERMS of the priceless gift of Subud, Pak Subuh, Bapak, is without doubt the most important person in my life. In terms of someone I have actually lived with, however, that person is Simone, my late wife.

Simone was born Hannelore Elfriede Margarete Zimmermann on March 4, 1931, in Roessel, East Prussia, Germany, now northern Poland. She beautifully retells the dramatic first fourteen years of her life in her *Voices from a Vanished Past—Memories of a Christian Childhood in Hitler's Germany*, the excerpted memoir she held in her hands exactly one week before she died. The point of that book was to show how, thanks to a caring family and her own strong, resilient nature, she managed to grow up mainly unscathed, inwardly and outwardly, during the Third Reich and ultimately escaped to West Germany with her family from the advancing Russian Army just before the end of World War II. Her mother, Mutti (later Oma) was the hero of the story, since she was able to cajole, bribe, or shame the German MPs into letting her and her two daughters leave East Prussia despite the general order requiring civilians to stay put. Thanks to Mutti's courage, the three of them arrived in the Munich suburb of Grünwald, Bavaria, in what would become the American Zone of Occupation in May 1945. There they would be safe.

Simone was a talented dancer and actress, whom the requirements of the post-War period kept from having a career in either field. Instead, she worked as best she could as a secretary/stenographer in Munich, while saving up for holidays in Paris, the Austrian Alps, Italy, or—in the case of our fateful meeting—Greece. Fortunately, she worked most of the time for a large Munich-based chemical company, Wacker Chemie. In the annual company cabaret, Simone was inevitably a star, singing, dancing, and showing a flare for comedy.

A formative experience was the year she spent, 1951-52, as an au pair to a family in England. While caring for their year-old son, Keith, she learned spoken English, a language she could already read and write, and got a respite from the stresses of early post-War Germany. She was 20 when she arrived and 21 on return. It was her good fortune that the family, the Millers, had an apartment in London, where they owned a fancy French restaurant, and a country house in Great

Missenden, Buckinghamshire. Simone got to spend time and care for Keith at both. The year she was with them, moreover, they wintered on the French Riviera at Juan-les-Pains, where she picked up some French as well as a taste for places with warm sunshine and palm trees.

By the time we married in November 1963, she was 32½ while I had just turned 24. Like our younger daughter, Christine, Simone was blessed with always looking younger than her years. So, except for family members and a few close friends, no one knew about or could see our age difference. That situation remained true throughout most of our marriage. Then, when she turned 70 and looked between 50 and 60, she started telling people her age, since she loved to see their shocked faces. The day before her seventieth birthday, in fact, when we were at the wedding of a young friend, a handsome man, perhaps 40, asked her to slow-dance. She was dressed in one of her best muumuus, well-made-up as usual, and had her hair down with Hawaiian flowers in it. Always beautiful, she looked stunning that night outdoors in the light of the full moon and the flickering tiki torches. When I came back from the bar with mai-tais in hand, she thanked the young man and explained she had been planning to share a drink with her husband. After, she told me in German, the language we generally spoke together, "*Na, Pappa. Pass' auf! Ich hab' noch Chancen.*" ("You'd better watch out, Pappa. I still can attract a man!") For any Freudians out there, I should note that, following the German custom, Simone and I referred to each other, once we had children, as "Pappa" and "Mama" or variants thereof. This was totally conventional, although a former student thought our addressing each other that way strange.

Simone was an excellent companion, easy-going and a good listener. All that helped since I was intense and talkative. Over the years we tended to flow into new situations well together, since as an academician I generally had to move to new jobs. She was used to moving too, since her father, who had refused to join the Nazi Party, was frequently transferred to new country schools as a form of harassment. Then, toward War's end, as I reported, the women in the family had to flee from present-day Poland to extreme southwestern Germany and start all over again.

Simone was not a linguist. Even though she, her mother, and sister Gerda arrived in Munich when Simone had just turned fourteen, she never learned the local Bavarian dialect and was made fun of in school as a "*Sau-Preuss*", a "damn Prussian"—the term Bavarians apply to any speaker of standard German. Later, despite living in the

United States for over 40 years plus her year as a young woman in England, she always spoke English with a marked German accent. Our kids' school friends, who loved to imitate her, would ask her to say "squirrel," which she inevitably pronounced *skvill*. She excused herself by saying she was always speaking German with her husband and mother. "Reinhold did not want to forget his German, you know, and Mutti cannot speak English."

Although primarily a wife and mother, Simone worked from time to time. While I was in graduate school, she was a secretary for two neurologists. She also babysat a few days a week and inherited my old job teaching German at the New Haven YMCA. Her earnings were essential to paying our bills. Once in Flushing she taught German for a year at the Berlitz School in Manhasset, Long Island. From the time Marianne was born, however, she became a stay-at-home mom, although she occasionally translated documents into or out of German for Berlitz. During our first years in Hawai'i, she did not work at all. Then, when Bapak began rallying Subud members to do enterprises, she set up Alohalani Batiks and the Batik Boutique with the Fongs.

In later life, Simone wrote a few articles that were published in Subud magazines or newspapers plus a notable story about her family just after World War II, "The First Christmas of Peace," which the *Minneapolis Star-Tribune* brought out on December 25, 1995, to commemorate the fiftieth anniversary of that occasion. The article later became the final chapter of her memoir. While none of these pieces brought in money, they did show she had a real talent for writing in English, where her language was absolutely accent free. Taught by her friend Ivy Olson to make bracelets out of safety pins, rubber bands, beads, and buttons with loops, Simone began in the early 80s to design and produce them for sale. Each piece was unique and beautiful. She made necklaces and earrings as well. She often worked at night, when things were quiet and no one bothered her. Soon she was earning enough from her handiwork to pay for all her birthday and Christmas presents and have pin money for her own needs. To this day people tell me they still wear Simone's costume jewelry when they go out on special occasions. Subud members add that wearing Simone's creations makes them happy.

Throughout her life, Simone was a dedicated Subud helper. She managed to find the time to explain Subud to interested people and test with members even though she was burdened with caring for her invalid mother during many of those years. Bapak had appointed her a helper in 1962, a voluntary job she worked at without a break until her final illness. She was also kind and charitable, someone who never forgot to send presents and birthday greetings or give food or money to people in need. She treated everyone with respect and didn't have a racist bone in her body. Finally, nothing impressed me more than how she faced the process of dying. So I'll conclude this brief description of my wife of 43 years with that story.

Simone's health was good throughout our marriage. She did have chronic digestive problems, though, which were somewhat alleviated in the late 1980s when her gall bladder was removed. The only other operation she had during our time together was gum surgery in Chicago. Even after her gall bladder was taken out, however, she was periodically bothered by abdominal pains. Therefore, when she had such a spell in spring 2006, neither she nor her doctor paid it much heed. It simply seemed like more of the same. By this time, I should add, we had been living in Honolulu again for ten years after moving from Saint Paul. When the pains did not abate after a time as they usually did, the doctor ordered an MRI. Kaiser's specialists found something in the pictures they didn't like, so Simone was immediately called back for a CT scan. The next day, June 22, 2006, which would have been Bapak's one-hundred-fifth birthday had he lived, found us on the H-1 Freeway bound for the Kaiser Hospital in Moanalua for the results. The sun was shining, and a bright rainbow floated just above our destination. All the signs seemed positive, so we were hoping for good news. But God's idea of good news and ours sometimes differ.

When we arrived, we went to the office of the young Japanese American surgeon who was Kaiser's pancreatic specialist. He showed us the pictures of Simone's pancreas; then sketched what a normal pancreas would look like. In Simone's case, he explained, the organ had been distended by a cancerous mass that had completely filled it. He next showed other pictures which indicated the cancer had spread to the large intestines as well as the liver. The good news, if we wished to regard it that way, was that surgery was unnecessary as were radiation and chemotherapy. He would be recommending palliative care only and told us our Kaiser membership included access to an excellent pain-management program. We did not think to ask how long Simone could expect to live.

On the way home, the sun was still shining as we descended from the Moanalua hills toward downtown Honolulu. The rainbow was now gone. Or if it was there, we were headed in the wrong direction to see it. Simone's mind was clear as the sky. As we drove, she told me her wishes. First, she wanted to die at home, where she could be surrounded by me, her friends, her things, and her cat. Second, she wanted the kids and our granddaughter to come sooner rather than later so that they would remember her looking as she always had. She did not want them there for her death. Third, she wanted to become Catholic so that she could die in the same religion as me. Much as she liked the people at Calvary Lutheran Church in 'Aina Haina, she felt a greater closeness to the members of our Catholic parish in Manoa Valley. Finally, she wanted to hold a copy of her memoir in her hands before she died.

When we got home, we both did *latihans*. Toward the end, as I was lying on my back on the floor, The Voice whispered in my left ear, "This is the right time for your wife to die. She will die in September." After, we decided to get a second opinion from my friend Dr. Bradley Wong, general surgeon at the Queen's Hospital and professor of Surgery at the University of Hawai'i Medical School. This he graciously provided without charge. Simone and I also discussed the fact that in a week Christine and I were booked to fly to Morocco for the Third Vittachi Conference, where we were scheduled to do a workshop together. Simone still felt okay and had received that it was important for us to go despite her new situation. What a woman! So I arranged with Dr. Wong for the second opinion while making sure that Simone would be cared for at home, primarily by our downstairs neighbor and friend Christine Heath, who was also a patient of Dr. Wong's. Soon enough he had confirmed the Kaiser doctor's diagnosis, had talked with Simone about how a Zen Buddhist approach to her situation might help, and had given her a CD of his piano playing, something as an accomplished classical pianist he often gave his patients. The girls and Halinah Busack as well as the local Subud members were notified, and our daughter Christine and I left for Morocco as planned, where we were well seen to by Sharif Horthy, executive director of the Guerrand-Hermès Foundation and Bapak's long-time secretary, and his wife, Tuti, Bapak's beloved granddaughter.

I remember encountering them soon after arrival in one of the courtyards at El-Akhwain University in Ifrane, in the mountains above Fez and Meknes, where the conference was being held. I told them about Simone; then started sobbing. They both hugged me for what seemed a long time as I cried and cried. It was very consoling. Tuti made sure to do special *latihans* with Christine, whom a beautiful English Subud sister and helper, Laila Armstrong, also took under her wing—going swimming with her on one occasion and doing special *latihans* with her also. Christine met and became friends with a lovely young Polish woman, Adrianna, a newly minted Ph.D. who taught English at a university in Vraclav, formerly the German city of Breslau. Later, during her Fulbright year in Germany, Christine would visit Adrianna and her husband in Poland, and the two women have stayed in e-mail contact ever since. As for me, I was able to do *latihan* with the Subud men at the conference, perhaps eight of us, in Simon Guerrand-Hermès's spacious quarters each morning and most evenings. That much *latihan* versus the usual twice a week proved an excellent preparation for the two months that lay ahead.

Upon my return to Honolulu, I contacted the Saint Francis Hospice Program. The intake nurse turned out to be the daughter of a colleague of mine in the local interfaith work. We were pleased to learn that Simone's Medicare would cover the entire expense of the program, and in fact the only thing we ended up having to pay for was the $25 rental fee for a portable adjustable table that fit above the hospital bed that would soon be moved into our living room. Even Simone's medication, mainly morphine in first tablet then liquid form, would be covered. I bought a shoji screen to match the one we already had. With the two screens, we could give Simone the privacy she needed in the living room, where she could watch TV or see videos if she wished. Later, toward the end, I slept on our pull-out couch that was perpendicular to Simone's hospital bed and only a few feet away.

During the time I was in Morocco, Christine Heath did a marvelous job of caring for Simone. She would cook gourmet meals downstairs, replete with wine, and bring them up for the two of them to eat by candlelight on our Rosenthal china, on a linen tablecloth with matching napkins. Fortunately, Simone maintained her appetite till six weeks before her death and enjoyed the meals and companionship. Christine also treated Simone to a top-of-the-line pedicure and manicure. Subud sisters came over regularly to do *latihan* with Simone, while others stopped by to visit, for example, our Vietnamese friend Quynh Nguyen with her Turkish Bulgarian friend Sibel Mestanova. The two girls, in their 30s, had just come from hula class, so they demonstrated what they had learned to Simone. She in turn taught them the Viennese waltz.

On my return from Morocco, we both worked on editing excerpts from her memoir. Fortunately, I had already keyed in and edited the primary chapters, which, once published, came to 250 printed pages. There was no time to do the remaining chapters, perhaps another hundred pages, so—time being of the essence—we decided to go with what we had and gave this version the title *Excerpts from Voices from a Vanished Past*. I could always do the remaining chapters later. Meanwhile, I had checked online and learned that the mean time for someone with stage IV-B pancreatic cancer, or a cancer that had metastasized to at least one "distant organ," was three months from the time of diagnosis. That meant that if Simone were anywhere close to the mean, we were looking at her dying two months from the time of my return from North Africa.

Although he had no time to do a foreword, we got a wonderful endorsement for the book from the noted Quaker educator and author Parker Palmer. Bishop Stephen Randolph Sykes had agreed to do the graphics and cover design as well as place the photos including the captions, all things in which he had expertise. And Jan Rumi, president of Wisdom Factors International, the nonprofit for which I was executive director, offered to make sure a pre-publication edition would be printed and bound in time for Simone to hold a copy in her hands.

So now Simone and I set to work selecting and captioning the photographs for the two sets of inserted pages that would eventually grace the book. She had had the presence of mind as a fourteen-year-old to grab the family's irreplaceable photo albums as she, her sister and mother fled on foot from the rapidly advancing Red Army. This joint effort was a good form of occupational therapy for us as well as a final collaborative project, recapitulating the many mailings, writings, translations, garage sales, and other things we had done together in the past.

Soon after my return from Morocco, Fr. Philip Chircop, S.J., the forty-something priest from Toronto, originally from Malta, came to town for a month or so. He had been in Honolulu several times in past years to do missions in our church as well as staff-development workshops for the priests of the Diocese. He was an incredible workshop facilitator and speaker, and in retrospect I am sure he is one of the main reasons Simone decided to become Catholic and I to remain one. Once a Catholic acquaintance, a woman, had given Simone something called "The Chaplet of Mary," a kind of Rosary that was supposed to substitute for Holy Communion for non-Catholics who were not permitted to take the Eucharist. Simone was upset by this gift, since she had always received the Host and the Cup at our church. Since she attended Mass with me even during the week sometimes, the priests all knew her by name and had never hesitated to commune her. Anyway, she asked Fr. Philip about this feeling of being shut out by our acquaintance. Fr. Philip's response was wise, to say the least: "Anything which separates is not from God." So, as soon as he heard about Simone's diagnosis, he stopped by the church office to pick up the specially sanctified oil for anointing the sick (*olio infirmorum*, in Latin), then drove up our hill to give Simone Holy Communion at home. When it came time to do the Our Father, he suggested we each do it in our own language—Simone in German, me in English, and he in Maltese. It was a special moment. After the oiling, we all had tears in our eyes. In less than a year, Fr. Philip's mother would die of cancer as well.

Several weeks later, Harper, Marianna,* and little Sarah, our granddaughter, arrived for their two-week visit. They had been in Hawai'i not too many months before for Simone's seventy-fifth birthday and would come again in late September for a week of memorial services and related activities. I am grateful to Harper for the financial sacrifices he made to enable his family to attend Simone's last big birthday as well as to ease her passing by bringing the three of them to Honolulu six weeks before she died plus for the special events thereafter. During this particular visit, he took Simone into my office and assured her privately that he would always take care of Marianna and Sarah and would never leave them—something his own mother, alas, had done to him as a child.

While the family was in town, we took Simone on her last outing to Waikiki, where she saw her beloved Pacific Ocean for a final time from the pool area of the Royal Hawaiian Hotel, the place the family was staying. The hotel management was especially sweet. The night manager, a woman who had gone to the same high school as Marianna at about the same time and who had just lost a parent to cancer herself, had put together a beautiful basket of tropical fruits, flowers, and chocolates—something they would ordinarily give a VIP visitor—and presented it to Simone. She was gracious as usual, and I don't know about the others, but I had to control myself to keep from crying.

One little story I need to interpolate at this time will give you some insight into Simone's skill as an actress. When the family first arrived, Marianna took me aside and asked, "Dad, are you sure about Mom's diagnosis? She looks so good." And that was the truth. Not only did she do an effective job of making herself up, but she exercised her

---

* The German pronunciation of Marianne is "Mary Anna," not "Mary Ann." In high school, Marianne changed the spelling of her name to Marianna so people would pronounce it correctly and in order to dissociate herself completely from a certain character in the old TV show "Gilligan's Island," of whose name she was not particularly fond.

considerable thespian skills to seem just like always—lovable, sweet, and charming. Somehow she managed to keep up her appearance and energy throughout the visit. It came as no surprise to me, however, that the moment the family left, she starting going downhill fast.

Two other noteworthy events took place during the kids' visit, which included Christine, who came a day or two after the Levines (Marianna and family) but stayed an extra five days with me after they returned to Sag Harbor. One was the Kim Gennaula interview, and the other was Simone's reception into the Catholic Church. These events came within several days of each other in early August. Both were scheduled so that the visiting family members could participate. Kim, the beloved local CBS-TV news anchor, was a friend. On hearing of Simone's illness, she arranged to video our kids interviewing their mom.

The other was that in early August Simone was formally received as a Catholic in our house. After, she would receive Holy Communion every day until her death six weeks later. Either a priest or deacon would come or one of the lay Communion ministers. Our good friend the Lutheran pastor Doug Olson, who had lost his own wife, Ivy, to cancer, came the afternoon of Simone's death to give her Extreme Unction. I should also mention that, besides being her default Eucharistic minister, I also prayed the Lord's Prayer in German with her each night. This ritual brought us even closer and is one of my fondest memories.

Let me now give you some insight into Simone's attitude during her final weeks. I already mentioned how clear and business-like she had become as we were driving home from her diagnosis. Then there was her insistence that Christine and I attend the Vittachi Education Conference in far-away Morocco, even though doing so would leave her on her own for two weeks during the last months of her life. When she spoke about her situation, moreover, she would say how lucky she felt. Unlike the 9/11 victims, she had time to finish up the things that were most important to her, see her family, and die at home. On the other hand, unlike some people we knew, for example Ivy Olson, she would not have to hang on for several years, suffer, undergo painful medical procedures, inconvenience others, and have spells of false hope while always knowing inside that her battle was ultimately doomed. Toward the end she told one of her care-givers, who reported it to me, that she was getting bored and wished the end would come sooner rather than later. Her prayer in this regard was answered.

The Saint Francis Hospice Program was excellent. Not only did we have a connection with the intake nurse, but we could select our friend Luisa Wyant as the Hospice social worker. She had recently joined the program, and Simone would be one of her first cases. I was able to find three individuals who were willing to come once a week for a few hours each to give me the chance to go swimming or shop. One even brought along her daughter, a massage therapist in training, who gave both of us massages.

During the three months between Simone's diagnosis and death, someone had lent me a few books on Padre Pio, now Saint Pio of Pietrelcina, the Italian Franciscan mystic who died in the 1970s. A stigmatist, he was famous for answering prayers and helping those in need, especially the sick. So I asked him to intercede so that Simone would be spared pain. I knew from my internet research that pancreatic cancer could be among the most painful of all the cancers, and although Hospice had promised to handle the pain through medication, I figured help from Saint Pio wouldn't hurt. Whatever eventually did the job, in the whole time of her dying, Simone never rated her pain as greater than a 6 on a 10-point scale and never cried out. Besides this, she never needed oxygen, which we had on hand in three varieties, and was sick to her stomach only once when she had taken liquid morphine on an empty stomach. After that, we knew better. And later, when she could no longer eat much except a little vanilla or butterscotch pudding, she seemed to have developed a tolerance for the medication, and taking the drops in a glass of water never upset her stomach even when the latter was empty. In any case, I hope to make a pilgrimage to San Giovanni Rotondo, Padre Pio's monastery, one of these days to pay my respects and thank him, so to speak, in person.

Simone did not have, nor want, many visitors during this period. In the beginning, though, she had more. In July my cousin Bill Feldman, the only other living Feldman relative besides our Uncle Allan, flew in from California for a few days to pay his final respects. Another visitor was Col. Mylene Huynh, a Vietnamese American physician in the U.S. Air Force. I had gotten to know her through my work at Aloha Medical Mission. A beautiful woman inside and out, she (and her husband) had made Wisdom Factors International a considerable donation to help get us started. She brought Simone a lovely little cactus plant in a costly oriental bowl and showed the compassion of both a good doctor and a good Buddhist. Yet another visitor was our friend Masago Asai, who has since translated Jan Rumi's and my *WisingUP—A Youth Guide to Good Living* into Japanese. She brought along her two elementary-school-aged girls, whom Simone gave two decades' old dolls she had from Germany, one to each. Masago for her part gave Simone a CD she had burned with a compilation of soothing Hawaiian songs. These we would play along with chants by St. Hildegard of Bingen and Mozart's adagios right up to the end just as we would watch, courtesy of Netflix, a series of Hollywood musicals. Perhaps five days before she died, we saw a double feature of *The American in Paris* and *Chicago*. These were the last things she would watch on the little screen. I was heartened as I caught a glimpse of Simone beating out the rhythm from a *Chicago* tune with her fingers on the sidebar of her hospital bed. By this point she was no longer able to speak or even write short messages.

I'm guessing her favorite visitor was Gen. Hank Stackpole. A retired three-star Marine Corps general who had commanded the Corps in the Pacific before retiring and who had acquired two Purple Hearts in Vietnam, Hank had agreed to come onto the Wisdom Factors Board. Jan Rumi had had a connection to him through Hank's work while still in the Marines to save as many as 150,000 Bangladeshis after one of the country's major floods. On orders from Gen. Collin Powell, Hank had taken a brigade of Marines on their way home from Operation Desert Storm on a humanitarian mission to Bangladesh. It became known as Operation Sea Angel. Hank was also a devout Roman Catholic. So when he visited Simone, now in her hospital bed full time, he taught her, a new Catholic, to pray the Rosary. I was on the other side of the shoji screens but could hear what was going on. It seemed as if Hank were comforting one of his dying troops. Before he left, he gave Simone a little wooden finger rosary, the very one, he said, he had used in Vietnam. Perhaps that was the best gift she got, along with the *Story of a Soul: Autobiography of St. Thérèse of Lisieux*, which she read soon after the diagnosis and which she said provided her great comfort.

As mentioned earlier, after the kids left in mid-August, Simone started to go down fast. Everything on her checklist had been accomplished accept holding a copy of her book in her hand. That came next.

Perhaps two weeks after the family left, Simone took a fall. Thank God for the thick carpets. Also, she seemed to fall in slow motion. I'm sure an angel was on hand to prevent her from falling harder. She certainly didn't need a broken bone at this point. When I reported the fall to Nurse Debbie, she said that from now on Simone would need to stay in her hospital bed and came by the next day to give Simone this instruction herself. That was the only time I saw a twinge of rebellion in my wife's otherwise impeccably accepting attitude toward death. It was as if she knew once she was in that bed, she was truly and irrevocably on death row. Debbie was gentle but firm. So in the end Simone did as she was instructed, but I caught a look of sadness in her eyes as she complied.

As the end got closer, Simone was able to eat less and less. Debbie told me that a death in Hospice was generally caused by starvation, which was a good, painless way to die. The body resisted taking in food and slowly but surely shut down. The person would eventually go into a coma and slip away. That's exactly what happened. On September 13th Jan Rumi arrived with five copies of the book. Simone held one for a moment and looked at a few of the pages as we held them open for her. By this point she seemed only partly here and apathetic even about the book. She was too weak to hold it or comment. A few days before, when she had tried to tell me something and I couldn't understand, I brought her pen and paper. Despite three or four attempts on her part, all I could make out was the initial "ess," after which the rest was unreadable. Now, after four-plus decades of good communication between us, the line had been broken. Henceforth I would simply have to guess.

From that Wednesday, the day the books arrived, until the following Monday, the 18th, she said nothing. Then, Monday morning she looked up at me and said *Mittwoch*, Wednesday. "*Mittwoch*?" I repeated, not understanding at first. Then I got it. She was telling me when she would die—on Wednesday, in two days' time. During that final week, she still tried bravely to help me turn her, as I was required to do periodically to keep her from getting bedsores. Sita, our cat, would sometimes snuggle into the arc above her hip. At one point, maybe the day before she died, I saw Simone's fingers moving very slightly to pet her. In retrospect, I now know that my wife was saying goodbye to her loyal cat.

On Tuesday night, the 19th, at about 8 p.m., I noticed that, although her eyes were open, she no longer responded when I called her name. I thought immediately she had gone into a coma. I called Debbie. She said my conclusion was likely. I also told her about the "*Mittwoch*" incident. Debbie thought Simone might well be right. The next morning Debbie came at 9 to check. Simone had certainly fallen into a coma, and from her vital signs, Debbie concluded she would not likely last out the day. At that point our Hospice volunteers Valerie and Sheana, her massage therapist daughter, arrived. I asked Debbie if Simone could still get a massage. A gentle one, she concluded, would relax her and be helpful. So Sheana, the most impressively mature 19-year-old I had ever met, set to work. My full-body massage, which came next, certainly helped me. A friend from Sacred Heart Church brought Simone her final Holy Communion, which she took by having the Host touched to her lips. I consumed the wafer. In the early evening a local Subud sister stopped by to see Simone and bring us dinner. Mariam Stephens, our Irish Subud friend visiting from California, had come the day prior for one of her three-week writing visits. She considered Simone a kind of spiritual replacement for her older sister, who had died a few years back of cancer. Now she would be with us to assist Simone as she did the same.

Linda Nishigaya, our Sacred Heart Church friend, returned and did a slow Rosary with Simone so the rest of us could have dinner. We anticipated a long night. In keeping with her considerate nature, Simone saw to it that we would not have to watch and wait with her too long. In the afternoon, her breathing had become labored. Indeed, the process did seem like the labor of childbirth. Periodically one of us would mop her brow. At perhaps ten to ten that night, her breathing became shallower and less labored. I felt relieved. There were six of us on hand: Aliman and Mirnah (now Karinah) Sears, Jan and Bithi Rumi, Mariam Stephens and me. I should say there were seven of us, since Sita stood watch at the foot of Simone's bed, loyal to the end. During the last hour I found myself playing little children's touching games in German, mainly, "*Die Maus, die kommt; die Maus, die kommt; da, da, da beisst sie!*" "Here comes the mouse. Here comes the mouse. Now she's biting you!" I also sang her German children's songs. Simone's face had been looking left the whole time with her eyes open and unblinking. Whether she heard me or not, I can't say. During this time I was doing things without intention. Mariam had gone into the bedroom to take a "little lie-down," as she put it. She was still jetlagged from her trip. Since Simone had gone into "transition" and we knew from Bithi, a registered nurse, that the end would not be long, Mirnah went into the bedroom to call Mariam back. Actually, Mirnah had taken on the role of coordinator, which she did very well. For my part, I knew I would be the one to close Simone's eyes. For whatever reason, the thought frightened me. I wondered if I would be able to do it. As it happened, there was no need to worry. In a final act of kindness, Simone closed her own eyes, or at least they fell shut by themselves several seconds before she died. Then, at 9:58 p.m. Hawai'i Standard Time, on September 20, 2006, Simone Zimmermann Feldman breathed her last. The Voice had been right—she had died in September. But she had been right too. She had died on *Mittwoch*.

As we shared later, the six of us around her hospital bed all felt like cheering and saying things like "You go, girl!" She had done so well and died in such a heroic yet peaceful manner. The whole thing had a feeling of rightness as well as inevitability about it. This was the way all of us hoped we would die, we agreed. A week or two later, when I described the process from diagnosis to death to our old landlord, Dr. Bob Hunt, who had been a psychologist for many years at the Hawai'i State Hospital for the mentally ill, he said that doubtless Simone's deep acceptance of her death was the main factor in how smoothly everything had gone. He had seen many deaths, he said, and the easiest ones had always been among those individuals who had simply surrendered themselves to their fate. As a footnote, I should add that the loyal Sita had stayed seated yet aware by Simone's feet until she passed. It was as though she had been on guard duty. My feeling in retrospect is that she really had been.

I had a sighting of Simone the night before her cremation. As I was coming out of our kitchen, I noticed her, dressed in her old rainbow-colored muumuu, the one she had bought soon after our original move to the Islands in 1967 and had especially liked. She was walking into the small corridor leading to our bedroom. It was just a split second, but she was radiant—it wasn't just the bright colors of her outfit—and she seemed to give me a glowing smile. The whole incident, brief as it was, showed me she was fine. I felt a warm sense of comfort from the experience.

And now one final story. As Simone was in her last months, she promised me, if it was permitted, to let me know from Upstairs that all was well. After she died, however, other than that momentary sighting, I had no other experiences. Finally, perhaps three months after her death, I had this dream. I called my own number in Manoa, the place where Simone had died. In the dream I thought it strange to be phoning home; after all, no one was there except Sita the cat. Unexpectedly, Simone answered the phone. "Why are you answering?" I asked. Then, with the bluntness often found in dreams, I continued, "You're dead!" "Yes, Pappa." She answered. "But I am keeping my promise. From where I am now, it is easy to get into the electrical system. That's why I am phoning you." She then went on to tell me she was fine and had already been assigned a job. She also described, with her usual enthusiasm, how things up there were. When I awoke the next morning, I remembered everything—except her descriptions about the situation in the afterlife. I suppose my security clearance wasn't high enough. In any case, I was comforted by what she did tell me and was surer than ever that she was okay. Now I just needed to figure out what God wanted me to do in my remaining time on the planet.

14
Back in Honolulu

MUCH AS she had disliked the long, cold Minnesota winters, in 1996 Simone was concerned about how we would make it in the expensive Fiftieth State. "Don't worry," I told her. "With a $1,000-per-month apartment at the Olsons', we'll be fine." Soon after our arrival, though, Ivy Olson gave us some bad news. Doug's oldest son and family would now be moving into "our" apartment, so we would be put up in the studio downstairs until we could find something else. It would be a good deal, Ivy reassured us: only $560 per month, including food. So, with most of our house proceeds still available, we began looking for places to buy. However, nothing in our price range was acceptable. Then, through an acquaintance, we learned about a rental in Kaneʻohe, on the Windward side of Oahu, with a yard, swimming pool, and views of both the Koʻolau Mountains and Kaneʻohe Bay. That weekend Simone and I made an inspection tour. We were immediately enchanted. There was a private master-bedroom suite upstairs with lanais (balconies) on both sides, half bathroom, and views all around. Downstairs there was a guest bedroom as well as a private office with a built-in desk and bookshelves. Also, the price was reasonable--$1,500 per month. To be sure, it would be a 30-minute drive downtown and another ten to church, but gasoline was still fairly cheap, so why not go for it? After speaking with the landlady, a Southerner living on the Mainland, we did. Having arranged for our furniture in Saint Paul to be shipped, we moved in on November 15, just seven weeks after our arrival.

Once in the house, when we added in the utilities, weekly pool maintenance, and other costs, it was not such a bargain. Because I would be away a lot in the Twin Cities, Simone requested that a burglar-alarm system be installed. Our landlady agreed so long as we paid for it. That improvement had a monthly maintenance fee associated with it as well. Also, we needed a new master bed, a sleeper couch for the living room, and two chests of drawers and night tables for the bedroom. The cost of wiring the whole house for the alarm was not insignificant. Slowly but surely our earnings from the Saint Paul house began to disappear. Still, so long as the Minnesota foundations kept giving me work each quarter, I felt confident we would be okay.

My former UH colleague and Kailua-based friend, Loren Ekroth, and

I began discussing a business idea for a professional newsletter for nonprofits on how to raise funds through social enterprise: how they could do good by doing well. We even coined a set of new terms—*philanthropreneurship* and *philanthropreneuring*. Simone was not convinced, but the two of us were enthusiastic. So she acquiesced. While we were still living in Saint Paul, Loren had introduced us to a businessman from Fresno who was in the coupon-fundraising business. Loren himself was in a related school-fundraising business and had been doing well, so we explored the possibility of a Twin Cities coupon book that nonprofits could use to raise money. Basically, there were hundreds of dollars' worth of coupons for something like $15 retail. The nonprofit would keep half the take and give the other half to us. The Fresno firm put together the basic book, and we tried, unsuccessfully, to market them to Twin Cities' nonprofits. Fortunately, the Fresno company had paid for the books, so all we had lost was our time.

The outcome of our proposed newsletter was not so happy either. Both Loren and I had put money into establishing a corporation, developing a sample and a first edition, and mailing them out to nonprofits around the country. Fortunately, my future son-in-law's father, Mark Levine, a successful New York magazine publisher, came to town to help plan Marianna and Harper's wedding. According to Mark, magazine publishing was a risky business which, given what we wanted to do, would probably require an upfront investment of $100,000. Neither of us had that kind of money, so we decided to fold our tents and dissolve the corporation. It wasn't a big deal, since we had to send subscription money back to only a few nonprofits—far short of the hundreds we would need to break even. Simone had proved right: we were no businessmen—or at least I wasn't—so we should have left well enough alone. By now I had spent most of our nest egg.

Still, things were looking up, since the Bush and McKnight Foundations kept coming through with plenty of grant applications for me to vet. Even with my tax-deductible roundtrip flights to the Twin Cities and car rentals there, we came out ahead thanks to the foundations' generous pay scale and the Gehrmans' hospitality. Then one day in 1999 I received a call from the Bush senior program officer with bad news. The Foundation, he said, had decided to hire a few new program officers, so there would no longer be work for me. They would keep some of their local program consultants on, but my distance and inability to attend Board meetings made it advantageous for them to reassign my work to the new staff. Then, not two weeks later, I received a similar call from the McKnight Foundation.

Simone's earlier concern had proved justified. Within ten days, 55% of our income had disappeared. The fundraising work from Angel Network was simply not enough for us to pay all our bills in expensive Hawai'i. To make matters worse, we had optimistically signed a lease for four years. What now?

I should have negotiated to get out of our lease and looked for a cheaper place. For whatever reason, I never did. Somehow, I thought we could tough things out. On the income side, we did make some progress. With Ivy Olson's permission, I started seeking other nonprofit work. By the time I left Hawai'i in 2007, I had contracted with some 30 different charitable organizations there. In 1999, moreover, I got myself a book contract from St. Mary's Press, the Christian Brothers' publishing arm in Winona, Minnesota, to bring out a sole-authored book entitled *Wisdom—Daily Reflections for a New Era*. This work appeared in 2000, and the Christian Brothers paid me a four-figure advance which helped with the bills. Interestingly, I was able to complete this long book in less than 100 days. Each day I would write from three to five reflections on some aspect of wisdom. I would sit in front of my computer, and one chapter title after another would come to me. Then I would find an appropriate lead proverb or quotation for each and start writing. The stream of words simply flowed. After, I would read the new chapters to Simone for her input. The analogy I used for this book was Hokusai's famous series of 18th Century woodcuts, "Thirty-six Views of Mount Fuji." In my case, the topic was Mount Sophia, Wisdom. I eventually had titles like parental wisdom, religious wisdom, know-nothing wisdom, karma yoga wisdom, the wisdom of sharing, wisdom and the middle way, even rat race wisdom. Each one-page reflection of about 300 words began with a proverb or a quotation. "Rat Race Wisdom," for example, had this quote from comedienne Lily Tomlin: "The trouble with the rat race is that even if you win, you're still a rat." At the end of each reflection, I provided a short written exercise to help the reader respond to the essay. In this case the question was, "How committed are you to the rat race? Respond in your Wisdom Journal."

Eight days ahead of the June 30, 1999 deadline, I sent everything by Internet to Michael Wilt, my editor. He in turn had the job of placing the individual essays, one for each day of the year. Some were easy to assign, like New Year's and Christmas Wisdom. The rest he clustered according to his sense of where things belonged. He did a great job. Later he told me the staffers at the press had organized a kind of pool on when I would run out of steam. Michael insisted I would submit the required 366 reflections, including one for Leap Year. And so I thought I had. However, the day after my triumphant e-mail with the final group of chapters, I got a panicked call from Michael. Apparently I had miscounted and was one short. Did I have another in me? I did. And so he won the office pool, and in April 2000 my second wisdom book came out. Ellen Kushner, host of Public Radio's *Sound & Spirit*, wrote: "With wit and humor, passion and personal revelation, insight and storytelling, Reynold Feldman offers us the world's wisdom in 366 pages. His sources are wonderfully diverse; a great collection from around the world and through the ages." Dr. Angeles Arrien, cultural anthropologist and author of *The Four-Fold Way*, wrote, "*Wisdom* is an invaluable resource and guide for strengthening, developing, and accessing our own inherent wisdom nature." And the famous Hassidic *reb* (rabbi), Rabbi Zalman Schachter-Shalomi, co-author of *From Age-ing to Sage-ing*, whom I had experienced as a Yale undergraduate at a memorable Friday evening Hillel service, added, "Having a daily inspirer to dip into when at your God space is a blessing. Reynold Feldman has produced such an ecumenical-transdenominational soul friend."

Alas, just as this book came out, St. Mary's Press decided to shift its publishing focus to Catholic religious books for young people. As a result, they gave short shrift to marketing *Wisdom*. Still, between bookstore sales around the country and my personal efforts through speaking and promotional tours, we managed to sell out the first printing of 3,000. Unfortunately, because of the publisher's new emphasis, a second printing was not to be. So, unless Wisdom Factors reprints and distributes the book, it will remain out of print. Still, at a time when our financial ship was slowly sinking, it was heartening to have a new book out which many people seemed to appreciate. One woman, a member of Sr. Joan Tuberty's Centering Prayer Group in Minneapolis, who had been fighting depression, told Sr. Joan she had taken the book home, read it through in a single sitting, and felt it had changed her life for the better.

In 2001, some months before the expiration of our lease, we were able to find a two-bedroom, two-bath apartment in town for $1,000 per month. Although our landlady let us out of our lease, she did not give us back the full deposit. Still, we would save enough on our new rent so that we didn't care about the loss. Unfortunately, we couldn't get anything back from our expensive burglar-alarm system. The more important point, though, was that we had begun to live from credit cards and credit-card checks—not for frivolous things but necessities like rent, food, and gasoline. Soon after we moved into the new apartment, it became clear we would no longer be able to keep up with our payments. So we sought out a nonprofit debt-counseling agency. The advisor, a retired businessman, said at my age, given the uncertainties of my income as a consultant and author, we should file for Chapter 7 bankruptcy. Since we had missed a few credit-card payment deadlines, we saw interest rapidly mounting at usury-like rates of 25%, even 30%. Simone and I hated the thought of not paying what we owed. On the other hand, the burden had become impossible. There was clearly no other way. So reluctantly we filed, and on February 22, 2001, the Bankruptcy Court of Hawai'i approved our case. We could now start over on a cash-only basis.

We stayed in the new apartment for 33 months. During this time our rent remained unchanged, and we only moved because our Swiss landlord, a retired executive chef, died, and his wife wanted to put the place on the market. Unfortunately, we were in no position to buy since we had used up all our savings before declaring bankruptcy. Thank goodness we found a two-bedroom apartment in Upper Manoa that was perfect for us. We were also blessed with a new landlord, Dr. Bob Hunt, who was more interested in who his renters were than in making money. So the initial rent was only about $60 more a month than our apartment in town. I am guessing that Bob could have asked and easily gotten $400 - $500 a month more. Once again, God was providing, including a short-term loan from a friend to enable us to pay our one-month deposit.

Two angels also appeared on the earning side: Dr. Myaing Tin Thein and Dr. Jerry Chang. Dr. Myaing, as she is called, a Burmese by birth and a prize-winning East-West Center grantee from before my time there, was my friend Marni Su Reynolds' mother. Marni had worked for me for a while as publicity director for Angel Network before going on to other things. Her mom ran a large, successful nonprofit in Honolulu called the Pacific Gateway Center. On Marni's recommendation, Dr. Myaing started giving me fundraising and grantwriting work, beginning with a major marketing study for her agency.

After I returned from running an international youth conference in Jakarta—yet another income source for me—I got a call from Dr. Jerry Chang, a retired diplomat, East-West Center administrator, and youth leader. He had led an international touring company of singing young-adult peace ambassadors for a large Christian charity and now wanted to create something similar that represented the world's major religions as well as regions and countries. He would pay me $1,500 per month to assist him with thinking through his ideas, doing research, and writing grant applications. Meantime, he had the idea to invite the next Parliament of the World's Religions to Honolulu. We became one of three finalists, although Barcelona won the contract. For 18 months this collaboration with Jerry held Simone and me over water financially.

Early in our work we held a well-publicized luncheon at Central Union Church, the state's largest mainstream Protestant congregation. Jerry was concurrently the moderator (chair) of the church council there and had led the parish's effort to build a multi-million-dollar, multi-purpose hall, where a few years later his memorial celebration would take place. One of my jobs that day was to staff the registration table. I distinctly remember a youngish middle-aged businessman signing in. He looked like an Asian Indian and had a beautiful smile that reminded me of Bapak's. He also seemed like a more suntanned version of my father's first cousin and one of my favorite "uncles," Jack August, an accountant. This gentleman, named Jan Rumi, was a Purdue-trained master's degree holder in management with a second major in information science. At the time he was chief of consulting for Grant Thornton's local office. His professional background notwithstanding, he was interested in interfaith understanding. Though an ethnic Indian, he was a Bangladeshi from Dhaka and a Muslim. As brief as our first encounter had been, I was able to tell him that, while I was a Jewish Christian (still a Lutheran at that time), I was attracted by Islam and had done the Ramadan Fast something like 30 times.

Jan had signed up to give electronic feedback on the application I was drafting with Jerry for the Parliament of the World's Religions to come to Hawai'i. When I found myself needing more work, I included him in my "Looking for Dancing Partners" e-mail. He invited me to meet for coffee. I brought along my two books to show him, and we spent the better part of three hours together that Sunday afternoon. We left the meeting with an agreement to write a youth guidebook together on living wisely. Along with that little book, which we initially self-published as *WisingUp—A Youth Guide to Good Living* (2003, 2005) and which we wrote almost entirely during the Ramadan month, 2002, emerged a new nonprofit organization which we incorporated as Wisdom Factors International. I remember how Jan, his wife Bithi, Simone, and I, the initial incorporators, met one afternoon at the Red Lobster Restaurant in Waikiki for our first Board Meeting in Fall 2003. Also, on November 11, an article Jan and I wrote appeared in *The Honolulu Advertiser*, "Hawai'i – Capital of the 21st Century." It began—

When we think of capitals, we think of geographical expressions. Honolulu is the capital of Hawai'i, Berlin of Germany, etc. Yet in the world after Albert Einstein, where space and time form a continuum, why not have places as capitals of eras also? You know: The Age of Rome? Of Paris? Of London? Those would be the places that epitomized the idea, the thrust, the theme of a particular period. In this regard, we propose that Hawai'i become the capital of the 21st century. . . .

Prior to these developments though after Jan's and my three-hour coffee meeting, we got to know Dr. Maeona Mendelson, a sociologist and nonprofit manager who had coordinated the first World Congress of Youth in Hawai'i in July 1999. Although I had heard about the Congress and had even met several young Moroccan participants at Calvary Lutheran Church with their host family one Sunday, this was when things were falling apart for our family in Kane'ohe, so I was not able to get involved. But God must have heard my intention, since in November 2002 I spent a week in Rabat, the Moroccan capital, to help plan the second such Congress, to be held the following summer for two weeks in Casablanca. Not only that but Jan and I along with Mae and her husband Gil, an elderly female Minnesota State Representative from Hilo, and a half dozen other adults accompanied 14 Hawai'i youth representatives to the event, among the latter the Mendelsons' daughter and Jan and Bithi's then 16- or 17-year-old son, Rushdi.

On my first trip to Morocco in November 2002, I remember walking into a spice shop in a village an hour south of Rabat. The international members of the planning team—I was actually representing Maeona, since her son was being married at the time and she could not attend—were on an inspection trip to look at possible sites for the intended Action Projects at the Youth Congress. Anyway, as I entered the fragrant premises on my own, I started crying for no apparent reason. Then the thought struck me that members of the Sephardic (Spanish Jewish) side of our family, kicked out of Spain in 1492, must have spent time in Morocco, maybe even several generations, before moving on and eventually settling down in Romania, where Grandpa Paul, my father's father, was born. I felt a strong, almost dizzying sense that this place had once been home. No wonder I have returned to Morocco three more times since then.

My next trip there was for the World Congress of Youth itself, in August 2003. The young Moroccan King, who turned 40 during the Congress, paid for all the ground costs, including housing us adult chaperons at a five-star hotel in Rabat. Our rooms—Jan's adjoined mine—were beautiful. The food was outstanding as were the pool, the spa, and the other amenities. Of course, most of our time was spent at the youth camp in Bouznika, but that was fine too. What the latter lacked in luxury was more than made up for through the presence of 1,500 young leaders from 150-plus countries and their 500 adult companions. Between the formal sessions, Jan and I hung out with people, young and old, from all over the world. We also did a small Wisdom Workshop. I ended up using all my languages including the little Arabic I had picked up. I also learned from an adult from Ireland about the Indigo Children, special souls who were being incarnated at this time, she said, as a way of helping the Earth stay in business. The job of sensitive adults, she said, was to keep these youth safe until they could grow into positions of influence. Then the world would change for the better. Just now, as I write this in late February, 2009, I read in a 2008 book on the subject that Nancy Ann Tappe, the woman who first wrote about these special children, considers Barack Obama an Indigo. If so, America now has its first Indigo president. I wouldn't be surprised. Anyway, my impression from the quality of the youth I met at the Congress was that our hope for the future did indeed lie in the hands of this genial generation, and I felt moved to focus more of my attention thenceforth on youth. Along these lines, Jan had financed the printing of 100 copies of *WisingUP*, which we gave to selected young people in exchange for their endorsement. Those received were later included in the book.

Several other memories from the Youth Congress come to mind. One has to do with climbing the large stone steps to Casablanca's Great Mosque. By 2003 my knees had become weak from doing six annual Honolulu Marathons in a row. Anyway, I couldn't quite make it up one of the steps and started falling backwards. Fortunately, the young men just behind me saw what was happening and prevented what could have been a nasty tumble. Thank God!

Another experience was even more dramatic, though less dangerous physically. The Moroccan King had not wanted youth representatives from Israel to attend the Congress. His reasons were probably political—maintaining good relations with other Arab and Muslim states comes to mind—but it was said he was concerned there might be an ugly incident between the Israeli and Palestinian participants. The English Congress organizers had none the less managed to get Israeli as well as Palestinian youth to attend, and in retaliation, the King had refused to open or close the Congress; he sent his brother to do the first and his sister the second. During the first week things went smoothly, and relative harmony prevailed. Then, at the beginning of the second week, the King's concern proved justified. Words had led to a fistfight. As an associate member of the Congress Planning Committee, I was called to an emergency meeting. Should we conclude the Congress immediately and send everyone home, or should a way be found to keep things going until the end? Everyone was upset and confused. I suggested we follow the practice, used universally at Subud meetings, of getting quiet for a few minutes before considering what to do. Everyone agreed. After a brief silence, our harmonious discussion led to an agreement to put the options to a plenum session that afternoon. On concluding our meeting, the Moroccan Youth Forum president, a young female attorney with a headscarf, wondered if I would ask for a similar period of quiet at the large gathering. I agreed.

Here was the scene. Close to 2,000 young people and their adult sponsors were crowded into a huge white tent under the hot sun. That day I happened to be wearing my green *kabiya*, or long Moroccan robe, together with my by-then trademark Hawaiian planter's hat. I had quickly memorized how to make my request in all four of the official Congress languages: Arabic, English, French, and Spanish. Raising my hands, I called for a moment of silence so that everything could be discussed calmly and quietly. Instantly, I felt a strong force, almost like electricity, flowing through me. After, there was once again a harmonious discussion. At the end it was decided to continue the Congress until the planned conclusion. As I was leaving the tented great hall, a distinguished-looking gentleman in a gray suit approached me, shook my hand, and said, "*Monsieur, vous avez sauvé notre Congrès!* "Monsieur, you have saved our Congress!" "*Pas moi*! I responded, pointing upwards. "*Lui*!" "Not me! Him!" "*C'est vrai. Lui!*" "That's true. Him!" Then he gave me his card. Of all people, he turned out to be the Moroccan Minister of Energy. In the aftermath, members of both the Israeli and the Palestinian youth delegations started coming to me. Word had gotten around that I was a Jewish-Christian who knew a lot about Islam and even fasted regularly for Ramadan.

Back in Honolulu, Jan Rumi became something like my manager. Indeed, he was responsible for my last salaried position until now. First, though, I had met the University of Hawai'i's creative new president, Dr. Evan Dobell, at an East-West Center event. It so happened I had copies of both *Wisdom* and *WisingUP* with me which I inscribed and gave to him. In his thank-you note, he said he liked my ideas and suggested I schedule an appointment. Actually, I had recently dreamed up a project which I thought might interest him. Called the Aloha Corps, it would be a Hawai'i-based type of Peace

Corps I envisioned doing cross-cultural community-development work in Asia and the Pacific. The University, I thought, would be a perfect place to supply the pre-service training as it had years before for the Peace Corps. Anyway, we did eventually meet, and I pitched my idea, which he found attractive. I would be happy to develop it for his consideration, I told him. The only problem was I would need funding for my work. The President didn't think that would be a problem. So I wrote and sent him a prospectus and work plan. The results were several months of income, a new friend in the University's president, and an interesting project, which I thought Wisdom Factors International might eventually manage. I subsequently completed my work and, through widespread interviewing, even managed to interest several of the State's major elected officials. Unfortunately, by that point the President had run afoul of his Board of Regents, and before long the University's most recent great hope found himself fired. Alas, with him went my project, stained by his suddenly tarnished reputation.

At the beginning of 2004, however, something more positive was about to happen for me. Once again thanks to Jan Rumi, I got to know Dr. Ramon Si, a Chinese Filipino ears-nose-and-throat physician who some 20 years before had founded the Aloha Medical Mission (AMM), a Hawaiian version of Doctors Without Borders. At first, all the missions went to the Philippines. That made sense because when Dr. Si started AMM, it was a project of the Filipino Medical Association of Hawai'i. Meanwhile, its mission had expanded to include Laos, Cambodia, Vietnam, Indonesia, and other countries.

AMM hired me to do a major strategic-planning consultation. My primary conclusion was that the organization needed a full-time executive director in order to grow. Now over 70 and still running a full-time private practice, Dr. Si in my opinion was not capable of providing the time or energy necessary even with the help of an unusually devoted group of directors. After a board planning retreat which I facilitated as the last act of my consultancy, the directors decided to offer me the position of full-time interim executive director. This had not been a unanimous decision, as I later learned, but Jan Rumi, there as a former board member, had gone all out to have me hired. He thought I would be perfect for the job, having just completed the strategic plan. Privately, of course, he knew how timely a full-time job would be for Simone and me. So, on January 5, 2004, a Monday, I began my new work. Still finishing the Aloha Corps Final Report for the University, I made a tactical error by showing up mid-morning during my first few days on the job. It turned out to be a mistake Dr. Si would not quickly forget. My rationalization was that I had begun working for free from late November by helping to plan a spring concert with the Board vice president, Dr. Jorge Camara, a well-known Filipino eye surgeon in town. Both Dr. Camara and three other AMM-affiliated physicians were classically trained pianists. In addition, there was a young, blind Filipino piano virtuoso, whom AMM had treated a decade before in the Philippines, who would participate. The benefit concert, called "Four Doctors and a Patient," grossed $250,000, around 65% of which was net proceeds. In the course of 2004, in fact, I oversaw an operation—a full-time secretary and me—which brought in $405,000 in contrast to $90,000 the year before. The board was happy with my work, and I had become friends with Dr. Camara. Unfortunately, Dr. Si did not like my work style and would periodically lose his temper with me. In retrospect, it must have been difficult for him to turn over some of his leadership responsibility to another person for his baby. After 15 months he told the board it was either him or me. When the board asked my response, I said Dr. Si was the organization's founder and had done thousands of hours of volunteer work to build it up. I thought the board had no choice under the circumstances but to get rid of me. So, beginning on April 1, 2005, I was back to Reynold Feldman, Consultant, with 26 weeks of Unemployment Compensation to help things along. This was the third of the three times in my life I had gotten canned and my last employment to the time of writing (February 2009).

As in the past, the weekly unemployment payments covered our food and gasoline. Fortunately, I had met a physician, a retired German plastic surgeon unrelated to AMM, who had set up his own one-man overseas medical charity. Much like Jerry Chang, he too was looking for someone to help him out. I named a half-time salary he found acceptable, and so, until Simone was diagnosed with terminal cancer in June 2006—i.e., for a little over a year—I wrote grant applications and did Public Relations work for him. Meanwhile, for the rest of our financial needs I was blessed with enough nonprofit work to keep the bills paid.

The other source of income at this time was Wisdom Factors International (WFI) itself. Through Jan Rumi I had become a member of the Honolulu Lions Club in 2003. The next year he was president, and the year after that, I was. This was a historic club, since it had been the first to break the color barrier back in 1926 by taking in Asian Americans, and it thus opened the way for Lions Clubs International to expand beyond the mainly white confines of North America to its present four-plus million members in 195 countries. I was able to persuade the District 50 Lions of Hawai'i, consisting of 64 clubs, to adopt *WisingUP* as a fundraiser. Over a period of several years some 3,000 books were purchased through this program, raising quite a bit of discretionary money for both the District and the clubs. For its part, Wisdom Factors could pay me an executive director's stipend of $1,500 per month for the same period. Yet another outcome was that *WisingUP* was reissued by a commercial publisher, Cowley Publishing (later a sales mark of Rowman & Littlefield), which brought in more funds for WFI. Meanwhile, the Chinese version of the book came out in Taiwan thanks to another piece of good fortune. One of the parishioners at Calvary Lutheran Church was an elderly Chinese gentleman who was chair of the board of the Commercial Press, a large Chinese publishing house now doing business in both Chinas. Although this translation hasn't yet produced great amounts of money, it did win recognition from the Republic of China's Ministry of Education and Culture in summer 2004 as one of the ten best books for Chinese young people to read during their vacation that year and opened our minds to the possibility of having *WisingUP* published in other languages.

How I made money during the short three months of Simone's final illness is a mystery to me. In fact, the period is a kind of blur so far as work goes. I must have done something, because all the bills got paid. I'm guessing that WFI continued to pay me, but that alone would not have sufficed. The main source was doubtless our combined Social Security. The cost of Simone's funeral was covered by personal donations. Meantime, people pre-paid for her book, *Voices from a Vanished Past—Memories of a Christian Childhood in Hitler's Germany*, which by January 2007 I was able to send out. Before long it was profitable, and I could make a four-figure donation in Simone's name to Subud USA for helper travel. Thanks to an admirable piece of foresight on Simone's part, perhaps two years before her death she had asked me to increase her term life insurance from $5,000 to $10,000. As a result, in January I received a check in the latter amount which helped things along while giving me a little respite from work as well as the opportunity to get some needed dental work done and buy a new computer.

In 2006, the Ramadan Fast started two or three days after Simone's death—very helpful timing. The focus on not eating, getting up before dawn, reading and listening to the Qur'an each day, and keeping myself from alcohol, criticism, gossip, scenes of violence, looking at attractive women, and even listening to the news on the radio or watching it on TV diverted my attention from my grief and allowed the first stage of healing to occur. I also flew to Los Angeles and drove up to Badger, California, to spend the last ten Fasting Days, the so-called Nights of Power, in that mountain community with Subud friends. It was exactly the right thing to do. I particularly remember a day of gathering walnuts with a group of brothers on a farm owned by one of the members.

I also remember a test a fellow Subud Honolulu member, Aliman Sears, and I had done after the first ten days of Ramadan that year. On a whim I asked Aliman if he wanted to test how we were doing with our Fast so far. He agreed. My answer proved another encounter with the Voice and something totally different from what I had expected. It said, "Reynold, you are always worried about not having enough money, but God has never let you down. In fact, on the Other Side you are a multi-millionaire. So from now on, it will be a sin for you to worry about money. In this world you will always have enough, and in the other you are already rich."

In late June, 2007, I attended the Subud National Gathering, a kind of spiritual retreat, held that year at Western Carolina University in Cullowhee, North Carolina, near the Tennessee border. The opportunity to be with old friends, do *latihan* twice a day, and sell lots of Simone's books buoyed my spirits. After, I spent a healing two weeks in her new log cabin on Mount Reynolds (!) in Asheville with my old Society for Values in Higher Education (SVHE) tennis partner Rachel Jones, and her dog Greta.

To be sure, man proposes and God disposes, as the old proverb instructs. And so it was in this case. I should mention that one of the factors in my move from Hawai'i in December 2007 was my new landlady's decision to raise the rent by half. She had kept it at the deflated level she had inherited from our original landlord, Dr. Bob Hunt, for over a year. But as she explained to me, her construction business had not been doing well and she simply couldn't keep the rent so far below the market. I knew this new arrangement would not be sustainable for me. Then came Ramadan 2007.

Just before the Fasting Month I got a phone call from my daughter, Christine. She was still in England and had spent a few days at an international Subud gathering in Ascot in August to celebrate 50 years of Subud in the West. During that time she had shared a room with a Danish musician and artist named Aisha. "Normally," Christine continued, "I don't do this sort of thing even with friends my age let alone my father, but I feel the two of you have so many things in common and in some ways she reminded me of Mom. So if you agree, I'll send you her e-mail address. Then the rest is up to you." Soon Christine's e-mail arrived with Aisha's contact information. At first I didn't do anything. My interest was piqued, however, because Simone had said she would try from the other side to send me a new partner. As she put it, "Pappa, you are still young, and I know you too well. You are not a person to be on your own for a long time." So when this call came from my younger daughter, I was interested. Then, on September 12, I received an e-mail from Aisha. She complimented me on having such a bright, beautiful and loving daughter and also on an article someone had forwarded to her with my ideas for creating a kind of wisdom community in Badger, California, where an American Subud friend of hers was now living. I responded immediately. From that acorn emerged a mighty oak of international communication, initially by e-mail and then by long, inexpensive telephone conversations. Aisha sent me her original CD, "Songs from the Heart," the album cover illustrated with an original painting. On it she sang beautifully in Danish, English, and Spanish as well as played the piano and flute. Our daily communications wove a strong connection. Could she be the one Simone had promised to send?

Not long after beginning our electronic communications, I headed to south Florida for my great-nephew Jason's bar mitzvah. During my three weeks there, I started thinking again about moving from Hawai'i. Suddenly I had another Voice experience. This time it wasn't my usual male baritone speaking American English in my left ear. Rather it was Bapak himself who told me that as Bapak's helper it was now time for me to work only for him, that I was to sell everything, leave Hawai'i by year's end, and travel the world. I can still hear the sentence, "From now on you work only for Bapak." And so, once back in Honolulu, I began to wind things up.

The two months from mid-October to mid-December, 2007, were hectic. Thanks to Craigslist and a mega-apartment sale, I managed to get rid of almost all the material accumulations of 43 years of married life. Items of sentimental value—photos, letters, and selected books, CDs, and DVDs—I shipped to my daughter Marianna on eastern Long Island. She also asked that our good Rosenthal china, which had been part of Simone's trousseau, be sent to her. At the last minute Dr. Myaing, my former client from the Pacific Gateway Center, decided to buy my old Honda, high mileage and all, at the full Blue Book value less $600 because the air conditioning didn't work. Then, after a no-host farewell dinner at the Wai'oli Tea Room on Friday, December 14, attended by around 50 friends, Sita the cat and

I flew off on the Continental nonstop to Newark late Sunday night, December 16.

15
New Worlds

THE DRIVE from Newark Airport to Sag Harbor, Long Island, was tough after the all-nighter on the plane, but somehow Sita, the luggage, and I made it. The money raised from the various sales had exceeded my expectation, so I was able to follow my heart and invite Aisha to fly to New York to spend Christmas with me and the family. My son-in-law, Harper, had generously found a furnished house in Sag Harbor village, 15 minutes by car from the Levine house in Noyack, where Aisha and I could stay and each have our privacy.

Aisha arrived at Kennedy Airport one evening a few days before Christmas. The wait seemed interminable, but finally she came through Customs. After two months of emailing and phoning on a daily basis, we met. On the drive back to Sag Harbor, I got lost, but eventually we arrived, and she was happy with our New England-style house. Getting lost on the way back was symbolic, since our relations in person proved not as harmonious as they had been at a distance. After 43 years of almost entirely smooth relations with Simone, I was doubtless expecting too much. As Aisha pointed out, we didn't really know each other. Simone and I had corresponded for four-and-a-half years before meeting. How could a mere two months compare?

Aisha was a relatively new Subud member, about seven-and-a-half years when we met. Still, her three years of living in Subud communities in Indonesia, I felt, had super-charged her *latihans*. However, while she lived at the international Subud spiritual center in Jakarta, something traumatic had happened. A mentally ill member of a distinguished Subud family had broken into her room, beaten her up, and dislodged her left retina. After she returned home, the Danish health system provided four operations in an only partially successful effort to improve the situation. While surgeons had managed to re-attach the retina, sufficient foreign matter remained in her eye, minute droplets of silicon oil, that a new, artificial lens could not be put in place. The ophthalmologists had done a test with a contact lens, but so much was still floating around that for Aisha it was like looking through a busy fish tank. The experience was totally disorienting. So the Danish doctors decided to leave her without a lens. In consequence, she was blind in her left eye. With only half her peripheral vision, moreover, she became accident prone, with falls, a concussion, and several broken bones resulting. Not only that, but she could no longer work as a musician because it was now too difficult for her to read notes. She was left to live on meager temporary-disability payments that never quite covered her monthly bills.

Between Christmas and New Years we drove to rural Maryland to consult with our Subud ophthalmologist, Dr. Jim Busack, who had consented to examine Aisha for free. He also referred her to a retinal specialist, a trusted colleague, who evaluated the condition of both her eyes at a discounted rate. (Talking about God providing, I had sold perhaps 20 of Aisha's CDs before leaving Hawai'i. The specialist's consultation fee came to exactly one dollar less than the amount I had raised. No wonder I think of God as a Hong Kong tailor, custom-making everything to order.)

The drive to Maryland and back had been difficult. With the weather shifting between rain and snow, visibility was often poor, and the whole thing seemed to take forever. In addition, I had come down with a low-grade flu and reacted badly when Aisha tried to cheer me up by clowning around. My reaction in turn upset Aisha who on several occasions began crying. She later told me she had wondered why she had agreed to travel thousands of kilometers to end up spending time with such a disagreeable semi-stranger.

Once back in Sag Harbor, my flu moderated and my mood improved. Our living in that house together thus became smoother, and Aisha accepted my invitation to stay a week longer than originally planned. In mid-January, she invited me to visit her in Denmark, although she told me once I was there she had been hoping for a longer interval than the ten days between her departure from New York and my arrival in Copenhagen. In the event, I stayed in Denmark three months, learned a little Danish, and saw something of the country. The language, positioned somewhere between English and German, proved much harder to learn than I had imagined. Reading and writing weren't so bad. It was speaking and understanding, since Danish like English and French (but unlike Spanish, Italian, and German) is not phonetic. Take two examples: *meget* (very, too) and *have* (have). The former is pronounced "mahl" like the first syllable of the composer Gustav Mahler's last name; while the latter is pronounced "hey." Or take the common expression, *I lige maede*, meaning "likewise" or "the same to you." You hear this said all the time in response to phrases like *have en dejlig dag* ("Have a nice day!"), pronounced "hey ain dye-lee day." It's pronounced "ee lee mool"!

Other impressions of Denmark included the fact that everyone rode bikes. No wonder this mainly tall, handsome people was also for the most part slender and athletic-looking. My eyes, used to the 60-plus percent of us Americans who are overweight or obese, had to adjust to the normal weights and forms I saw on every side. Another thing I learned was that Danes represent the highest percentage of atheists and agnostics in the world, 80% of the population according to some surveys. Yet one researcher at the University of Leicester, England, ranked the Danes as the happiest people in the world.

During my initial three months in Denmark, I functioned for Subud as a *helper without borders*. Although Subud has a group of people called "international helpers" who build up Subud in different parts of the world, limited funds keep them from traveling to all the places requesting a visit. So, since Bapak stated that a helper anywhere was a helper everywhere, individuals like me, long-standing helpers traveling abroad to countries where Subud had a small or no presence, could be deputized to assist the International Helpers in their work. Because Denmark, which had had three Subud groups in the 60s and 70s, now counted only seven active members, the International Helpers felt I might be useful to them there. For my part, this work seemed to agree with what Bapak had told me, so I made an official application and was approved.

Shortly after my arrival in Copenhagen, I contacted the helper couple Ruslan and Hamidah Jelman in England. The men I was speaking about Subud to there were transplanted Algerian Berbers, and since Ruslan was one also, I felt he and his French wife might be able to assist me in my work. When I phoned them, they were immediately willing and less than two weeks later flew to town at their own expense for four days. Before I left, two of the Berber men were opened in Subud and a third expressed interest in joining. Fortunately, a long-time Danish member and helper, Ludvig, who was 77 years old at the time, committed to making the drive from Odense, Denmark's third largest city, to the capital to *latihan* with Madjid and Makhlouf on a regular basis and also to speak with Youcef, the third Berber who was not yet opened.

Another major thing that happened while I was in Denmark during the mild winter of 2008 were my two visits to Aisha's brother, Rune, a history teacher at the innovative Frie Laererskole, or Free Teachers College, in Ollerup on the island of Funen (Fyn). While staying with Aisha in the Noerrebro District of Copenhagen, I was a mere three blocks away from the well-known Assistenskirkegaard, a large cemetery housing the remains of two of Denmark's most famous sons, Hans Christian Andersen and Soeren Kierkegaard. I soon learned about a third famous son, not buried there, whom few have heard of outside Denmark except for Lutheran clergy—a 19th Century pastor, theologian, politician, and educator named N.F.S. Grundtvig (pronounced "Grun-vee"). Grundtvig had started out as a conservative clergyman in the early 1800s. Then he had a transformational experience related in part to his reading Deuteronomy 30:18-20, where God tells Moses and Aaron, "I have put before you life and death, the blessing and the curse. Choose therefore life. . . ." It suddenly struck Grundtvig that religion, education, politics, even family life in Denmark at the time were more death oriented than life affirming and that he was part of the problem. Out of this dark night of the soul, he found himself working for new directions in all these domains. His special interest however became education. Rather than intellectually oriented classical instruction for the few, he now favored practical training for the many. Rural farmers often had no schooling outside religious school, so Grundtvig came up with the idea of rural residential schools for them and their sons during the winter months when the weather prevented work in the fields. This program, he believed, would respond to what they needed to know as both farmers and human beings. Above all, these schools would be democratic in spirit, with the teacher simply first among equals. What was to be learned would be determined in collaboration with the students.

The first "free" schools were founded by a farmer-educator named Christian Kold in the 1850s. Soon one of Grundtvig's main disciples, a Jewish convert to Christianity and Lutheran pastor named Ernst Trier, established others. Today there are thousands of such "free schools," "folk high schools," and a newer innovative called "after schools" throughout Denmark, Norway, and Sweden plus some in Finland, Germany, and a few economically less developed countries in Africa. And the Free Teachers College, where Aisha's brother taught history, was the only college that prepared faculty to work in these schools, which were funded by the state much as American school districts now fund charter schools.

At DFL (*Den Frie Laererskole*), a small residential facility in a beautiful part of south-central Denmark, some 250 students spend five years in a combination of academic study, creative work, and practical experiences. Storytelling is a required subject as is wood-working. Field trips to different parts of the world, where students and faculty often camp to save money, are included in the curriculum. Three languages are offered: Danish, English, and German. During my first visit in February 2008, I addressed the English class, taught by a puckish Liverpudlian named Ed Morris, on the arcane American primary and electoral system. By that point many of the students were hoping Barack Obama would become America's next president. I also spoke to Rune's class on the American educational system, another mystery for the Danes. Unexpectedly, I found myself participating in the fourth-year German seminar, where one of the students was a local politician and jazz player and another the beautiful mother of three boys with a husband who taught Danish merchant marines the fine points of sailing. (DFL is located only a few miles from the Baltic Sea.) On my second trip to DFL in April, I decided to pitch a proposal to return in fall to lead a faculty-student study group on how schools could prepare global citizens for the 21st Century. Monika, the talented German teacher, had just concluded a study group on The World Citizen, so what I proposed would be a continuation of her project. My idea was to facilitate the group for free in exchange for a dorm room and two meals a day. By June my proposal was accepted and in mid-October I returned.

The third important thing that happened that winter in Denmark also came through Aisha. She clearly observed me going through my grief. When I arrived in Copenhagen, I was planning to write a fictionalized account of my junior year in Germany. Why not do an autobiography like Simone's? Aisha suggested. In my case, it could cover my life to date and focus on my spiritual and religious experiences. The moment she mentioned the idea, it seemed right to me, and now that I am almost done, I can confirm the soundness of her idea, at least for me.

An important part of my healing in Denmark came from two other sources, again thanks to Aisha. One was hanging out with the Berber kids—Madjid and Fazia's then nine-year-old son, Jonas, and five-year-old daughter, Louise, as well as Makhlouf's daughter Maya, who was nine. Of all these, Louise, or Lulu as we all called her, was my main "therapy." She spoke Danish and a little French but no English. With Jonas and Maya I could get along in French and some English. Lulu sometimes became frustrated with my defective, mispronounced *dansk*. She told me in no uncertain terms, *"Hawai'i, du er en stor baby paa dansk!"* ["Hawai'i"—her nickname for me—"you are a big baby in Danish!"] She couldn't comprehend how an adult could speak Danish so poorly when all the other big people she knew spoke it perfectly. Still, she played with me several times a week when Aisha picked her up from pre-school and took her home while both her parents were at work. Since I was so obviously a big baby, she mothered me by combing my hair, buttoning my shirt, and once even shaving me. I was petrified of course, but with the total concentration of a five-year-old permitted to do an adult thing, she did the job with no mishaps, *Gud ske lov!* "Thank God! We would also watch TV together on the Disney Chanel. Although the Danes use subtitles versus dubbing for English, German, French, and other Scandinavian-language programming for movies and television, they did synchronize shows for little kids unable to read. So I watched "Anders And" (Donald Duck) quack out his lines *paa dansk.* At least *he* was no big baby in Danish!

Lulu had three favorite games she liked to play with me: *Nomselei, Sorte Per*, and *Hest.* The first was that universal favorite of little kids, Chase. I would play the stupid old man, put the my right hand above my eyes as if searching for something, and say in an old man's voice, "*Hvor er Lulu*?" "Where's Lulu?" She would sneak up from behind and give me a good whallop on my rear end. I would scream and jump up and down while she laughed hysterically and ran away. Then I would chase her as we went round and round through a set of doors in Aisha's small apartment that made the circle route possible. Once in a while I would reverse course and catch her. This did not occur often. Then I would gently get my revenge by patting her rear end and she would scream with a mixture of delight and horror.

The second was a kids' card game I knew from my German days. It was played exactly like Old Maid, where the person loses by getting stuck with Black Peter, a European-style chimney sweep, when all the other cards have been discarded. Lulu of course never wanted to lose. So to insure victory, she cheated like crazy. I pretended not to notice, but when she won, as she inevitably did, she would give off a triumphant smile while I screamed and cried out over the injustice of it all. Of course, I would occasionally cheat a little myself, since it was so much fun to see Lulu's face when she found *Sorte Per* in her hand. Then she would say, "*Nej, Hawai'i. Det er ikk' retfaerdig*!" "No, Hawai'i. That's not fair!"

But where would grandparent-grandchild-type play be without that old standby, Horsy? We played it in two versions: *Store Hest* [Big Horse] and *Lille Hest* [Little Horse]. Which we did depended on how worn out I was. Lulu naturally preferred the former, where she got to ride on my shoulders. Although she didn't enjoy Little Horse that much, it being more for "babies," if I said in my self-defense Danish, "*Jeg er meget traet, Lulu.*" "I'm too tired, Lulu.," she'd accept it as the best she could get. Still, she preferred when I bucked and lurched in a rarely successful attempt to unseat her. That at least was some action and not as babyish as slow plodding around Aisha's living room so close to the hardwood floor.

Another piece in my healing-from-grief puzzle was going to Melina Christiansen, a hands-on healer and kinesiologist who had been treating Aisha for free during the past year. She gave me a pensioner's discount for an hour treatment. It was money well spent. I always came out of the sessions feeling calm, happy, and in some way restored. Since her English wasn't as good as Aisha's, she would also speak Danish with me, and somehow we managed to communicate, although we each would have to say "*Hvad saaru*?" "Come again?" more than once.

Possibly the most important thing I did in Denmark was help Aisha find a doctor to do one more, hopefully final, operation on her bad eye and then raise money to pay for it. Fortunately, we could send the Maryland specialist's detailed evaluation around by e-mail along with a write-up of how the damage had occurred. One person I thought to send it to was my former Aloha Medical Mission colleague and friend Dr. Jorge Camara in Honolulu. He replied by e-mail that the sort of retinal surgery Aisha required was not something he did. However, with her permission, he forwarded the information to his Honolulu colleague Dr. Michael Bennett, principal of The Retina Institute of Hawai'i. Within a day he sent us Dr. Bennett's response that the latter believed he could do something to improve Aisha's vision and secondly he felt moved by her story to do the operation without a fee. Aisha and I were overjoyed. After Dr. Bennett gave us numbers on the cost of the other aspects of the operation, we worked out a budget to cover round-trip airfare, room and board in Hawai'i, and the balance of the operation. Then I put on my fundraising hat and got to work. Aisha had already raised US$2,000 from the International Subud Emergency Fund. Within a month I received commitments from friends and family, hers and mine, for the other $9,000. In early September, she flew to Honolulu, where I met her, and stayed for two-and-a-half months. Dr. Bennett performed not one but two operations, for, according to him, Aisha was going blind in her "good" eye also. So, two weeks after a three-hour surgery on her left eye, he did a shorter but still complex operation on the right one. By then I was back at my daughter's place on Long Island, soon to be on my way to Denmark, where Aisha returned on November 22nd. The amazing thing is that Dr. Bennett performed both surgeries absolutely free. That is, he got one colleague to donate the use of his ambulatory surgical unit twice and another to provide free service as the anesthesiologist. Dr. Camara's office supplied the free artificial lenses. And Nurse Debbie Shimabokuro, the surgical coordinator, and other members of Dr. Bennett's staff provided both technical expertise and tender loving care—all without charge.

My search for female companionship began three months after Simone's passing. I just wasn't cut out for the single life. Also, to be honest, it wasn't the sex; rather, it was the absence of physical touch and companionship that I found difficult. Suddenly I felt like half a person. I'll spare you the list of women who entered my life during this interim. You've already heard about the most important one, Aisha, but at this point, after further contact in Denmark, we seemed headed for a long-term friendship, not an intimate relationship. We have helped each other a great deal, and for that we are both grateful. But gratitude alone is not enough to build on. There needs to be a fit, and either that does not exist in our case or hasn't yet emerged.

In one sense I am reliving the time of my life when I normally would have been dating. I missed all that, as you'll remember from the Graduate School chapter. After only one serious girl friend, Jane Tompkins, I married Simone, and that was it for 43 years. So, here I am, 69 years old—not quite 67 when she died—a total neophyte in the dating game. Not only that, but having had just one intimate partner in a harmonious relation for nearly half a century can spoil a person. So I guess what I am really looking for is, in one of my favorite lines from W.B. Yeats' poem "Among School Children," "a glad kindness." I want mutuality, a sharing of lives, physical intimacy, and fun. In the past 29 months since Simone's passing, I have met or spent time with 28 different women, from a day together to ongoing e-mail exchanges. I have not been intimate with any of them. It's as if God has taken a vow of poverty, chastity, and obedience on my behalf. No need to become a monk. I am one already. And the reality is, I have not yet been ready for a significant new relationship with a woman. To use the Biblical phrase, "my time has not yet come." On the other hand, I feel more and more that as Simone's One Thousandth Day celebration nears on June 22, 2009, I am being readied to be open to and available for a new partner. Needless to say, I've had a few serious discussions with the God of my understanding over the last two-plus years. And "He" has indicated that when the time is ripe, the right person will emerge. May it be so!

While I would like to say that I have totally surrendered on this point—you know, "not my will but Thy will be done"—the whole project is still a work in progress. Who knows? Maybe by the time this manuscript finds a publisher, I'll have something different to report. Yet on my better days, I feel a sense of adventure and am looking forward, like Sloan Wilson's hero in *The Man in the Gray-Flannel Suit*, to see what happens next.

16
Denmark Again and Ireland

MY TWO months (October 19 – December 20, 2008) at the Free Teachers College, Denmark, exceeded my expectations. Aisha and Rune had sent sheets, towels, blankets, pillows, candles and candleholders, not to mention original art by Lulu to improve my little room-and-bath in the so-called "Hilton." That was the wing of the building containing the dining hall, kitchen, and administrative offices that housed two classrooms and five rooms for visitors. Mine was Hilton 5. Right outside my door was a little "tea kitchen" with small fridge, stove, and pantry shelves equipped with plates, mugs, bowls, pots and pans, and cutlery. All I needed was to walk or bike— Rune had provided me with a used *cykel*—to *Brugsen*, the one and only store in our picturesque village of Ollerup, stock up periodically, and I was set for my evening or weekend meals.

I didn't have to wait long for my life at DFL to ramp up. I had arrived on Sunday; our first Study Group meeting, replete with a delicious class-prepared vegetarian meal, began 6 p.m. that Tuesday. My original intent had been to discuss how schools could prepare "global citizens" for the world of today and tomorrow. By the end of the first class, however, the topic had morphed into "Better Schools for a Better World." We also shifted our meeting day to Wednesday evening in hopes of attracting more people, but without luck. We also staged an all-day workshop during *Faguge*, "Professional Training Week," the third week I was there. Some 14 people showed up, including a fair representation of women and individuals from outside our study group. We used the day to name and prioritize the characteristics of a "better world" and had small groups recommend teaching-learning strategies to help bring such a world into existence. It proved a successful six hours together.

By the fourth week—the Group met weekly—we had gone from all working on the same project to doing individual ones. Mine was to survey my network by e-mail on what they thought the main characteristics of a *better world* were and, if they were so inclined, to sketch out a teaching-learning activity to help instill or strengthen a top characteristic in students. Some 126 individuals from 16 countries voted on their top five characteristics from a composite list of 80. Here, for your information, are the eleven highest vote-getters:

1st	Universal peace.
2nd	A healthy, sustainable environment.
3rd	Humor and laughter.
4th	An end of racial, cultural, and any other kind of discrimination.
5th	Widespread respect for all life.
6th	Universal free education for all.
7th	Universal love, compassion, and empathy.
8th	Acceptance and celebration of human diversity and individual differences of all kinds.
9th-11th	Global health coupled with universal affordable medical care.
9th-11th	Universal economic security—no homelessness, hunger, poverty, or large differences in wealth.
9th-11th	The presence of at least one caring individual in everybody's life.

A memorable experience at DFL that fall was sitting up late with a room full of Danish students as they watched the results of the American presidential election. I was asked to present my take on things and once again tried to explain our convoluted electoral system. The next day, November 5, people applauded me as I entered the *spisesaal*, dining hall, while others wished me *tillykke*, congratulations. Several expressed what was probably a widely shared sentiment: Obama's not only your president; he's our president too. He's really the president of the world. I was of course overjoyed that Barack had won. I cried for Florine and all the African Americans who had not lived to see this day. Plus, I was convinced that he would be one of our great presidents and couldn't have come at a better time.

All in all, a lot happened during my two months at DFL. For me the most important experience, however, was being among young people and making new friends. Although I didn't *feel* lonely, I am sure I have been desperately so since Simone's death. Being at the College helped me taste the richness of life again. As a group the DFLers were a poised, frisky, creative bunch. No stereotype stiff

Scandinavians here. Lots of action each day and for me lots of healing.

※

After spending Christmas with Ludvig and Aisha in Copenhagen and New Years with Ludvig in Odense, I flew on January 5 to Dublin. For most of my three weeks on Erin's green isle, I stayed with Syna Horton and her husband Lucas in Shercock, County Cavan. Ireland is not a large country, but it still took 90 minutes to drive northwest from Dublin International Airport to the Hortons' alpine cottage on Lake Sillan. On the way, we stopped off for dinner at an excellent Italian restaurant in a town called Ardee. As Syna explained, this area was close to the border with Northern Ireland, and in the bad times I.R.A. members would hide out here between cross-border attacks. Fortunately, that was a thing of the past now, and many families in this region would head across that same border on weekends to shop, since prices tended to be lower in the North. Thank you, Ambassador George Mitchell, for helping establish peace.

Syna had been my daughter Christine's friend before she was mine. I had initially met her in Portland, Oregon, where she was a massage therapist. Then I saw her during two different visits to Badger, California. The first time she was still single, Ms. Bornazos; the second time I met her new English husband, Lucas (then Latif) Horton. During a long walk in the Sierra Nevada mountains, I learned that Lucas was an architect and project manager with international experience. He had headed the British Subud hotel project for a while until, despite its promise, it failed for lack of adequate capitalization. Here in Ireland he was the senior architect in a national firm located in Castleblaney, one of the closest larger towns. Like me, Lucas had lost his first wife to cancer, so we had an important bond. For her part, Syna was still working part-time as a massage therapist in both Castleblaney and Carrickmacross, although the focus of her practice had switched to cranial-sacral work and a therapy called *ontology*, a term which up till then I had only heard as a division of philosophy.

The weather during my three weeks in Ireland was, for the most part, sunny and not too cold. Also, I noticed that the fields stayed green in winter even though the trees were all bare. Maybe that year-round greenness is a partial explanation for the importance of the color in Irish culture, from the flag to the shamrock to the name Kelly green. Where I stayed with the Hortons was in the midst of rolling hills and farmlands sectioned off by hedgerows. Speaking of the latter, they often lined the roads, where there were typically no easements. Often they grew tall and looked like they were made of iron, not wood. Syna commented that many of the hedgerows were ancient. I could believe it.

As beautiful as my room in the Hortons' alpine cottage was, there was no Wi-Fi. Maybe, as Aisha thought, that was a good thing, since I was forced to focus on the book. Also, I was chilly all the time. Fortunately, the Hortons had placed an electric space heater in my room, which was constantly on; the duvets kept me nice and warm at night; and once in a while I sought refuge in the Jacuzzi. Periodically I would walk around the gated community containing a dozen or more similar cottages. When I did three brisk circuits, I got my 30 minutes of exercise, lowered my blood pressure, and improved my circulation.

Prior to my arrival, Syna had fixed me up with three gigs: two wisdom workshops and a job facilitating a meeting of alternative therapists in the area. For the first workshop, I spent 90 minutes with approximately 30 women, including Syna, who were called "The Blaney Blades." This event took place at a nonprofit community center in Castleblaney—hence the name of the group—called Iontas (pronounced "Intis") directed by a late-middle-aged nun, Sr. Celine ("as in Dionne," she explained). It was a good group, all women except for one poor husband who had been carted along. We had a lot of fun, and at the end Sr. Celine was quite pleased. On the way home, Syna compared my facilitation style with Solihin Thom's, a real compliment because I knew she had studied with him and had a high opinion of his skills. She also said that Sr. Celine didn't often give praise and she had just given me in effect an A+. At the session I had offered my usual silly derivation of *wisdom*, the word, as stemming from "wise" + "dumb." The women had fun assigning one of the two categories to hypothetical situations I reeled off, like continuing one's education (wise) or diving into an empty swimming pool (dumb). I then gave Dr. Salk's (and my) definition of the word and ended by talking about our BIG versus our little selves. The idea, I said, was for me to be *REYNOLD* as much as possible and *reynold* as infrequently as possible and for all of us to strive to be our biggest selves as well. Even *ReYnOlD* was better than *reynold*, but still we should try, to borrow an old recruiting slogan for the U.S. Army, to be all that we can be, our B & B (BIGGEST & BEST) selves. In between, I read a selection from *WisingUP* and the concluding chapter from Simone's memoir in which she described the first Christmas of peace after World War II. As usual, I didn't manage to get through it without crying. After, a number of people bought books. So all in all, it proved a productive outing.

To keep me from getting on my high horse, no doubt, for the next workshop, scheduled at the Solis Holistic Health Centre in Carrickmacross for area educators, nobody showed up. Not only that, but I got an upset stomach from my one-and-only experience of wolfing down fish and chips at a local fast-food restaurant beforehand. The third experience, facilitating a group of alternative therapists, again including Syna, was somewhere in the middle: not a rousing success but not an abject failure either. About ten people attended, mainly women. As a non-therapist I played traffic cop and strived to keep the discussion going and anyone from dominating. All that worked out fine. At the end there was a good-will collection, and I split the €40 with the hosting organization. But I was not done. Iontas called and asked if I would be willing to be the guest speaker for a group of women they were training to re-enter the work force, from late teenagers to individuals close to my age. This was a voluntary assignment, but again I was free to sell books. (I sold one *Voices*.) This was an all-morning gig with some twelve to fifteen participants. The time went fast, and we laughed a lot. At the end I taught the ladies the *Hukilau* hula. That might have been the highpoint.

During my visit with the Hortons, Syna, ever direct in her manner, told me she thought my occasional attacks of high blood pressure might stem from the internal stress caused by my not having a home base. All this traveling might be fine for a younger person, but at my age she felt having a fixed place to return to would make a positive difference. After laying her ideas out during one of our 20-minute car trips to a nearby town, she suggested that Honolulu might be my best bet because I had such a good network there. I told her I would think about what she said and possibly test about it with some helpers when I was next with a larger group. For his part, Lucas and I did some *latihans* together. He told me how, when he had been a helper in a Scottish Subud group, he had begun doing short *latihans* after the regular ones with men who had particular needs. For example, there was a long-time bachelor who kept saying he wanted a female partner but would never do anything to get one. So in his case, the special *latihan* had the intention of helping him find a suitable mate. Then there was another brother who had severe agoraphobia. He refused to leave his home town for fear of the unknown. He wanted to get over this problem, so in his case that was the intention. Lucas said in the first case, the man soon found a suitable girl friend whom he eventually married and they are still together some years later. And in the second case, Lucas one day received a call from the man who said, "Guess what? I'm in London having a fabulous time!" So naturally, I was eager to experience such a special *latihan* with the intention of finding my new life partner. Lucas was happy to oblige. I can report that I have since done several such focused *latihans* on my own but as yet without results. Again, maybe by the time this book finds a publisher, I can update you and say, "Guess what? I have a fabulous woman in my life and we are planning to get married." We shall see.

There's a well-known early-19th Century novel by Clara Gaskell called *North and South* illustrating the differences between the cultures of northern and southern England. I can't speak for Ireland, but I did get to see something of the South as well as the North. After less than a week, I was invited to spend five days with Ireland's *de facto* Subud elders Michael Heaslip and his wife Raphaela in their beautiful house near the Cork Airport. Thanks to Michael, now in his early 70s, we visited some of the most interesting parts of Cork and did a day trip to Kilkenny. On one of the other days, Raphaela was going to a therapists' meeting in Limerick, the writer Frank McCourt's hometown, so I got to spend a good five hours walking the streets there, playing photographer, visiting churches, and taking advantage of some of the January sales, all the more dramatic because of the financial crisis.

Before visiting these cities, I accompanied Michael to Cove, Cork's historic port town. In a former train depot there is now an emigration museum with wonderful exhibits documenting the millions who had left Ireland for the New World and Australia during the Great Potato Famine of the 1840s and 1850s. Not only that, but there was a whole room dedicated to the *Titantic*, whose final stop had been Cove. After the visit, we went to the nearby historic harbor hotel, where we refreshed ourselves—in my case, with a Jameson's (Michael pronounced it "Jamm-ison's") Irish whisky—and debriefed. Getting to Cove and back required taking a car ferry across the river. The foggy afternoon and evening lent an air of mystery to these brief rides.

Michael was the son of a well-known animal-feed merchant in town, with a large facility in Cork's harbor district. He had sold the business and now used his time to advise young entrepreneurs. I thought it interesting that both Michael and I had been sons of men in the grain business, with my father at one point the manager of a large complex of grain elevators in Chicago harbor. Raphaela for her part was the daughter of a philosophy professor at University College-Dublin, a Protestant institution. As a matter of fact, both Heaslips were raised members of the Church of Ireland, which is part of the Anglican Communion. So although they looked and sounded as Irish as could be and their family trees went back hundreds of years in Erin, they were both Protestants. That version of Christianity in all its variations comprises only about 5% of the Irish population yet represents some of the most distinguished names in Irish history. I had known, for example, that that most Irish of poets, William Butler Yeats, was Protestant but learned only this trip that the Guinness brewing family was too. In fact, many well-to-do families in Ireland, Michael told me, were Protestant, and they played a role in Ireland similar to that of the Jews in the United States.

Speaking of Yeats, the Butler in his name related to one of the first families of Ireland, the Butlers of Kilkenny Castle. They had been butlers to the English Tudor kings and for their efforts had been rewarded with a small but imposing Norman castle in Kilkenny. I especially wanted to visit the castle, which Michael and I did, to honor Mother M. Joseph Butler, an early leader of the Religious of the Sacred Heart of Mary Order and foundress of the Convent where I had stayed in Tarrytown, New York, who had come from a Catholic branch of the family.

The hour trip the next day with Raphaela over to Limerick gave us a good chance to converse. Her professor father had been an expert on the idealist philosophy of Bishop George Berkeley (pronounced "Barkley"), the Anglican (Church of Ireland) Bishop of Cloyne, not far from Kilkenny. He is the namesake of the city and world-famous university near San Francisco. I had a connection with him too, I told Raphaela, since as an undergraduate I had lived in Berkeley College, one of now twelve residential colleges at Yale. Our emblem was in fact the Bishop's family crest, and on a roof near our dorm suite one could see a miter, or bishop's hat, indicating which college this was.

On reaching Limerick, after having agreed with Raphaela on a pick-up point, I did what I liked to do in new places and allowed the Spirit to guide my feet. Once again, the *latihan* in action! I was not disappointed. I found several great bargains, had a nice lunch in a bakery, and even came upon a religious-articles shop named Knock after the town in northwest Ireland where the Blessed Virgin had appeared in the 19th Century. There I was able to replace my broken rosary with a beautiful new one; buy a half dozen medals for gifts with St. Patrick on one side and the Patroness of Ireland, St. Brigit, on the other; and even be given a whole bunch of free postcards and holy cards from Knock when I told the cashier I had a sister friend in the States from Knock. Moreover, as I was checking out, the cashier asked if I wanted to have my new beads blessed. Indeed I did. It so happened that the genial middle-aged man next to me at the counter was a priest from Tipperary. "Here now, Father will bless 'em for ya." When the beads are ready, the priest will appear! Maybe it's not as long a road from Tipperary as to it.

One of the things I absolutely wanted to do in Ireland was go to Mass. I mean, next to Rome, Ireland is the motherhouse of the Catholic Church in the West. Still, despite my best efforts, nothing availed. Nevertheless, I had some quiet minutes at beautiful St. Michael's Church, where I could light a candle to the Blessed Virgin and send up some petitions for family and friends.

I had such a good time in Cork and the two nearby cities that I almost hated to go back north. But not to worry, the Heaslips had invited the Hortons and me for the following weekend. This time we drove down in Lucas and Syna's car, stopping for lunch at a nationally famous pub, Morrissey's, halfway between Shercock and Cork. Ireland, it struck me, is a country of many churches and even more pubs. The smallest village may have one store and one church but two or three pubs. Or so it seemed.

On January 27, I found my way on a bus from Castleblaney to Dublin Airport. SAS took me back to Copenhagen, after which I went by train right from the Airport to Odense, where, at one in the morning, "Uncle Ludvig," my now 78-year-old Subud brother and ever-generous host, met me on the platform and drove me to his bachelor apartment. He too was a widower, in his case for decades. His wife had died very young after a debilitating disease which had left her blind for the final year of her life. A retired school Latin and Danish teacher, Ludvig was the last remaining helper of the old Danish Subud group. He was also an expert in grave rubbings. While I was there, he learned that his large, illustrated book on the subject—the project of a dozen years—was now set to be published. The next day he drove me down to Ollerup, where I stayed two nights at Rune's place and said goodbye to my DFL friends. Then, on February 1, after a quiet farewell weekend with Aisha in Copenhagen, I got on SAS once more for the smooth flight back to Newark, thirteen-and-a-half months after I had first arrived there from Honolulu.

17
The Beginning of Wisdom

HOW THE concept of *wisdom* entered my life, I can't say for sure. But I do have a theory. It came from getting fired. To date I have been fired from jobs three times. The first, in 1970, was technically a *reorganization*. I had been working for the better part of a year at the East-West Center in Honolulu as the intercultural activities officer. Under the leadership of Chancellor Everett Kleinjans the ten-year-old Center was undergoing a major restructuring. Beginning in 1971, it would have up to a half-dozen "problem-oriented institutes," not the Institutes for Student Interchange, Technical Interchange, and Advanced Projects, as it had had from its beginning. Degree students, technical trainees, professional researchers, and diplomats on study sabbaticals would henceforth be clustered by topic, be it population, environment, or cultural affairs. Under the new configuration, an office like mine, headed by a Ph.D. and staffed by three other full-timers to deal with orientation, debriefing, and activities fostering an intercultural worldview, would no longer be necessary. Instead, there would be a lower-paid position for orientation and debriefing and a certain amount of moral support for degree students only. A masters-prepared person with a student-affairs background would be sufficient. The Personnel Director told me I could apply for the new position but went on to say I was overqualified and would probably not be happy with a technical position that left little room for creativity. Ah, industrial psychology!

The reality is that I had been a thorn in the flesh of the higher, almost exclusively Caucasian American administration. (Of course, I wasn't much different in background, only that I was a middle manager.) My point, which I repeated publicly, was that our Center for Cultural and Technical Interchange Between East and West, shortened to East-West Center or even the Center and EWC, was in reality a Center for Technical Exchange from West to East. In my view, true *interchange* was a two-way street, and as the only humanist on staff besides my boss, a Harvard-trained theologian, I argued that the cultural side really did come first and not just alphabetically. Another problem, from the top administration's perspective, was that I was popular with the students, who found the higher-ups distant and theoretical while I hung out with the "participants" and valued their opinions, which I surveyed and took into account in our office's policies and practices.

So when word got out that our office was being eliminated and I would not be staying on, the students staged what I believe was the first protest in Center history. In other words, they understood what I understood. Being "organized out of a job" was just another way of saying, at least in this case, I was being fired.

As it happened, I still had a contract as an assistant professor of English across the street at the University of Hawai'i's Manoa Campus. Technically, to protect myself, I had taken a one-year leave of absence from my academic job. My plan was to see how things worked out before burning any bridges. That turned out to be a wise decision. The second time I was fired, however, was more traumatic. I've already told that story in Chapter 12. Suddenly there would be no regular income, no medical or other fringe benefits, no job title, nothing. But as you may recall, the Voice assured me that all was well, that "He" had never let me and the family down before and had no intention of doing so now. And thus it turned out. The third time I got fired, from the Aloha Medical Mission in 2005, was described in Chapter 14. Meanwhile during that interim year of 1990-91, two important new developments occurred: Blue Sky Associates and a course called The Literature of Wisdom—A Cross-Cultural Exploration.

In fairness I should first mention another source of my interest in wisdom. In 1978, my Subud mentor, Varindra Vittachi, invited me to a weeklong conference in England on Education for the Coming Era. At the time Varindra was already working at the U.N. as director of information for the United Nations Development Program's Population Program. This was one of several conferences he was co-facilitating with Dr. Jonas Salk on the future of the world. By this point in his career, Dr. Salk was spending much time and energy on his new nonprofit, The Epoch B Foundation. According to him, Epoch A was the present world; Epoch B would be the more sustainable world of the future if we human beings had the wisdom to create it. In this conference series, Dr. Salk and Varindra were attempting to reach leaders in various fields as well as journalists to discuss what such a better future might consist of and how we could achieve it. Varindra wanted me there as a forward-looking American *educationalist*. He also suggested I bring Simone. My roundtrip transportation from Chicago plus room and board for both of us at Farnham Castle, Surrey, the meeting venue, would be covered. I needed only pay for Simone's airfare. As it happened, Air France was having a roundtrip special from Chicago to London via Montreal. We jumped at the chance.

Not long before Varindra's call I had picked up a 1973 book by Jonas Salk entitled *Survival of the Wisest*. In this work he argued that Evolution (a term he capitalized throughout) was calling for the birth of more and more people with the capacity to make decisions that over time proved beneficial to self, others, and the planet as a whole. That was how he defined wisdom. Unless a critical mass of such persons were born, sooner rather than later, he didn't extend the planet much hope. So Epoch B, per Salk, would be the direct result of the emergence and activities of wiser human beings.

When I met Dr. Salk in England—he insisted we all call him Jonas—I gave him my copy of his book to sign. His flattering inscription said I had already been putting into practice the very things he (and Evolution) had been calling for. I then asked him how I could help my students become wiser. For me his book was talking in more global terms. He looked at me very earnestly, and for a moment I thought I might have offended the great man. Then he replied, "I think that's your book to write, Reynold." So, his words may have planted the seeds for my later initiatives to foster wisdom throughout the world. Meanwhile, after the conference, Varindra asked me to submit an article on "the educated person cross-culturally"—my topic at the meeting—which he brought out in the U.N. journal *Populi* in 1979.

Let me tell you briefly about our encounter with a ghost, actually THE ghost, at Farnham Castle, where Simone and I were staying. The Castle had initially been constructed by Etienne, or Stephen, the grandson of William the Conqueror, in the early 1100s. So the oldest part of the structure was the castle keep, a round stone affair typical of Norman architecture at that time. Soon it had become one of the seats of the Catholic Bishop of Guildford, whose headquarters was in the nearby city of that name. In Elizabethan times, a second section was added to Farnham, and later Queen Elizabeth I stayed there during one of her Royal Progresses. Finally, Bishop Morley, the now Anglican bishop, had added a third section during the Restoration. It was there we conference participants were housed and Simone and I had our spectral visitor.

On our first night in the Castle, we sat up in bed for a while to read. At about midnight the lights flickered and went out. Although old castles aren't noted for the quality of their heating, an especially cold wind came up out of nowhere and blew over us. I figured there had been a short. Anyway, we didn't think anything of it and went to sleep. The next morning, the lights worked fine. At breakfast I wondered to the manager if there had indeed been a short circuit during the night. "Not at all," he said. "You were simply honoured by a visit from the Bishop [Bishop Morley]. He took great pride in the wing he built, including the Great Hall, and is sometimes known to visit guests in his addition." The next night or two, a few chills ran down my spine as I went to the loo in the dark, stone hallway. Nonetheless, we had no further encounters until the last night, when the Bishop visited us again. This time Simone and I were prepared. We wished him a good evening and prayed for his well-being. Then we told him we would be leaving the next day and thanked him for having received us in his castle, where we had had rich, informative meetings. During the stay we had also put together a wine-and-cheese reception for the entire company to honor our fifteenth wedding anniversary on November 30. Varindra, Jonas, Jim Rose (publisher of Penguin Books), and others attended and had wished us many more years of happiness together. I wonder if the good bishop joined us for that occasion as well.

To get back to Blue Sky Associates and The Literature of Wisdom class, both *arrived* in my consciousness and came to life at about the same time. Simone and I had won a free weekend at Ruttger's, a resort an hour north of the Twin Cities by car. The time was May 1990. Simone's mother was in the hospital for an operation to place a stent in her kidney the following week. She was resting quietly, so, after getting the doctor's permission and leaving our phone number at Ruttger's with the nursing station, we decided to cash in on our good luck. It mainly rained that weekend, but we were exhausted from the stresses of the last weeks and were happy to see videos and rest. During the weekend I wrote up an idea for a professional association—once again of innovators and change agents in education. This was not something I had been thinking about. Instead, it came to me like a hologram out of nowhere. Unlike Interversitas in my Northeastern days, this new organization would include any kind of human-development activity, formal or informal, from cradle to grave. The name which came to me was *Blue Sky Associates—Catalysts for Educational Change.* Despite the negative connotation of blue-skying in business, my initial colleagues in the venture agreed to the name. After all, the idea had come out of the blue, and were dreary gray skies really better than blue ones?

Several days after our return to Saint Paul, Oma died. I guess her soul decided she didn't need the discomfort of an operation when it was her time to go. I had begun my transitional 15 months after the Metro State firing just six weeks before. Soon I began sending emails out to colleagues around the country outlining the proposed new organization. I received enthusiastic endorsements, with people stating their readiness to pay the $100 initiation fee I had suggested. This time, moreover, we would focus on conferences, meetings, and consultancies—i.e., go beyond issuing directories, which was all I had been able to do with Interversitas—and we agreed to hold a planning get-together at Mundelein Seminary, the Chicago Archdiocese's now hardly used training college for priests. That summer several dozen showed up for an exciting weekend including talk, games, rituals, good food, and an amazing level of conversation and fellowship among individuals, most of whom had been strangers to one another. The campus was lovely as was the early-summer weather. Soon enough I got Blue Sky Associates (BSA) registered as a Minnesota nonprofit corporation, and not many months later we received our official federal tax-exemption from the Internal Revenue Service. Thenceforth, we held something like a half dozen meetings, seminars, and conferences until Simone and I relocated to Hawai'i in September 1996. Each had a different focus. Soon we worked it out with the Society for Values in Higher Education to include our conferences within their annual Fellows Meetings. In this way, the Society made all the arrangements with the college campuses for room and board, and all we had to do was show up, pay the reasonable costs, and hold our meetings with the 15 to 30 participants who had come for Blue Sky. We gained additional members this way too so that by 1996, BSA had around 80 associates. Also, our own conference fees generated income for BSA and paid for both some of my time plus copying, mailing, and other office expenses.

One of the highpoints of our achievement came in July 1996, a mere month-and-a-half before our move to Honolulu. Associate Kaia Svien, an educator, therapist, and ritualist in Minneapolis, and I co-coordinated a major national conference that was held at St. Olaf College in Northfield, Minnesota, about 45 minutes' drive south of our home in Saint Paul. Some 150 – 200 people registered for the three-day conference on "Teaching from Within." Our keynoter, the well-known author, educator, and consultant Parker J. Palmer, had been so interested in the topic that he had invited Kaia, me, Jane Tompkins (our featured speaker), and a few others for a day at his home in Madison, Wisconsin, to plan the conference. Not only that, but he refused payment for his talk—a great boon, since he was in huge demand and could command high fees. At the conference, he generously encouraged conferees to become Blue Sky associates. (In the same spirit of helpfulness, Jane Tompkins also declined to be paid for her talk.)

From the SVHE Fellows Meetings I had learned to mix fun and play with work, so the conference, besides major talks and concurrent interactive sessions, included rituals, entertainment, and even a dance party with a live band. Afterwards, we held a long-weekend retreat at a nearby Catholic retreat center for 17 conferees, including three nuns. Again, food, fun, and ritual—including a Mass—were mixed in, and the sessions were genially led by one of our Associates, Dr. Rosemary Broughten, a former nun, professor of Religion, SVHE Fellow, and experienced retreat leader. To this day, I consider that weekend the best professional gathering I have ever attended. When the time came to go, the retreatants, most of whom had been strangers to each other, laughed, cried, and hugged. No one wanted to leave. Later, I thought that weekend had been like an X-1 rocket launched from a specially converted Boeing 747. Once the big plane had reached its maximum altitude and speed, the test pilot fired his rocket engine and went on from there, building on the altitude and speed already achieved. So our retreat built on the wonderful conference just concluded and became a truly amazing time of community-building, intimacy among human beings, learning and teaching.

While our move to Hawai'i didn't kill BSA, it made developing the organization harder. Despite help from cutting-edge electronic technology, I was still in the middle of the Pacific Ocean. Having board meetings wasn't the only challenge. I also got busy flying back and forth to the Twin Cities to do consulting work, so my paperwork for BSA became a casualty of my need to earn a living. Membership thus did not grow during this period, and I provided a bare minimum in terms of services. Still, we were able to hold several more SVHE-related conferences, including arguably our best in 1998 at Reed College in Portland, Oregon, which Simon Guerrand-Hermès and Sharif and Tuti Horthy attended all the way from Lewes, England. By this point I made sure always to include some Subud participants, up to a third but usually less. I called it "Subud homeopathy," some drops of people who practiced the *latihan* in the midst of others who did not. The Guerrand-Hermès Foundation for Peace delegation, concluding this was a powerful model, would help fund two subsequent youth conferences BSA fielded in Jakarta, Indonesia, and Crestone, Colorado, in 2001 and 2003, respectively.

First, though, we put on our largest activity to date, a Wisdom Weekend on Salt Spring Island, British Columbia, a ferry trip of several hours from Vancouver. With attendance from as far away as the East Coast of the U.S. and Western Australia, the gathering involved hundreds of people on the Island and had keynote addresses by the founder of the Virtues Project, Linda Kavelin-Popov; a well-known First Nations chief, Leonard George from Vancouver; and me.

Included were a church service at the United Church of Canada's sanctuary in the Island's main village, Ganges; a radio interview of me on the Canadian Broadcasting Corporation's British Columbia affiliate on the meaning and importance of wisdom; lots of concurrent sessions; entertainment, including comedy performers; a night of dancing; and even an experience of the "wisdom of sailing." The idea was to introduce the idea of wisdom and "wising up" to an entire small community. Out-of-town guests were put up at local B & B's and in some cases people's homes. The United Church of Canada minister of the Ganges church, a Subud helper and artist named Rohana Laing, was the chief local organizer.

Getting back to the Jakarta and Colorado Blue Sky conferences, both were named for Varindra Vittachi. When I helped fund-raise for and subsequently attended the Subud World Congress in the Andes Mountains in Colombia in July 1993, he was already in the last stages of liver cancer. He had become so slender that, with his glasses on, he greatly resembled one of his heroes, the Mahatma Gandhi. When I visited him in his quarters, where he was confined to bed, he marveled at how "these underdeveloped Colombians" could build an entire Subud Center with a *latihan* hall capable of seven or eight hundred people doing our spiritual exercise at a time. "But what have you Americans done? You are the richest people in the world, but when it comes to Subud, you have nothing to show for it—no great halls, no impressive centers, no major enterprises, nothing!" Although I didn't say a word to him at the time, I decided I would do something to make him proud. That was the last time I would see him. He died that October in London. So I created the Varindra T. Vittachi Conference Series on Educating for a Human Future within the framework of BSA. The first one took place in late June 2001 in Jakarta as part of the Jakarta Arts (JakArts) Festival, a Subud production. Like our conference, Vittachi I, JakArts was part of a long list of activities and projects honoring the centenary of Bapak's birth on June 22, 1901. Incidentally, June 22nd was also the birthday of the City of Jakarta, so the mayor's office was happy to have the Arts Festival at that time.

Vittachi I, which attracted some 200 participants from 22 countries, took place at the Hotel Atlet Senayan in downtown Jakarta. Because the hotel was also the JakArts headquarters, we got the great room rate of $25 per night including a gourmet breakfast. Since two attendees could share one room, the per-person price was even cheaper. The Guerrand-Hermès Foundation subsidized what we were unable to raise through donations or from conference fees, so we could help individuals from economically poor countries attend. The conference theme was "Educating for a Human Future." The former Indonesian Education and Culture Minister, Dr. Fuad Hassan, together with Varindra's widow, Sarojini Vittachi, an Indian Subud member who had been an executive at UNESCO and later directed the U.N.'s peace-keeping initiatives in several dozen South and West Asian countries, including the Middle East, shared the honors of giving keynote speeches. We were also able to show a commencement address on "The Educated Person" Varindra had given at Metropolitan State University during my time there as academic vice president. Beyond that there were the usual concurrent and plenum sessions, rituals from different cultures and religions, and lots of music and singing. I had engaged Subud members from all over the world to serve as small-group facilitators plus had recruited a number of international Subud youth, in town for Bapak's Bicentennial Celebration followed by the Subud World Congress in Bali, to attend the Conference. So, as Tuti Horthy later shared with me, the whole event had the feel of a Subud meeting with Bapak present. To help things flow smoothly, not only did the conference staff meet daily, but we did *latihans* together every morning. Perhaps the high point was the near-professional-quality show Hugh Lynn, the half-Maori Subud member from New Zealand, produced and directed with talent exclusively from the participants and staff. (Hugh had been a rock-concert producer in his native country.) As the evaluations showed, Vittachi I was a great success.

The second Vittachi Conference, on Educating for a Sustainable World, was much smaller, with only 50 people attending from eleven countries. This time the venue was Atalanta, a 40-acre sustainability and community-development project of some Subud members in the 8,000-foot-high San Luis Valley of southern Colorado. One reason for the reduced size was the difficulty of getting visas for non-First-World students in post-9/11 America. It was now August 2003. Our on-the-ground director was Illène Pevec, a prize-winning community gardener and environmentalist with projects in British Columbia and Brazil. Once again, the Guerrand-Hermès Foundation was our main funder; however, this time, thanks to Illène, we also received a sizable grant from the Lewis Foundation, the family charity of the founder of Progressive Insurance. As at Vittachi I, we had a good mix of workshops, talks, food, fun, and activities. Our keynoter was Chief Orville Looking Horse, the Seventeenth White Buffalo Woman Pipe Carrier and spiritual head of the Sioux Tribes. We also continued our tradition of having Subud members as small-group facilitators. Two differences were that Vittachi II took place more outdoors than indoors. For example, just as the sun was setting over the surrounding desert, a Native American woman professor led us in building a Medicine Wheel on the highest point at Atalanta. Moreover, our main common activity was constructing a green amphitheater complete with a gazebo-like stage. Our materials were desert sand, chicken wire, and empty, misprinted 75-pound rice bags, which green-buildng guru Kelly Hart, our project coordinator, had acquired cheaply. Three teams of 15 – 20 took turns shoveling sand into the bags, wheel-barrowing them to the site, then hauling them to the top of the rising structure. We dug the sand in such a way as to create steps for an amphitheater. By the end we had a completion ritual in which everyone planted the rocks we had brought on top of the adobe arms on either side of the entrance to the gazebo. The only thing we could not finish was the adobe work, which later a team of itinerant Mexican workers did over a weekend. The entire project cost less than $1,000. Also, having an international, cross-generational team of 50 do the building brought us together as a community.

Vittachi III was originally supposed to take place in Nova Scotia, Canada, in summer 2005. The Guerrand-Hermès Foundation had even called a meeting of the likely conference organizers, including me, to spend some cold January days looking at the Lester Pearson Peace Center there as the possible venue. For whatever reason, people failed to register, and at the eleventh hour, the conference was cancelled. So, the Foundation planned Vittachi III, and as mentioned in an earlier chapter, that conference took place in late-June 2006 on the American-style campus of Al-Akhwain University in Ifrain, Morocco. The chief conference organizer was Dr. Scherto Gill, a Manchurian-born woman, also a Subud member (one of the first from the Peoples Republic of China), the Foundation's executive secretary. This time there were plenty of people on hand, perhaps 150, and the mix of Subud members—professionals in education, for the most part—and the concept of having small home groups were continued from Vittachi I and II. We also had Moroccan entertainment and time for sightseeing. As a conference participant, small-group facilitator, and co-workshop leader with my daughter Christine, I did not have the responsibility I had borne for the first two Vittachis. Since Simone had just been diagnosed with terminal cancer, I was in no state to do something like that.

Technically, both the Vittachi activities and Blue Sky's wisdom gatherings fell under what we called The World Wisdom Project. Later, that project would be re-established as a new nonprofit organization, Wisdom Factors International (WFI), founded in 2003. Eventually, Blue Sky Associates would lapse into inactivity as more things were done under WFI, whose board of directors all lived on

Oahu. Hence, there was no problem having face-to-face meetings.

The other major wisdom activity to emerge in 1990-91 was my course, the Literature of Wisdom—A Cross-Cultural Exploration. Once again, like Blue Sky Associates, it had just shown up in my mind. I don't know where the idea for this course came from beyond my growing interest in wisdom. Initially, wisdom was simply a thematic thread on which to string literary works from around the world. My plan was for course members to read the selections for form and content in the usual way. However, once we got started that very first of twelve times, student interest quickly shifted to how we as individuals could become wiser. As it happened, that first quarter course became the template for the other eleven times the course was offered. We began by introducing ourselves, learning our names, and discussing what wisdom meant for each of us. I then introduced the course and what my operating definition of wisdom was. I would then go over the works I had chosen for us to study.

We began by considering an international assortment of proverbs. Then we would discuss classics from the ancient world, both sacred and secular. At some point we would look at a "wisdom" film. The very first was *It's a Wonderful Life*, the Frank Capra classic. Like the books, I would change the movie each time. After the proverb unit, I would have us all write a letter to a real or hypothetical person with advice on living the good life. As with all our written work except our journals, students ran off enough copies so class participants could benefit by everyone else's wisdom. Over the six years this course was offered, there were some phenomenal letters. In retrospect, I should have published an anthology with the best. Oh well, it was a missed opportunity. Anyway, in the class when the letters were due, I had us divide up into eight groups of three. (The class always reached its enrollment limit of 25.) Individuals then read their letters out loud, discussed similarities and differences, and nominated one person's composition to be read to the entire class. After, we began as a large group listing out and numbering non-repeating characteristics of the good life. Generally, we would come up with 25 to 40. I next showed the class how to prioritize the items by having us each note down on a slip of paper the numbers of the five we considered the most important. I mentioned that this technique was an effective way for groups to prioritize anything. It turned out that some class members had written their letters to real people, and many actually sent their letters off.

Another exercise was my asking everyone to point to the teacher. At first, everyone pointed at me. Fair enough, since I was the teacher of record. Typically, several students would remember their orientation course, where they learned that as adult students they already knew a lot and would learn from each other. So, a few creative souls began pointing at other students—something the rest quickly took up. Then everything exploded. Some pointed up: One learned from God or the Universe. A few others pointed down: Mother Earth too would teach us. Finally, people pointed to themselves. They would of course teach themselves. By now a kind of dance emerged in which all of us were pointing all over the place. If we were open to it, learning would take place in many ways, and everybody and everything could be our teacher. Being open was the key. I would mention Harold Taylor's book *The World as Teacher* in this context.

Once the Literature of Wisdom class got started, it developed a life of its own. Because I couldn't find a truly cross-cultural proverb book in paperback, I got the closest thing to it—a collection of mainly Anglo-American sayings with a few Latin, Greek, and Chinese ones for flavor. Not only that; but the language in all the books I could find was masculinist. I started calling these the "He Who" proverb collections, since so many, like "*He who* hesitates is lost," were in that format. Therefore, to live up to the course's subtitle, "A Cross-Cultural Exploration," I created a list of a hundred supplementary proverbs in inclusive contemporary American English, ten each from ten different traditions. There were African, Arabic, Russian, Chinese, Japanese, Jewish, and others in my handout. Many were funny. After we completed our work with the proverbs, one of the students raised his hand. "Reynold," he said. "Your list is much more interesting than the proverbs in the book." "Well," I responded, "I just couldn't find an affordable book in modern inclusive English with proverbs from all over the world." "Okay," he continued. "You're a college professor, right?" I nodded. "Professors write books, right?" I started to suspect where this line of questioning was leading. "So why don't you create a collection of your own?"

After class, a woman my age named Cynthia Voelke came up and said if I really wanted to put together a book of proverbs, she had a research background and was interested in working with me on the project. Long story short, we met that week and mapped out a strategy. After I wrote our ideas up, I happened to share them with the Rev. Roland Seboldt, our choir director at the Germanic-American Institute. Though now retired, he had been the long-time head of book publishing at Augsburg-Fortress Press. What I didn't know at the time was that he was still active as an acquisitions editor at Harper San Francisco, a part of HarperCollins Publishers. Two months later Cynthia and I had a contract for a small hardback called *A World Treasury of Folk Wisdom* which Harper published in spring 1992. It had 100 topics containing 1,000 proverbs from 135 cultures. The language was inclusive. Many of the sayings were funny like "If a thief kisses you, count your teeth" (Yiddish), "Don't call the crocodile big mouth till after you cross the river" (West African), and "Love is blind but not the neighbors" (Mexican). By 1992 I no longer had a job, so every source of income became important. As fate had it, that little book sold 20,000 copies, brought Cynthia some much-needed income, and helped me pay for Christine's college. From then on I used it in all the remaining offerings of the Literature of Wisdom. When the devil slams the door, God opens a window. Here was proof. I had lost my job and couldn't seem to find a new one. Yet out of nowhere, I was the co-author of a minor bestseller put out by one of the largest houses publishing in English. Not only that, but I was earning money twice a year by teaching a course that had emerged unasked.

Besides the readings and occasional exercises, class participants were required to keep a journal on all the readings as well as the class discussions. I wanted to see how everyone engaged the material and what they got out of class discussions and readings. Several three-hour sessions toward term's end were dedicated to group-project presentations, each of which the teams had discussed and refined with me before getting started. The projects provided more wisdom resources for the participants. Team members also had to give me one-page summaries of their contributions, a document requiring the signatures of the others in their group. I wanted to avoid situations where one or two individuals did most of the work and the others freeloaded.

For the final exam, the questions were printed in the syllabus and remained the same for all twelve course offerings. It wasn't about the questions; it was all about the answers. I wanted students, in a letter to their fellow class participants, to answer the following: (1) What do you think wisdom is now? (2) What are you sure wisdom is not? (3) What are three important things you learned from this course? (4) What three things do you plan to do after this course to become wiser? And (5) What final comments do you have for your colleagues in this course?

As with all other written work in the Literature of Wisdom, students were requested to make three-ring-punched copies to share with everyone else. The final class was inevitably a pot-luck at our house, with Winston the cat in the thick of things and Simone as hostess and audience member. In the spring term we would sit outside in the gazebo; in winter we used the family room. First, each person read his or her paper out loud. We then had dinner, where the food was generally as good as the letters. Finally, we had a concluding ritual, which ended in a group hug. Community had been achieved on a small scale in a short academic quarter. People laughed and cried, and as many as ten hung out for an hour or more after the class had officially ended.

On June 30, 1991, my formal employment with the Minnesota State University System ended. Twenty-six weeks of unemployment compensation didn't do much to make up for the loss of a $75,000-a-year salary plus benefits. Actually, it barely paid for the now-more-expensive medical insurance I had to carry for Simone and me. But the Voice was not wrong. While I continued looking for a new academic job, several things happened that launched my career as "Reynold Feldman, Consultant." First, Chuck Graham, my boss during the transitional 15-months at the State University Office, created a consulting project for me to survey the international programs in the System's seven universities. This was a considerable undertaking which paid well. Then, another colleague asked me to prepare the System's request to the Archibald Bush Foundation for a three-year $640,000 faculty-development project. Meantime, my unsuccessful attempt to become the president of the School for International Studies in Vermont yielded an eight-month grant-writing assignment that had me going to Brattleboro every month. The timing was impeccable, because concurrently Marianna was attending Bennington College, likewise in Vermont, so when I finished my work, I could visit her. These three projects, besides launching me on a new career, covered half my lost salary. But what about the rest?

Well for one thing, my nationally known colleague Dr. Jerry Gaff, who would later hire my daughter Christine as his assistant while she was studying for her master's degree at Georgetown University, sent higher-education consulting jobs my way. One I particularly remember during this period was to assist with a general-education-reform initiative at Gallaudet University in Washington, DC. Because Gallaudet is a federal institution for the deaf, I had two sign-language interpreters with me at all time. For me the challenge was to think about what a generally educated deaf person would need to know and be able to do to live effectively in the majority culture. What universal values, attitudes, knowledge, and skills as well as curricular objectives would best serve the needs of non-hearing people? Along the way, I learned about "deaf culture," including deaf theater.

But even these many sources of income were not sufficient. However, God really did provide. I had applied for a program-officer job at the Archibald Bush Foundation in Saint Paul in 1991. Although I became one of two finalists, the person who ended up getting hired had served Bush as a program consultant in the past, was well liked by the staff, and seemed the better fit. Nonetheless, once on board, he had what some of my later colleagues there described as a personality change, was unable to keep up with the work, and was soon asked to leave. I meantime had been doing a number of post-grant evaluations for Bush. So when the newly hired program officer left, I received a call from the senior program officer, asking me whether I would like to become a program consultant. The Foundation had determined not to replace the newly fired program officer but instead to farm out his work to several program consultants. The latter would make site visits, review grant proposals, write critical project analyses, and together with program officers make recommendations to the Board of Trustees on whether the proposals in question should be funded or not. For this activity, all my expenses would be reimbursed, I could keep accrued airline mileage for my personal use, and I would be paid $60, later $70, per hour for work, including time away from home. John then went on to say that, if I was up for the job, he had a whole dump truck of proposals ready to assign me.

From 1991 until 1999, by which time we were already in Honolulu, Bush was very good to me. Indeed, before I knew it, I was earning as much as I had before as a university vice president. In addition, I soon found myself flying around the country, since although Bush was a regional foundation making grants primarily in Minnesota and the Dakotas, it funded educational projects at tribal colleges and historic black colleges and universities nationwide. As a long-time postsecondary educator, I was their consultant of choice for many of these proposals. The Bush program officers moreover were a wonderful group of professionals and human beings. I always enjoyed working with them, and for their part, they kept finding additional work for me such as coordinating their post-grant evaluation program and doing a five-year retrospective analysis of the outcomes of various grants. At one point, in fact, the McKnight Foundation in Minneapolis called their Bush colleagues in Saint Paul to see if any of the Bush program consultants might have time for additional work. So in a matter of weeks, I was vetting grant applications for the two largest foundations in the Upper Midwest, not to mention a major, well-paid evaluation of the Blandin Foundation's state-wide effort to improve schools around Minnesota and some pre-grant evaluation work for the Saint Paul Foundation. In short, out of nothing I was guided to a means of supporting Simone and me and keeping our beautiful home near the Mississippi River in one of the most desirable districts in Saint Paul, and that remained true until we left the Twin Cities for Hawai'i in early September 1996.

Why did we move to Hawai'i? Well, in 1995 I was able to write a successful planning grant that brought me to Honolulu for a number of short stays of a week or two to assist Ivy Olson with the development of Angel Network Charities, Calvary Lutheran Church's backyard ministry to the homeless. In that same period, I managed to get Ivy named as one of the first President Bush's 1,000 Points of Light for her volunteer leadership. During these trips to Hawai'i, I began to feel it would be good for Simone and me, now that we were older, to return to the Fiftieth State to live. No ice and snow plus a consistent temperature of 70 – 85 degrees year round were no small incentives. Although Simone had concerns about giving up our house and moving thousands of miles away from the girls, the prospect of returning to Hawai'i, being with old friends, belonging to the Subud group we had helped found in the late-60s, and rejoining Calvary By The Sea Lutheran Church, where we had spent so many enriching hours during my 1980 sabbatical, finally won out. Ivy Olson was delighted at the prospect, but everything depended on (1) my raising some $40,000 in foundation grants to pay for my services and (2) our living inexpensively in the two-bedroom apartment on the first level of the Olsons' large house in Hawai'i Kai. Well, Ivy promised the latter, and once the two grants came through, I negotiated with the Bush and McKnight Foundations for continuing work. I told them I would pay for my flights to the Twin Cities. Meantime, friends from Pilgrim Lutheran Church in Saint Paul, the Gehrmans, said they would provide me with free room and board whenever I came to town. And so, by July our house had sold at a nice profit after less than two weeks on the market.

On September 4, 1996, having put our furniture into storage, we hosted an outdoor party for our friends at the Germanic-American Institute and indulged ourselves in one final meal of hamburgers, onion rings, and malteds at our neighborhood's renowned Snuffy's before driving off into the future. And so, on September 26, 22 days after setting out from Saint Paul, we arrived once again in Hawai'i. If you've read Chapters 14 through 16, you'll know the rest of the story.

18
Judaism

GRANDMA IDA Litsky Feldman came over from her Central European *shtetl* in the years just preceding the 20th Century. How she and Grandpa Paul could ever have gotten together is a mystery to me. They were the original odd couple. While she was Orthodox and observant, he was an affable ne'er-do-well, a kind of Jewish Zorba the Greek. Her father had been a scribe, not one of the New Testament kind that formed a political party generally opposed Jesus but the literal kind who copied out a few Torahs a year in beautiful calligraphy with specially blessed stylus and ink. Because he worked in proximity to the sacred text, Great Grandpa Litsky, who died long before I was born, was considered a holy man. Consequently, he was often consulted by individuals and families in the community about matters both sacred and profane.

Later I heard Bapak had told some of his followers that in order for someone to come to Subud, they had to have had at least one spiritually advanced ancestor within the prior five generations. Whether or not he had actually said this and whether it is true I do not know. Should that be the case, Great Grandpa Litsky was likely that person for me. What I do know is that he ran a strictly Orthodox Jewish household, with four sets of dishes, two for Passover and two for the rest of the year; one each for dairy and for meat products, and that for all of her 94 years, Grandma Ida continued his regimen by keeping kosher and striving to follow the 613 rules and regulations (many do's and many more don'ts) comprising the Orthodox Jewish Halakha, or required observances.

When we went to Grandpa's and her apartment in the Hotel Newton on Upper Broadway in Manhattan, we would inevitably be served chicken matzo-ball soup with noodles and a few floating pieces of parsley. I would later laugh at the Woody Allen film where he commented that his mother would typically put the chicken through "the deflavorizer." I always had to beg for pepper, possibly the start of my love affair with spicy foods, to do something, anything, to make Grandma's soup less bland and more edible.

Grandma had contracted TB as a young woman, and although she had recovered, she became a lifelong hypochondriac. According to my father, she had been "dying" as long as he could remember, even though she outlived a whole string of doctors. If I as little as coughed at her place, she would look at me with a worried face and tell me to wear rubbers, dress warmly, and sleep enough to stay healthy. "Paul, get the boy some cough medicine," she would shout to Grandpa. "Leave him alone, Ida. He only coughed." He would respond. "I know," she countered. "But you can never be too careful."

Grandma Ida was also a Jewish cultural nationalist who would frequently talk about the accomplishments of famous Jews, from Supreme Court Justice Brandeis to Albert Einstein, who was still alive at the time and busy solving universal puzzles at Princeton's School for Advanced Studies. She liked the fact that she and Grandpa were staying in their little efficiency apartment at the Hotel Newton. She was so convinced that the great 17th Century British mathematician, Sir Isaac Newton, was Jewish—his name was Isaac after all—that she had named my father Jacob *Newton* Feldman after him. Later, when I learned that Newton had been an Anglican theologian of note as well as a scientist, I could never bear to break the news to Grandma. In spring, 1956, on my acceptance to Yale, my mother had bought me a tie-pin and matching cufflink set—men still used both back then— with the Yale insignia on them. There one read *Lux et Veritas*, light and truth, as well as the Hebrew equivalents, *Urim* and *Tumim*. When Grandma Ida caught a glimpse of the latter, she was ecstatic. "So you're going to a *yeshiva* [Jewish theological seminary]," she said, gleefully. If she only knew what kind of ultra-*goyishe yeshiva* Yale was, she would have had a spasm for sure. I spared her the disappointment. "It *is* some kind of *yeshiva*, I guess, Grandma," I replied without much enthusiasm.

Five months before I was to turn thirteen, my parents enrolled me in an American Baptist boarding school in Central New Jersey, a mere twelve miles East of Princeton. Since I had had no formal religious training except for a year in a Reform Jewish Sunday School (sic!), where I hardly memorized two or three of the basic Hebrew prayers, I was nowhere near prepared for being *bar mitzvah* [made a son of the Commandments]. In a Jewish *bar mitzvah*, even a Reform one, the *bar mitzvah* boy had to chant correctly from the Torah, where one found vowel-less Hebrew words, then give an appropriate sermon on what he had read. Being *bar mitzvah* for a Jewish boy is equivalent to the Christian confirmation. It means for Jews becoming a religious adult who can take part in the ten-person (or more) conference call to God required by Orthodox Judaism. Grandma Ida had apparently told my father that if the Boy, i.e., I, were not properly *bar mitzvah*, she would die and curse him (my father) from her death bed. Although not superstitious, my father took no chances.

On or around my thirteenth birthday, I remember going to Grandma's Orthodox *shul* (synagogue; literally, school), Temple Shaare Zadek I think it was called, somewhere on the Upper West Side of Manhattan. Facing the morning minyan (congregation) of prayer-shawl-covered men who came each day and could chant Hebrew at 60 miles an hour, I lamely read my transliteration of the prayers said before and after the rabbi himself read *my* Torah portion. Some of the men glanced up at me as if encountering a foul odor. It was obvious I was clueless, a disgrace to *Eretz Yisroel*, the long-suffering Jewish people, and likely a symbol for why our people were going to the dogs. After, I saw my father slip a large bill into the rabbi's hand. Then, at least in religious matters, I did become a man. The Voice, the one that had comforted me when I was small and couldn't fall asleep because of a sudden fear of death, told me in no uncertain terms that I could be religious or not. That was my choice. But if I chose to be so, it could not be a farce like this. It needed to be real, or else it was better if I remained secular and forgot about religion altogether.

Throughout my years at prep school, Yale College, and Yale Graduate School, I corresponded regularly with Grandma Ida. She always wrote the word *God*, frequently invoked in her letters, as *G-d*. For Orthodox Jews, spelling out the Deity's powerful name was never done. One always used an abbreviated form, Anglicized as "Yahweh" for "Jehovah." Generally, she signed her letters "I'm with loads of love, Grandma Ida." These were sweet letters that actually cheered me up and gave me courage as I navigated my way through the sometimes rough waters of college and graduate school. Later, I became orthodox in another way, even if not Jewish. But I can't help feeling that where Grandma Ida and Great Grandpa Litsky are today, they would not be altogether displeased.

Grandpa Paul was an entirely different sort of person. Born Pinchas ben Sviaria ben Somebody Else Feldman, a Sephardic (Spanish) Jew in faraway Galati (Galatz), Romania, he arrived on Ellis Island, New York, as a 19-year-old in the last decade of the 19th Century. He was what was called a Greenie, a clueless immigrant with no relatives or resources in the New World. He and a friend the same age had been recruited by a Jewish benevolent society which had paid their way from Romania to Denver, Colorado—Grandpa always referred to it as "Colorado, Denver"—which needed two more *bar mitzvah*ed young men, per Orthodox Judaism, to make up the ten-man quorum, or *minyan*, required to send legitimate prayers to God.

On Ellis Island, the Jewish charity safety-pinned train tickets onto Grandpa and his buddy's shabby overcoats and shipped them off to Penn Station for their trip to Denver. Neither one spoke a word of English. Once in Denver, according to my father, Grandpa Paul (the English equivalent of his Jewish name) was housed with a successful Jewish businessman who owned a thriving general store. This man also had several marriageable daughters. Grandpa in those days was later said to have looked like a young Errol Flynn. Anyway, his host wanted him very much to marry the eldest daughter. "I know she's not very attractive," the man told Grandpa, "but since I have no sons, you'll inherit my business and become a wealthy man." Grandpa was unimpressed. He told my father later that the daughter had been "a real dog." So, he finished his contract and headed back to New York City via Chicago where he "worked" for a while in a bordello, Lord knows doing what. Had he married the daughter, he would have inherited incredibly valuable real estate in today's downtown Denver. But then, knowing Grandpa, he would have squandered the property long before it had attained its full value.

Once back in New York City—he didn't care for the cowboys, Indians, and other *goyim* in Denver either—he got work as a streetcar conductor. According to my father's next oldest brother, Murray, Grandpa had a special game he would play. He would stick pieces of chewing gum just above where he stood to collect fares. When arriving passengers gave him their nickel, he would flip it up to the ceiling. If it stuck to the gum, he would scrape it off at the end of the day and turn it in to the company. If it fell to the floor, he would pocket it for himself. On an ordinary day, Grandpa came home with a nice piece of change in his pocket, a self-created bonus.

When my father and Uncle Murray, three years his junior, were in elementary school, the family lived in Haddonfield, New Jersey, just across the Delaware River from Philadelphia. Then as now, Philly was one of America's busiest ports. Grandpa and one of his brothers owned a men's haberdashery shop near the waterfront on the Philadelphia side. When a sufficiently drunk sailor or merchant marine would stagger by, one would guide him in, sweet talk him, then lay him down on a piece of cloth. The other would draw the man's outline on the cloth with tailor's chalk, take a deposit for a suit that would rival the best Saville Row in London could offer, they said, then push him out the door and on his way.

During this same period, Grandma arranged for a rabbi to come from Philadelphia several afternoons a week to prepare the boys for their *bar mitzvah*. Apparently, there were few Jews and no temples or rabbis in Haddonfield at that time. My father and Uncle Murray were not into their religious studies and could not understand what God could possibly have against their playing baseball with the other kids after school. According to the story, the rabbi was handy with his ruler, and when the boys were not prepared, which was usually the case, he gave them some Old World motivation. He was also a little man. So my father and uncle decided the next time he hit them, one would hold him and the other would grab the ruler and give him a taste of his own medicine. And that's exactly what they did. The rabbi of course went complaining to Grandma in another room. So she got Grandpa's leather belt and gave my father and uncle the appropriate punishment for laying hands on a holy man. When Grandpa came home after a busy day at the clothing store, the boys told him what had happened. To complete the cycle, he in turn took the belt and beat Grandma for punishing his boys.

My father said that although he was *bar mitzvah*, he decided once he was no longer under his parents' control, he would turn his back on Judaism and live a life without the dogma and cruelty of religion. Also, he would never force his own children to suffer as he had because of his mother's fanaticism. Consequently, my sister and I were raised in a secular home. Only in his later years did he become interested in having Passover Seder in the apartment. But he consistently stayed away from synagogue services.

Grandpa reminded me of David Janssen's role in the long-running TV series "The Fugitive." As the announcer would intone at the beginning of each episode, the Fugitive had to "toil at many jobs" as he fled the relentless pursuit of the police inspector bent on capturing him for a crime he hadn't committed. In Grandpa's case, to be sure, he probably got fired from many of his jobs for incompetence, laziness, dereliction of duty, or pilfering. One job he held again and again was cook on merchant steamers. Occasionally he would tell the boys, "Your mother's just too tough for me. I can't stand it. I'm going to sea." He would be gone for months, though now and then he would send money to keep the household afloat.

He was also an entrepreneur of sorts. According to my father, he had co-owned and served as executive chef at a Mafia-financed restaurant in Miami in the 20s. His card, which Grandpa later showed me with pride, stated, "Paul Feldman, Chef de Cuisine," which my father mispronounced "chef dee kewzine." Like many another New York, my father also said "beauteeful" his whole life long.

My favorite of Grandpa's exploits, though, was his traveling Yiddish vaudeville show. Ever inventive, he had recruited a black female singer he knew from a bordello in Chicago, whether the same as the one he worked at in 1900 or not I don't know. He taught her to sing half a dozen Yiddish songs and called her *De shvartze Chasante*, the Black Chanteuse, which my father pronounced "chantoozie." He then added other acts and took the show to Jewish communities around the East. Apparently it was a big success. But Grandpa was not satisfied and wanted to do even better. So he would sometimes write checks on accounts he didn't have or on banks that didn't exist. One night my father and Uncle Murray got a call. "Boys," he said, "I'm in the Scranton, Pennsylvania hooskow." (Lots of Grandpa's English had a Western flavor thanks to his years in Denver. For example, he never said *railway station*. He would always say *depot*.) "Come bail me out." He had passed a bad check. His two sons drove all night to Scranton, made good on the check, paid Grandpa's fine, and took him home.

By the time I knew Grandpa Paul, he was an old man who had quieted down from his younger, more adventurous days. I liked going to the Hotel Newton because, though the food was bad, Grandpa would always have something interesting planned for me. For example, he would play a risqué Yiddish song called "Cockeyed Jenny" on a scratchy old 78 RPM record. Grandma would protest, "Paul, how can you play that smut for the boy?!" (Grandma, for all her accent, read a lot and, ironically, was a big fan of Bishop Fulton Sheen's radio and TV talks. So she had a very developed vocabulary of moralistic invective.) I didn't have a clue what the song was about. It was in Yiddish after all. But the words, music, and performance all struck me funny.

Grandpa also had an ear for languages even if he himself spoke accented English. Maybe he had picked words up in the multicultural environment of the merchant vessels where he cooked. One day I remember standing in the lobby of the Newton with him. He would talk Spanish with this one, Greek with that, Yiddish with another, and explain it all to me in English. I was impressed. In addition, he could speak and understand Romanian, Russian, and the Sephardic Jewish patois called Ladino. I'm sure I got my interest in learning languages from him.

Grandpa Paul died soon after my sister married. I was twelve. He called my father and Uncle Murray from the Newton one afternoon. "Boys, I don't want to cause you no more trouble," he said. "Take me to the hospital." The Old Man, as my father called him, was as good as his word. He passed away that night in his sleep. Grandma Ida lasted into her ninety-fifth year. After Grandpa died, my father found a little apartment for her in Liberty, New York, in the Catskill Mountains, the heart of the so-called Borscht Belt, where New York Jews would go on vacation to play golf and *tumul* (Yiddish for socialize). Of greater interest to Grandma, her apartment was less than a block from the *shul*, so she was able to go there regularly on foot.

I saw her one more time. One Sunday, Uncle Alan, who owned a driving school in Yonkers, drove my father, my recently arrived fiancée from Germany, and me up to see her. She looked frail. To her credit, she was nice to Simone, though we made sure not to stress the latter's nationality. Years later when Grandma died—she had been a victim of Alzheimer's in her final years—checks from my father and uncles along with $20 and $50 dollar bills were found scotch-taped to her body. Like others suffering from senile dementia, she was afraid she would be robbed. Apparently, she lived such a Spartan existence that she never missed the money.

✺

For my first 28 years I was technically Jewish. I say "technically" because my family was non-observant—they were what is known as "bagels-and-lox" Jews—and I had little training and less interest in discovering and following the religious aspects of our tradition. We identified with elements of American and East European Jewishness. The way my parents, especially my father, used the occasional Yiddish word or phrase was unmistakably New York and Jewish. Moreover, their friends and, with one exception, our extended-family members were all Jewish. Most, like us, were secular Jews. A few, like Grandma Ida and Uncle Sol, were observant.

Besides the occasional "required" Passover Seder at Grandma Ida's and the year at Reform Jewish "Sunday school" in White Plains, New York, during Seventh Grade, I had little contact with Judaism until, ironically, I went to Peddie, my Northern Baptist boarding school in New Jersey. Mainly of course we encountered a version of Protestant Christianity there, but after parents of Jewish students began to complain, a weekly prayer service was arranged for us in the local synagogue on Sundays. To be sure, it was merely a daily service, since Saturday is the Jewish holy day. Still, Sunday it was, since something Jewish had to be done with us while the Christian boarding students were required to go to their denominations' local church.

At Yale I would sometimes attend the Friday night Shabat service. Rabbi Israel, the University's Jewish chaplain, was a bright, articulate, and kindly man, and there was at least one outstanding guest, Reb

Zalman Schachter-Shalomi, the Hasidic rabbi, who left a lasting impression on me. But with one exception, I didn't make any friends there, and my attendance after a while became spotty. On joining Subud in 1961 and returning to Yale for graduate school that fall, I somehow found myself getting involved in the Conservative Jewish youth organization, *Atid*, the Hebrew word for "future." How I ended up becoming a Conservative Jew after hardly ever being a Reform one—the most liberal kind—is a mystery to me. I think it probably had something to do with a female friend I had made in the community, Marilyn Brown, who was active in the local *Atid* chapter. Marilyn was never really my girlfriend, but we did hang around together, and as I recall, she attended Simone's and my wedding in 1963. I went to a few Conservative retreats and read several books on the faith, but my main memory from my year in *Atid* was meeting and spending a weekend with Rabbi Abraham Joshua Heschel, the well-known theologian and anti-Vietnam activist, who in his book on the Sabbath said the main point of that special day was to spread its influence around to the other days of the week. In other words, we as Jews, or even as human beings, were not called to be religious only one day out of seven but were to act like God's creatures all week long. The way he put it was pithier: "You know the Sabbath is working when it infiltrates Wednesday."

My most important Jewish experience wasn't religious at all, although it was deeply spiritual. That was, as you'll recall, my visit to the Dachau concentration camp, or what was left of it, in fall 1958 and the dramatic encounter with the two German men on the train the next day. From then on, I fully accepted my Jewish personhood and identified myself as a Jew, a member of a distinctive people though in my case not a religion. Over the years, I have attended the occasional synagogue service—a bar mitzvah, wedding, or funeral—but my orientation has not changed.

In fall 2007 I was asked by my nephew as the oldest male in the family to read the Hebrew prayer before and after the bar mitzvah boy, his son Jason, recited his Torah portion. A linguist and a ham, I practiced my words to make them sound authentic. Afterwards, several people congratulated me on how well I had prayed. The best response in this regard, though, was when I presided over my mother's funeral in 1999. After the service, where among other things I had chanted the Mourner's Kaddish (the traditional Jewish prayer for the dead) in Hebrew, again from a well-studied transliteration, one of Mother's friends from her Jewish daycare for the elderly congratulated me on the inspiring service and proclaimed, "I never knew Estelle's son was a rabbi!" "*Oy!*" I thought to myself. "If this lady only knew what kind of rabbi I really was!" But then, another thought came. I remembered how, as a little kid, when my Uncle Sol had asked me what I wanted to be when I grew up, I told him without a moment's hesitation, "A rabbi." Now, with 64 or 65 years' hindsight, I can see that in one sense I had been prophetic. For *rabbi* like *guru* means a religiously or spiritually based teacher. Come to think of it, in my attempt to follow and imitate Jesus and in everything I have done professionally, that's exactly what I have become.

19
Lutheranism

I HAVE already shared a little about my Christian role models before my actual baptism in March 1967. First and foremost there was Florine, our wonderful African American housekeeper. Then there were Miss Sally and Miss May McAuliffe, the Catholic spinster sisters who lived next door to us in Great Neck's Old Village. My four years and two summers at the Peddie School of course played a major role, what with daily chapel, Sunday evening Vespers, and monthly Sunday morning convocations all required. I was the top student in religion class, which wasn't a latter-day politically correct survey of the great world religions but a Christian reading of selected key books and passages from the Hebrew Scriptures and the New Testament. How upset I had been at feeling unable to like Jesus best of all the characters in the Bible because he belonged to the Christian team from which I, even as a nominal Jew, felt excluded! I should probably also recognize my favorite prep-school teacher and academic role model, Al Watson. Even though he was not religious in the sense of Florine or, later, Alec Witherspoon at Yale, he was mainly responsible for introducing me to classical music including liturgical choral works and Gregorian chant. He also opened me to nature mysticism, New England Transcendentalism, and the transformative possibilities of Romantic poetry.

Probably the biggest Christian influence from prep school, though, was my senior-year roommate, Jim Culver, now a retired orthopedic surgeon from the Cleveland Clinic. Jim was a real Christian human being—kindly, helpful, never judgmental. In retrospect, these were unusual qualities for testosterone-driven high-school males. He was also one of the first in a series of three impressive Methodists I have met in my lifetime. The second, Chuck Graham, was the last outstanding university president I served under. The third was Jim Beddow, at the time president of Dakota Wesleyan University in Mitchell, South Dakota, and later an unsuccessful Democratic candidate for the governorship of that state. I worked for him as a consultant at Dakota Wesleyan after our move to Minnesota. The other major influence, first encountered at Peddie, was Christian hymnody. I just loved certain hymns, words and music both, and still do. I would give the signing of hymns a big place in my conversion.

At Yale College my primary Christian role model by far was Professor

Alec Witherspoon, a true Christian gentleman if ever there was one. Even when he read literature, his voice contained something of God in it. I can't quite explain it, and of course a lot of what we read in his course, like Milton's *Paradise Lost*, was religiously oriented. He was simply a man of great faith and kindness whose Christianity was not merely a religious affiliation or Sunday activity but had to do with who and how he was all the time.

The high Anglican services at Christ Church, New Haven, also touched me, even if there was pretentiousness associated with the church. I learned without a doubt that when it came to religion, I was inescapably high church. The more ritual, the better. Even before Subud, there had to be something in religion for me beyond ethics and morality. It wasn't merely a matter of a preacher talking about the mysteries of the faith. I had to *feel* the mysterious. Liturgical music, especially if old; special language, as in the King James version of the Bible and the Episcopal Book of Common Prayer; stories of recent or present-day miracles; impressive architecture; and all the other sensory accoutrements of a worship service—incense, candles, bells, hymns, chants, and holy water—had to be there to put me into another reality, the one in which Jesus cured the sick and pardoned the sinners and 1,900 years later made it possible for there to be followers like Florine Tolson Bond and Alexander McLaren Witherspoon.

My junior year abroad, mainly in Germany, gave me the opportunity to attend many concerts of holy music at local churches. I could write several pages on the importance of Bach, Handel, and other Baroque and earlier composers on my formation as both a Christian and a spiritually oriented person. I also used my relatively flush monthly allowance there to buy myself a multi-band radio, which was usually playing classical music, the earlier the better. Often I would attend church services too, Catholic and Protestant alike, sometimes with friends but more often on my own. To this day Baroque music transports me to that special place, and when I hear Bach or Archangelo Corelli, I think, "Now there is music that believes in God."

A major factor in my Christianity, however, was undoubtedly my wife, Simone. I don't mean I became a Christian for the sake of our relationship or in order to present a solid religious front to our kids. I'm sure some of my friends and even family members thought that. But that was not our case at all. Simone, it is true, had a stronger religious upbringing than I. However, she never put any pressure on me. We had Subud in common and were committed to it and each other. Actually, my becoming Christian had to do with yet another encounter with the Voice.

My wife had inherited a practice from her female line of reading the cards—regular playing cards from the number seven up (no jokers)—every New Year's Eve night, after midnight. It was just a party game. Sometimes, though, she could be quite accurate in predicting major events in the New Year. On New Year's Eve 1965/66, for example, she had laid the baby card, the Seven of Hearts, for us both. That is, the card showed up next to the card representing each of us: the Queen of Hearts for her, the King of Hearts for me. Then in her case, she randomly laid out a Jack and Queen of Diamonds just under her card. Uh, oh! Twins! This outcome was not implausible, since my mother was a fraternal twin, which meant we had a statistical chance of 1 in 64 of having twins too. In January, Simone missed her period, and on September 1, 1966, our first child, Marianne Michèle, was born. So what about the twins? Well, in a sense, we did have twins, since on September first my doctoral thesis was due at the Yale English Department. So that could be our girl and boy: Hers a real human baby; mine a brainchild—both the products of labor and love.

Since Simone had had a difficult delivery, I got permission to wait till September second, assuming Simone and the baby were okay, to deliver the dissertation, *The Dynamics of Innocence in Henry James: A Guide to the Jamesian Vision*, to the faculty. The next morning she and Marianne were in sufficiently good shape that I could leave. Also scheduled was a 3 p.m. meeting with the Rev. Richard Olson, the Lutheran Campus Chaplain at Yale who had married us. I would ask him to baptize Marianne with the water Francis von Kahler had brought back from the River Jordan.

I arrived in New Haven before lunch, picked up my dissertation copies from the bindery, and quickly took them to the Hall of Graduate Studies, where they were officially received. I had made the postponed deadline. If the faculty approved, I would have my Ph.D. by Christmas. After lunch at Mory's, the famous eating club, I went to the Old Campus. When I reached Dick Olson's office, I was 30 minutes early. So I kept going another hundred yards to Dwight Chapel, the place where he had married us nearly three years before. Since the Yale students weren't back yet for fall term, the campus and chapel were deserted. I intended to enjoy the quiet of the latter until 2:55 p.m.; then head to Pastor Olson's office.

After sitting for five minutes, the Voice visited me once again. "You should be baptized with your daughter," it said. "What?" Although I had great respect for the Christian religion, I had no intention of becoming Christian. Apparently the Voice was prepared for my reaction. "Do you see those books over there?" It asked. I noticed a pile of small prayer books which, by their size, I recognized as the 1928 Episcopal Book of Common Prayer. "Go over there, pick up a book, and open it at random. You'll be given a confirmation that what I am telling you is correct." Quickly praying to Moses, Jesus, and Bapak, I asked to be prevented from doing something stupid. Then I got up, went over to the prayer books, and followed the Voice's instructions.

When I opened the book, I saw the two pages containing the rite for the admission of new Christians to the church, a special service for adult baptism. On checking afterwards, I found there were over 750 pages, with only two of them containing that rite. I began sobbing. My body shook, and it seemed like I was making a lot of noise. It didn't matter. No one was around. Eventually I stopped and felt as if I had been thoroughly washed, inside and out. It also seemed as if a heavy knapsack had been cut from my back. I checked my watch—five to three.

Drying my eyes, I went over to the Lutheran Chaplain's office. Dick Olson was waiting for me. "Hi, Steve," he said with a friendly smile. "How are Hannelore and the baby?" "Fine," I answered, still not able to say much. "Did you get your dissertation in on time?" "Yes, thanks." "Sit down, and let's talk about the Baptism." We did, except first I blurted out the story of what had just happened. He listened attentively, puffing on his pipe. A few weeks before, he had been in the South campaigning for civil rights with Martin Luther King and other liberal clergy.

"I'd like to be baptized together with my daughter," I concluded. "Also, like Sts. Peter and Paul, I'd like a new baptismal name, *Reynold*." I didn't tell him where the name had come from, and he didn't ask. I may have mentioned the German equivalent meant "pure" and "chaste." He was silent for a moment and then explained: "Here at Yale we chaplains have an agreement that when any student wants to convert, the chaplains of the sending and receiving faiths, so to speak, get together with the student to test the individual's determination and see how carefully he or she has thought their decision through." Then he paused again. "But somehow in your case, Steve, I feel there are grounds for an exception. I'll talk with Rabbi Israel and give you a call. I'm a third-generation Lutheran pastor. I can't speak about my grandfather in Norway, but my dad never mentioned having had an experience like yours, and I can tell you I've never had one. I know from the Bible and more recent accounts that such things happen. I envy you having had one yourself. Anyway, I'll get back in touch soon." While he was speaking, I saw the disembodied head of Bapak, black *peci* [fez] and all, floating above and behind the pastor's head. Bapak had a huge grin from ear to ear. Then the apparition disappeared.

Well, apparently Rabbi Israel agreed, because on March 4, 1967, Simone's thirty-sixth birthday, Marianne and I were both baptized in Branford College Chapel, Yale University, at the base of Yale's iconic Harkness Tower. Pastor Olson used the water from the Jordan, and one of my sponsors was the legendary Francis von Kahler. That is how I became a Christian.

Once I was baptized, Simone and I barely managed to make it to church for Christmas and Easter. We did do all the German home rituals for both feasts, however, from an Advent wreath to dishes full of fruits, nuts, and candies (*bunte Teller*) and a reading of St. Luke's Christmas Story at Christmas, to self-colored eggs and hidden presents at Easter. From Simone I learned the mysteries of turning off the electric lights, lighting candles, and then, on Christmas Eve for example, carefully illuminating the real wax candles from Germany on our tree while singing a host of German Christmas carols, always ending with "*Stille Nacht*" ("Silent Night"). To this day, I have trouble singing that hymn known round the world in any language except German.

During our two New York years, 1965-67, we continued our scanty church attendance. In retrospect, I don't remember going to church in Flushing, where we lived, even once. After moving to Honolulu, I did join the inter-faith campus ministry as a nominally Lutheran faculty member, but if we went to church at all, it was to Church of the Crossroads, a radical United Church of Christ parish near the University presided over at the time by the brother of a Subud member in Chicago. I remember giving two guest sermons there, both on mystical themes. They were politely received; however, the Crossroads members seemed more interested in social activism than spiritual development. In any case, we never became members and probably attended only seven or eight services. Still, it was our church during our first Hawai'i years.

In 1978 or 1979, however, an event occurred which turned us into regular churchgoers. We had been living in Chicago since September 1973 but still attended a Protestant or Catholic service only once a year on Christmas Eve. One day our Honolulu-based friends, the

Keighers, asked us to be godparents to their five-year-old, Michael. The service would take place in the Methodist Campus Chapel on University Avenue, where our second daughter, Christine, had been baptized seven or eight years before. The event was to occur during our planned family trip to Hawai'i.

During the brief service, Michael became so wild that four of us men had to hold him in order for the ritual to be completed. The Keighers like us scarcely went to church, so the little boy must have thought he was about to undergo some kind of torture. Simone and I both got a wake-up call from his reaction. So, on our return from Hawai'i, we searched the yellow pages and found Trinity Lutheran Church in South Evanston, about ten minutes from our home in Lincolnwood. We did not have anyone's recommendation. At the time, moreover, we had no idea about the different varieties of Lutheranism. In fact, we went there because it had the latest Lutheran service in the area, beginning at 11 a.m. Soon, however, the joke was on us, since Simone and I were quickly recruited into the Senior Choir and found ourselves getting to church Sundays, to our children's dismay, at 7:00 a.m. so we could warm up and sing at both the early and late services.

Trinity proved a good choice. Before long we found out it was part of the ALC, the American Lutheran Church, comprised primarily of Scandinavian (mainly Norwegian American) families. Later, when we were old hands in Lutheranism—Simone was really an old hand, going back to her childhood in Germany—the parish would be amalgamated into the largest Lutheran synod in America, the ELCA, or Evangelical Lutheran Church in America. We soon learned that although the Lutheran Church, the oldest major Protestant denomination, was founded by Martin Luther, a German, the German American Lutheran Church, known as the Lutheran Church Missouri Synod, was the strict, narrow-bore version of the faith, so much so that members of more liberal Lutheran churches like ours were not allowed to receive Holy Communion in their precincts. Before long, Simone, the kids, and I learned about *lutefisk* (cod marinated in lye), *leftsa* (Scandinavian Christmas pancakes), *krumkake* (crisp Christmas cookies), the Sons of Norway social clubs, *akavit* schnapps, and the Christmas carol "*Jeg er saa glad. . .* ," which the choir and congregation dutifully sang every Holiday season.

More importantly, we found a group of friendly, caring people, mostly of Scandinavian descent, who liked to have a good time. The congregation thus provided a counterbalance to our Subud group, where people tended to get together only for *latihan* and then go home. We had some good occasions there too, but definitely lacking in the Lutheran gusto we had come to know and love at Trinity. For our kids Trinity was okay. When Christine was an early teenager going through her punk phase, the occasional "church lady" would approach Simone and hope our daughter wasn't on drugs. Simone assured her Christine was not and as long as her acting out consisted of no more than dressing up and using lots of dark eye make-up, that was just fine with her mom. The girls didn't make close friends at church as we had, but at least they had some good Sunday-School teachers and learned the fundamentals of the Christian faith.

Trinity Lutheran Church was really the place where I learned about Christianity. It was there that I received my adult Confirmation, taught adult Sunday School, served on the Church Council, represented the congregation once at a Synodal meeting in Springfield, Illinois, co-starred in a Christmas play "The Birthday Party" two years in a row, and of course sang in the Choir. When things got tough at Northeastern Illinois University, Subud and church were my escapes. It was at Trinity, moreover, I learned that for me Subud alone was not enough. As Bapak often said, "Subud is not a religion." And it had now become clear to me that I needed an everyday religion as well as an inner mystical practice like Subud.

After moving to Saint Paul in winter 1987, we joined a new congregation, Pilgrim Lutheran Church, in the Kings Maplewood District, not far from Macalaster College. It was a short ride from the house we bought in summer 1988 near the Saint Paul side of the Mississippi River. Now Minnesota, and especially the Twin Cities, comprise the mother house of Scandinavian Lutheranism in America and were at the time the home of the ALC, our old synod. (The headquarters of German Lutheranism and the Missouri Synod was and is St. Louis, Missouri, and the amalgamated ELCA has its offices in Chicago.) We never became as involved in this congregation as we had been in Trinity. At Pilgrim, for example, we didn't join the choir. By this point we had become active in what was then called The Volkfesthaus of Minnesota, later renamed The Germanic-American Institute. Simone and I enjoyed singing with the Institute's German-language chorus; getting involved in German cultural activities; making new German-culture-oriented friends; drinking wine, beer, and Jaegermeister; and dancing the Friday nights away in the pre-World-War-I-style Rathskeller. Simone could also go to her *Deutsche Damen,* or German ladies, club meetings, where the members, many of whom had married G.I.s after World War II, would reminisce about the bad times during the War, the good aspects of the European life they had left behind, and the fact that things were not so bad with their respective "Ami" husbands. Simone was probably the only one there who spoke radio German. Most of the others came from southwestern Germany, the former U.S. zone, where dialects were common. They would sometimes say, "*Aber Simone. Du sprichst so ein scheenes Daitsch*!" "Simone. You speak such a beautiful German!" pronounced with a South German accent. Given speech lessons as a teenager by a retired actress to help her overcome a childhood lisp, Simone did in fact speak an excellent German.

Now you might wonder what all this has to do with religion. Actually, the Germanic-American Institute, or GAI, took the place of the social side of our life that Trinity Lutheran Church, and especially its choir, had played in Chicago. In recruiting people, I used to say the GAI was the cheapest therapy one could have. Indeed, as I was getting fired from Metro State and establishing myself as a consultant, singing, dancing, and clowning around with our friends and acquaintances at the GAI helped keep me psychologically and emotionally on an even keel.

Also, I could see the appeal German folk culture could have as a quasi-religion. As I had learned from Simone, the house aspects of this culture lent an aura of the sacred to daily life. I'm talking about turning off the lights, lighting candles, and being quiet together as the evening turned to night. Or singing Advent and Christmas songs over the candle-lit Advent Wreath while the kids ate seasonal cookies and drank hot chocolate and we had a cup of good coffee. There *was* something religious, something sacred, to all that. Too bad Hitler and his minions had to ruin it by exploiting these rituals for his anti-life Nazi agenda.

Moreover, the GAI had no trouble moving into the world of Christianity. It was not after all a publicly funded institution required to maintain separation of church and state. Decorations were always in evidence for Christmas and Easter. German articles for those seasons were on sale in the gift shop, and Holiday meals and events were scheduled. In the last few years of our stay in the Twin Cities, the German choir director, the late Rev. Roland Seboldt, a retired liberal Missouri Synod Lutheran minister, arranged for a nearby Lutheran church to offer German-language Christmas and Easter services which German-speaking GAI members, both Protestant and Catholic, participated in and attended, including us. These were always quite moving for me. After, there would be refreshments and fellowship, again with candlelight, flowers, and the full measure of Germanic Holiday *Gemütlichkeit*. When it comes to Easter, moreover, there is probably no hymn stronger than the one Luther himself wrote and Bach later used as the chorale melody in one of his famous Passions: *O Haupt voll Blut und Wunden* "O Sacred Head Now Wounded."

I encountered Lutheranism Hawaiian style at Calvary By The Sea Lutheran Church in Honolulu. After six years at Northeastern Illinois University, I was permitted as an administrator to apply for a sabbatical, a paid academic study leave. I did this in 1979. My project was to research and, to the extent possible, write a book on the concept of the educated person across cultures. My former colleagues at the East-West Center on the Campus of the University of Hawai'i had offered me an office where I could work. My project interested them, so I reported before I left on what I had learned.

I had checked with Pastor Ted Fritschel, still the University Lutheran chaplain in Hawai'i, if there was a Lutheran church out towards Hawai'i Kai. We had been able to find an apartment to sublet in that area for our six-month study leave. He recommended Calvary. On our first Sunday in Honolulu, we visited the church, and it was love at first sight—for the whole family. It was not the usual by-the-book Lutheran service, and the church didn't put all its energy into Sunday worship. As Ted Fritschel had correctly observed, the pastor, the Rev. Douglas R. Olson—known familiarly as Doug or Kahu (Hawaiian for "Pastor") Doug—had a magic way with kids. Leader of the parish for nearly 15 years, he had managed to build up a large, enthusiastic youth group. Activities included practice communions with Oreo cookies and cokes. Then there were movie nights, after which the kids and Doug would return to the parsonage for a pizza party to discuss the relevant points of the film they had just seen. Also, they had volleyball games on the beach, weekend hikes, camp-outs, lock-ins, slumber parties—you name it. Whatever it was, it worked. Whereas our kids went more or less unwillingly to church in Evanston—they felt it was an okay place for us but not too appealing for them—here we never had to coax them to get up on Sunday mornings. As a matter of fact, both we and other parents could discipline our kids by saying, "Now look. If you don't behave, you can't go to church on Sunday." And they would behave. How many religious congregations, I wonder, can you say that about?

Calvary was a great place for adults too. Doug would say things like, "I train the parishioners to be leaders and take initiative, and then things happen by themselves." He had refined several programs, available perennially, to do leadership training in a church context.

One was the multi-year Bethel Bible Series, a three-year program: two dedicated to the Old Testament and one to the New. Simone and I managed to take and complete the course the last time Doug offered it before retiring. Another was called A.C.T.S.—A Commitment to Service—where teams of parishioners basically ran the church services for eight weeks while committing to other forms of servant leadership at home, at work, and in the community while participating in a weekly theologically based leadership course. We signed up for A.C.T.S. also. A parishioner who said his life had been changed by this program used to remark, "Once in A.C.T.S., always in A.C.T.S." By that he meant that someone who had been through the program would jump in where needed—if there were not enough ushers, if no one had set up Communion, if the coffee hadn't been made. In other words, A.C.T.S. trained a growing core of individuals willing to do what it took to make the congregation run smoothly.

Another activity Doug established was perhaps his signature program. Called "Tuesday Night Live," it was a kind of group therapy session which he ran from a high, movie-director-style chair. If people came in late, they would have to state that they took responsibility for their tardiness. Both Simone and I went to several sessions, but when our older daughter, then thirteen, started going, we stopped in order to give her the opportunity to say things she might not have with her parents present. I remember one time she came home and told us about a youngish middle-aged woman in the group who had been diagnosed with terminal cancer. The woman's situation had really impressed Marianna (as she called herself by then), who seemed to get a new perspective on her own difficulties at the time. In fact, that may have been a main reason the group helped people, for they got to experience others who had even worse situations to face than they did.

One of the big positive factors in Calvary's full pews was without doubt Doug's second wife, Ivalene "Ivy" Olson. Doug and Ivy—the child of a Seventh-Day Adventist missionary-teacher family, a single mom, and a former high-fashion model who stood five feet eleven in her stocking feet—were a dashing couple. Just 39 at the time, Ivy played an active role in the congregation by working with the teenage girls and women in general as a kind of consultant on how to be successful, feminine women. At Calvary at the time, you often heard the phrase "DougandIvy" pronounced as a single word. Someone would say, for example, "Has anyone seen DougandIvy? After we returned to Chicago from Honolulu, Ivy started a backyard ministry called Angel Network Charities, a housing-and-self-development program for Hawaiʻi's homeless which was later named one of the first President Bush's Thousand Points of Light and for which Ivy personally received a Presidential Voluntary Service Award from President Clinton.

For our family, though, Calvary's greatest contribution came the following year, 1981, when our older daughter, Marianna, was attending Chicago's private performing-arts high school. She enjoyed the performing-arts side but had difficulty with her biology teacher, whose class happened to be the first of the day. Eventually she stopped going to that class and soon to the school, but since she was not yet sixteen, she was still required by law to attend. Fearing a scrape with the juvenile justice division of the State of Illinois, we arranged to have Marianna live with Doug and Ivy at Calvary's parsonage in Honolulu. She finished her sophomore year, reached her sixteenth birthday, but—most importantly—under Doug and Ivy's tutelage managed to mature to the extent that she was able to tolerate and eventually graduate from public high school in the Chicago suburb of Skokie without any further problems. To this day I feel gratitude to Doug and Ivy for this amazing gift of Christian charity to Marianna and us. Their unconditional love was doubtless a main reason why Calvary Lutheran Church, *anno* 1980, was a growing and thriving Mainline Protestant church.

20
Catholicism

SO, AFTER 37 years as an engaged Lutheran, why did I become Roman Catholic on Epiphany Sunday, January 4, 2004? As I look back from the perspective of November 2008, it may not be so mysterious. Among my first Christian witnesses had been the McAuliffe sisters, who lived next door to us from when I was a toddler until I completed Kindergarten. Their house introduced me to statuettes, crucifixes, and the smell of frequently used candles. They were also sweet elderly women who treated me like the little boy they had never had. Somehow my post-toddler brain must have put together nice aunties with the sights, sounds, and smells of their home, since I never remember them saying anything to me about religion. If so, here is a good example of evangelism by example rather than talk.

My next encounter with Catholicism was courtesy of my sixth-grade girl friend, Tottie De Silva, in Scarsdale, New York. I knew she wasn't Jewish, but then, we weren't religious and she was nice. Still, our friendship outside school was soon curtailed by both our parents. There were plenty of nice Jewish girls around, my parents told me, and she was told something similar about "nice Catholic boys" by hers. It wasn't until I got to boarding school that I experienced my first Mass. I went once with my Venezuelan classmate, Umberto, who gave me a blow-by-blow explanation along the lines of "Okay, Feldman, this is where the priest changes the wine into Jesus' blood." I remember the incense, bells, genuflections, and crossings of oneself. The service was performed in Latin, this being a half dozen years before the Second Vatican Council. Since I was taking classical Latin and Spanish at Peddie, I could understand the language with a little help from the English in the missalette.

During freshman year at Yale, I mainly accompanied my friend Douglas to Christ Church, the Anglo-Catholic Episcopal church in town. Except for the missing Latin, it seemed to outdo the neighboring St. Thomas More Catholic Chapel in Roman-style ritual. So much incense poured from the sensor it was sometimes hard mid-church to see past the rood screen separating the chancel area from the nave. When the Yale Dramat staged its occasional medieval play or even *Murder in the Cathedral*, guess where they did it? Not in

Catholic St. Thomas More's, where they didn't even have a rood screen. The elders of the Brideshead family would have felt right at home in Christ Church. For my part, I loved the ritual. All Christ Church lacked was Latin and the Pope to be Catholic. The way Fr. Kibitz intoned the Elizabethan plainsong of the liturgy had something special in it which I later found in the occasional Catholic High Mass.

Just as hymns at Peddie had become a powerful force for my conversion to Christianity, what we heard and saw in my freshman histories of art and music courses must have drawn me toward Catholicism. I loved Gregorian chant, later liturgical music, Gothic architecture, illuminated manuscripts, and the countless great works of Catholic Christian art such as the many pietàs and paintings of the Madonna and Child. During junior year in Germany, I would go to both Protestant (Evangelical Lutheran) and Catholic churches for concerts and, on occasion, services. As I recall, I would go mainly to Catholic churches for the latter. Why, I don't know. Also, as you may remember from the chapter on my year abroad, when asked about my religion, at least until the episode on the train back from Munich after our visit to Dachau, I would usually tell people I was Catholic. In retrospect, it was a real case of be careful what you say—the angels may be listening.

During senior year I became friends with a Norwegian classmate, Per Halvorsen. It was then that he became Catholic—quite a move for a Norwegian, whose country is essentially all Lutheran and pretty non-observant at that. Per reminded me of my senior-year roommate at Peddie, Jim Culver, in how nice a person he was. Although I was still in my intellectual-skeptical phase and would occasionally wonder what a bright, young Norwegian could possible see in Roman Catholicism, Per was so kind and committed that I generally suppressed my urge to criticize or tease. A week ago I happened to Google Per, since I am in Denmark as I write this and not really that far from Norway. Within a few minutes of searching, I found him. Alas, he had passed away a year and a half before. There was a photo showing a white-bearded, white-haired man in white Holy Day vestments. In his eyes was the look of illness, even death. Where was the blond young man I had known back in 1959-60 in New Haven? Farewell, Fr. Per, O.P. You were a light along my path, although at that time neither of us knew it.

In graduate school, especially after Simone and I married, we acquired two friends, colleagues of mine in the English Department, who were Catholic priests, one a Jesuit, the other a Dominican. When they stopped by for coffee and cake, we would discuss all kinds of things, from literature to politics to theology. We generally invited the two fathers to our parties too. They never had a problem combining a few good drinks and articulate conversation with their religious commitments. I am pretty sure, recent Yalie that I was, that their balanced worldliness impressed me in those days and still does today.

After beginning my career, I would often have a religious student or colleague who turned out to be Catholic. Moreover, Simone and I would occasionally attend Midnight Christmas Mass at a nearby Catholic church rather than a Protestant, let alone a Lutheran, service—at least, until we joined Trinity Lutheran in Evanston. Later I met five Catholic nuns and a priest who collectively changed my life. I'll start with the one I met first. The only one who has since passed away, she had the biggest impact on me: Sister Eileen Rice, O.P.

We met in the late 70s at the Shakertown Conversation on General Education in a restored Shaker village an hour west of Lexington, Kentucky. The Shakertown Conversation was a weekend of intellectual exercises and fellowship on the theme of improving the general—versus the specialized—aspects of American undergraduate education. I had read about the Conversation in an article in *The Chronicle of Higher Education* soon after the meeting's first run. Before finishing, I knew I had to attend the following year, which I did. When I arrived the first time, I found myself in the company of fascinating educators, for all of whom the whole formation of their students was the priority, not simply the students' intellectual or pre-professional training. Education for the Shakertowners was at its core preparation for life. This opinion was of course the minority one in the higher-education community at the time, not just among the country's students, but even most faculty. Never mind! We Shakertowners were on a mission, just as Mother Lee, the Shakers' charismatic English foundress, had been two centuries before. The Conversations would go on for another sixteen years. I was fortunate to attend until the end, caused in large part by the deaths of the two founders and Sister Eileen.

I immediately noticed Sr. Eileen at that first meeting, in part because, as she liked to say, she had "gotten out of the habit." Okay, the real reason was she looked young and was extremely pretty, with an oval face; large brown eyes; and long, beautiful hair that went well down her back. She spoke with a wry, slightly tilted smile and was one of the most articulate people I had ever met. Despite her youthful appearance, she had already been the principal of her Congregation's academy, held a Ph.D. in mathematics from the University of Michigan, had been a Woodrow Wilson Scholar at Princeton in math, and had published a remarkable handbook on "ideas tasting"—introducing undergraduates to the Great Ideas through brief readings and exercises. In short, she was a knockout, and I was down for the count.

Besides our yearly meetings, I would often see and hang out with Sr. Eileen—just plain Eileen to me by this point—at academic conferences, since we both seemed to go to the same ones. She also visited us in Chicago and Saint Paul, and my entire family, even my Protestant-oriented mother-in-law, fell in love with her. At one point our daughter Marianna, then in high school, told us she was thinking about becoming a nun. After all, Sr. Eileen was one, and she was, in Marianna's opinion, very cool. While we were still in Chicago, Sr. Eileen was one of the sponsors at my adult confirmation at Trinity Lutheran Church. To his credit, the pastor, Waldo Johnson, had no problem that one of my sponsors was a Catholic nun.

In her Christmas card one year she explained—she was 49 at that time—she had been diagnosed with breast cancer and would be undergoing surgery. Later she called to say the cancer had spread and was now terminal. The way Eileen shared this news was as if she were reporting on plans for a trip abroad. It was simply personal news like any other, important but not to be dramatized. With that came her invitation to come to Siena Heights College, her institution in Michigan, to make a documentary video about her life. She knew our younger daughter, Christine, had just received a degree in filmmaking and culture studies and wanted her to be the videographer. I meantime was the president of Blue Sky Associates—Catalysts for Educational Change, to which Eileen belonged. She wanted Blue Sky to produce the film and me to direct it. So Christine and I, with later editing help from a friend in Saint Paul, flew to Michigan, stayed in Siena Heights' president's house, and taped hours of interviews with Eileen, some of her current and former students, and colleagues. Two months later she was dead.

Another memory is my fortieth birthday, November 6, 1979. Eileen, Tom Maher (the co-founder of the Shakertown Conversations), and I were attending a higher-education conference in Rochester, New York. Eileen asked me what I wanted for my birthday. She was thinking of treating me to lunch. "Please take me to Mass, Eileen," I said. She obliged. We found a nearby Catholic church that had a noon Mass. It was a Saturday, and the conference sessions had concluded at 11:30 a.m. I remember kneeling next to Eileen and feeling the strength of her belief. She had an incredible mind, but it did not seem to obstruct her simple, direct faith. In retrospect, I knew that was what had really impressed me from the first.

Other Eileen memories have to do with things she told us for the video. For example, she was a great cat lover. Her whole family was. Cats seemed to sense that and would simply show up at the Rice Family's house for treats they knew they would receive. "It was like during the Great Depression," Eileen explained, "when hobos and others would make little signs near houses indicating that vagrants were welcome there." She normally had two or three cats at any given time in her office. When parents would bring their new freshmen in the fall, she would often place all her cats. "You give us a kid, we give you a cat!" She would tell the parents. By the time she died, Sr. Eileen had placed something like 175 cats in this way.

Eileen was a conscientious teacher. For example, on her frequent trips to conferences, she would take along a stack of student papers. Since she never turned friends like me away who wanted to hang out during those occasions, she frequently worked into the wee hours to get her correcting done. She believed it important to give students feedback as soon as possible. Later, when she was undergoing chemotherapy for her cancer, the University of Michigan Hospital insisted she come at a particular morning hour for treatment. (Ann Arbor, where the facility was located, was a good 45 minutes by car from Adrian, the home of her college.) "I'm sorry," Sr. Eileen explained to the scheduler; "I teach at that time." "But Sister," the scheduler replied, "Everyone adjusts their schedule to make it to their appointments." "Not me," Eileen told her. "You'll simply have to give me a time that doesn't conflict with my teaching!" And guess what! The nonplussed scheduler did.

Eileen's attitude toward her illness and death was not only objective; it was playful and filled with humor. During her final term teaching, after her hair fell out—it would grow back before she died—she bought herself three wigs. One looked like her natural hair—long, straight, and brown. Another was blond. And the third she called "big hair." On the first day of class that term she did a fashion show to model the wigs. Using the old "applause-meter" approach known to us from early TV days, she asked students to clap their rating for each. All the classes unanimously selected Big Hair as their favorite. Later, during the taping sessions, Eileen told Christine and me that after she informed her friends of her health situation, many of them came to Adrian to visit her. Fortunately, her stomach was still working, and she had retained her appetite. So they would typically take her to dinner at one of the better restaurants in the area. "Jesus got only one Last Supper. But to date I've had about 25!" She told us with a big smile.

By all accounts, Eileen was a demanding teacher. Her current and former students loved her and quite a few shed tears for her during the interviews, but without exception they noted how she piled on the work and had notably high expectations. She always gave copious constructive suggestions for improvement as well as plenty of positive praise. As Siena Heights' Teacher Education Department, as she liked to say, she was, according to her students, a model teacher. Several of her alums, now experienced teachers themselves, said they had learned everything about being a good teacher from her. Not only that, but once a student of Eileen's, you remained so as long as you kept in touch, which many of them did. "She was our teacher, our mentor, our example, and our friend," one woman told us. "I've never known another person like Sr. Eileen and don't think I ever will." The College chaplain, a Catholic priest, added, "Eileen makes everything seem so easy. She must have a secret. I wonder what it is. I've got to find out!"

Eileen died on a Monday morning, early in the new year. She was not quite 50. On the preceding Thursday I had called her. She was at home, a house near the campus that she shared with three other nuns. Her biological sister, a family-practice physician, had been giving her steroid injections to keep her alive so she could finish the NCATE self-evaluation for the school's accreditation in teacher training. Eileen had taken on the responsibility for the self-study and intended to see it through. Anyway, she had now finished it, she said, and would go off the steroids. Once that happened, according to her sister the doctor, she would die in three days. I bid her farewell, thanked her for her friendship, and told her I loved her. Then we said goodbye. I barely got off the phone before I started sobbing.

Two days later, on Saturday morning, I was at Centering Prayer in downtown Minneapolis. As usual, Sr. Joan Tuberty, our instructor, was in charge. (You'll hear about Sr. Joan next.) In Centering Prayer as in Subud, I rarely if ever *saw* anything. This time however was different. During one of the two sitting-meditation periods, I suddenly found myself looking at the inside of a church from the back. It was as if I were a TV camera panning ever closer to the front. From the first, there was a nun in white habit who was throwing what I initially took to be a boomerang, although it was shaped more like a white Frisbee. She would toss it away from her with all her might, but it kept coming back. As I zoomed in closer, I saw it was a white bird. She would fling it away from the area near her heart, but it would immediately flap and flutter its way back. The whole time she had a big grin as if to say, "Why am I stressing myself by doing the same thing over and over? That bird won't fly away until it's good and ready." By this point I was close enough to see that the nun was Sr. Eileen. Also, I understood that she was trying to die but her soul wouldn't leave her body for good until the time was right.

That Monday afternoon I got a call from one of the sisters who shared the house with Eileen. She had died that morning and could I bring the special 20-minute version of the video documentary I had made at Eileen's request for showing that Thursday night in lieu of a homily at her memorial service? (Eileen's funeral Mass would be Friday morning, but with many of her former students and friends only able to attend after work, her Congregation of Adrian Dominicans had decided to hold a memorial service in their chapel Thursday evening followed by an actual funeral Mass the next morning in the College Chapel.) I said I would be there with the video. Once again, I stayed in the president's house. Christine must have been out of town, since she didn't come along this time.

The sister continued. "It was so interesting. Sunday during our noon meal we heard hysterical laughter coming from Eileen's room. We all charged up the stairs to see what was going on. Knowing Eileen, we thought she had had a death-bed remission and had awakened from her coma. Lord knows, there were enough people praying for that. But when we got there, we found her laughing in her sleep. She was still comatose. I asked her, 'Eileen, are you okay?' And these were her last clear words before she passed the next morning: 'This is fun here!'"

When I arrived on the Siena Heights campus early Thursday afternoon, old Sr. Miriam, an eighty-something-year-old Dominican who prided herself on being the first female to gain a Ph.D. in psychology from the Sorbonne in Paris, came up to me and confided, "Reynold, things are happening here since Eileen died." "Things?" I asked. "You know," she replied, "people are asking Eileen for something, and well, they are happening." At this point my voice was all but gone, and I knew I would have to give a short oral presentation before showing the video. So, as soon as I got to my room, I closed the door and said to Eileen in a loud stage whisper, "Eileen, can you please do something about my voice?" By the time the 8 p.m. service rolled round, my laryngitis was gone, and I could speak in my normal voice to the 800 or so people packing the place.

Also, when I entered the nuns' chapel that afternoon to make sure the video projector was working, I was shocked to find it the very church I had seen in my vision during Centering Prayer the preceding Saturday. I had never been inside that chapel before, but I now recognized certain features in the chancel area that had been in my vision.

My meeting with Sr. Joan Tuberty, a Franciscan nun, also came about through work. By this point I had begun teaching the course "The Literature of Wisdom—A Cross-Cultural Exploration" at Metro State in the Twin Cities. During this particular time, five of my students, one of them a Catholic, did their term project on Centering Prayer. It was something I had not yet heard of. They went down to Sr. Joan's Saturday morning sessions at St. Olaf Church and also interviewed her. For their class presentation, they gave handouts, explained the history of the practice, and then led us in an actual sample session. After class the students said, "Reynold, you really have to meet Sr. Joan. She and you have so much in common." One of them, a fiery redhead, added, "It's a match made in heaven." Then they all laughed.

Well, before the term was over, I did manage to call Sr. Joan and arrange to attend a Saturday session. Forty people were sitting quietly in a circle. The room was lit by flickering candles. At a certain point, Sr. Joan, a tall, strongly built woman with a strong but kindly Irish-American face, rang a Buddhist meditation bell, which signaled the first of two 20-minute sessions of meditation. Each armed with a "sacred word" of our choice—Sr. Joan had mentioned some possibilities—we were instructed to allow any thoughts that emerged to come. If we began to indulge ourselves in these thoughts, we were to gently return to our sacred word. In between the two 20-minute sitting meditations, we were to walk around our circle of chairs. That too took 20 minutes. Sr. Joan led and went v-e-r-y slowly. I was afraid I would fall, no doubt a residue from learning to walk as a toddler. Yet somehow this course of walking meditation, because we needed to concentrate on simply going slowly, was very powerful. When we got to sit for the final 20 minutes, somehow that course proceeded on a higher, finer level for me. After, some members shared their experiences, Sr. Joan offered a few comments, and then we watched a video of the Centering Prayer founder, Fr. Thomas Keating, a Trappist priest from Snowmass, Colorado, describe how and why Centering Prayer works. Later in that same church I had the chance to spend a two-day workshop with Fr. Keating. A tall, strapping man in his 70's at the time, he asked how many of us were grandparents. My daughter Marianna had just given birth to her daughter, Sarah. So I proudly raised my hand along with perhaps a third of the audience. Fr. Keating continued, "When I think of God, I picture a new first-time grandmother looking with unconditional love at her grandchild." Not bad for a Catholic priest! I thought. To this day, Sr. Joan and I stay in touch. She is one of my strong Catholic role models.

Next I'd like to tell you about another nun and also a priest. Both belong to the Order of the Holy Cross and have long-time connections with well-known higher-education institutions in South Bend, Indiana: Fr. David Burrell, the emeritus Hesburgh professor of Philosophy and Theology at Notre Dame, and Sr. Elena Malits, the retired professor and chair of Religious Studies at nearby St. Mary's College. We first met at a Society for Values in Higher Education get-together at Vassar College in summer 1980. Let me talk about Fr. David first.

He was ruggedly handsome and, to my eyes, a Henry Fonda look-alike, right down to the short, gray hair, aviator sunglasses, accent, and laid-back style. My favorite memory of him is from an SVHE Meeting a few years later at The Evergreen State College in Olympia, Washington. Fr. David had announced a Mass to be held that afternoon in a wooded area and invited those interested to attend. Five of us, including Simone and me, showed up. Fr. David asked me to assist and handed out readings for each of the others. When the time came, he communed each of us by name. Interestingly, none of us was Catholic. Now only Roman Catholics in good standing are supposed to receive the Host sanctified by a Catholic priest. In other words, it's a closed club. Strictly interpreted, being in good standing means that one accepts and follows all the dogmas and doctrines of the Church. So, here was a distinguished Catholic theologian from one of the world's pre-eminent Catholic universities willing to commune non-Catholics like my wife and me. Had he denied us the Host, I wonder whether we would have become Catholics later on.

I immediately liked Sr. Elena. Besides being head of Religious Studies at Saint Mary's, she was trained in Jungian therapy, had published a biography of Thomas Merton, and put on periodic Merton Conferences at St. Mary's. A bright, articulate intellectual, she was also a loving person one could pour one's heart out to. With both Elena and David, it was about inclusion, not exclusion—unconditional love, not the conditional love characterized by shaming and blaming. When you got to know her, you could truly believe in a

Jesus and a God who were "nice guys," not the grim-faced policemen in the sky just waiting for us to mess up so they could zap us. Nothing about Sr. Elena would cause one to confuse the Christian deity with Zeus or Jupiter.

※

The two other nuns I'd like to mention are Sisters Helene Louise Zimmerman and Joan Chatfield. Sr. Helene Louise belongs to the Religious of the Sacred Heart of Mary, a 19th Century French order, and Sr. Joan is the Maryknoll superior in Hawai'i. Maryknoll is also a 19th Century order, founded in the United States. These two women, who showed me Catholicism with a human face, were both part of my becoming Catholic. Sister Helene I first met and became friends with at the conference I helped coordinate at St. Olaf College in 1996. She came to two more Blue Sky conferences after that and joined the organization. She is one of the nicest human beings I have met—another instance that when it comes to evangelism, walk trumps talk every time. Also, to give you a sense of her personality, she told me she had once ordered a cab to go from the Convent to the Tarrytown, New York, train station. During the five-minute trip, the driver kept looking at her in his rear-view mirror. (She was still in her habit at that time.) Finally, on reaching the station, he turned around and said, "Sister, you'll have to forgive me, but I just have to ask you this. How did a nice Jewish girl named Zimmerman get to be a Catholic nun?!" With a smile, Sr. Helene, who is half German and half Irish American, explained that not all Zimmermans are automatically Jewish and that she had been born and raised in a New York Catholic family. On the point about Zimmermans, I should know, since that had been my wife's maiden name too, and she was brought up in a Lutheran family in Germany. In fact, *Zimmerman(n),* which means "carpenter" in German, is a common surname like Schmidt [smith] or even my name, Feldman(n) [farmer], which can be Catholic or Protestant as well as Jewish.

The final nun I want to mention, Sr. Joan Chatfield, M.M., is also from New York, where her mother was a career actress on Broadway. A cradle Catholic, Joan eventually received her Ph.D. in sociology and had been a professor and dean at Chaminade University of Honolulu. Having served as the diocesan ecumenical liaison, she is currently chair of the board of the All Believers Network (Belnet), where I am also a member. Prior to that she spent five years as her order's official liaison to the United Nations. I remember how she invited me to her house which she shared with three other Maryknoll sisters for my first birthday a mere month and a half after Simone's passing. She was thinking I might not want to celebrate that occasion on my own. How right and considerate she was! Thank you, Sr. Joan.

※

If you now conclude that I became Catholic because of all these significant encounters together with my love for ritual and the mysterious, you would be right, but not totally. Our every-four-year Subud World Congress in the summer of 1997 took place in Spokane, Washington. Some 3,000 Subud members from 60 countries attended the two-week event. Simone, the two girls, and I were fortunate to spend the entire time there and participate in many of the workshops. One of the most popular was entitled "Subud and Religion." Perhaps 50 people showed up at the first session, when we went around the room and briefly told how as Subud members we did or didn't participate in a formal religion, which religious community if any we belonged to, and how we threaded the needle of being both a member of Subud and a church. After lunch, when we continued, another 30 or 40 showed up. Eventually, we split up into smaller groups and practiced Subud's distinctive discernment method, testing. As usual, men and women tested separately. After *latihan* for 20 minutes, someone posed the question—one of two we had agreed to beforehand—"Is it necessary for you to practice a conventional religion in addition to Subud? Receive!" Since I had my eyes closed, I couldn't tell the breakdown, but some of us got yes, others no. As one of the yeses, I went on to test the second question: "Could God please give me an indication as to which my correct religion might be?" Without a moment's hesitation I began chanting snatches of the Latin Mass. This was no miracle, since I often listened to Catholic liturgy and knew whole sections by heart. Still, the indication was clear.

Almost exactly seven years later, I was chatting with a bunch of Subud members after *latihan* in front of the Honolulu YWCA. I was telling this very story to an active Catholic Subud member from southern California on business in Honolulu. A Catholic member from our group, a daily communicant and retired administrator from New York City, overheard me and interrupted: "Reynold, How many times have I heard this story! What's the point? You tell it over and over but never do anything about it. As far as I'm concerned, you should either become Catholic or stop telling your story." She was absolutely right. Then, in typical New York fashion, she continued in a softer voice, "I have a wonderful parish priest. He's half-Jewish and half-Japanese. Like you he has a doctorate, has studied in Europe and speaks half a dozen languages. In case you'd like to go, he's presiding over the 6:30 morning Mass tomorrow at Sacred Heart."

Starting the next morning I began attending Mass there. In due course Fr. Marc and I met and spent two-and-a-half hours together. I told him about my background including Subud and some of my experiences. He was intrigued. "You should start one of those groups in our parish," he commented. "Our people need to experience a little more of the contemplative dimension of religion." By the end of our meeting, he said I was good to go, that in all likelihood the Chancery of the Honolulu Diocese would accept my baptism and confirmation as a Lutheran and I could become a Catholic as soon as we received their blessing. I appreciated his offer but felt I had gaping holes in my knowledge of Catholic doctrine and practice even if I had read some of the Church Fathers and the Bible. I didn't even know what "ordinary time" was. So I wanted to go to the Rite of Catholic Initiation for Adults (RCIA) class, at least for a while.

I went for perhaps four months. It took place every Monday evening for two hours under the competent leadership of Dr. Sid Townsley, a retired Biology professor from the University of Hawai'i and our parish's deacon. The first night I walked in, Sid greeted me in an unusual manner: "This, I believe, is Dr. Reynold Feldman. He was my daughter Mary's favorite professor years ago at the University." He had me. I was in. The program was a good one, well thought out as I later found many things in the Catholic Church were. In any event, the bishop did accept my Lutheran baptism and confirmation. So on January 4, 2004, Epiphany Sunday, a day before I was to start my new job as executive director of the Aloha Medical Mission, I stood in front of the congregation at St. Pius X Catholic Church in Manoa Valley and recited the Nicene Creed. Simone stood beside me as did two Subud sisters, both cradle Catholics. I had informed all my close Catholic friends, including ones you just heard about, and they later told me they had prayed for me or had even had Masses celebrated in my honor. Thus I became a brand-new 64-year-old Roman Catholic. Since then I have attended daily Mass; participated in Rosaries; gone on retreats; attended mission talks; participated in Christian Passover Seders; functioned as a lector, cantor, and Eucharistic minister; served as a hospital visitor bringing prayers and Holy Communion to the sick and dying; taught eleventh-grade A.P. English in a Catholic school; and spent time at both a Benedictine Abbey and a Religious of the Sacred Heart of Mary Convent. My life as a Catholic layperson has been rich.

21
Universalism

MY RELIGIOUS interests were never limited to Judaism and Christianity. I spent a good part of 1961, for example, as a regular worshiper at the Vivekananda-Vedanta Hindu Temple in Chicago. As fate would have it, I have had something to do with Hindus ever since: my Subud friends Kasi and Raji Ramanathan in Chicago; our graduate-student friend Tutu Lahiri, now living in Spain; my dissertation advisor Dr. A.N. ("Jaja") Kaul; and most recently Dr. Dharm Bhawuk, a Nepal-born professor of Business at the University of Hawai'i. Although I never became a Hindu, my commitment to the importance of spiritual practice for any religion to be effective plus a gut-level belief in reincarnation, despite the official teachings of Judaism, Christianity, and Islam, continue to this day.

Then there are the Chinese religions. I first read Confucius's Analects when I was in high school. Later, in college, I read Lao Tzu's *Tao Te Ching*. Again, I have had significant encounters with Chinese people, from my graduate-student roommate, Phyllis S.Y. Sun, to my Chinese teacher in Chicago, David Li (Li Gucheng) and family, to Simone's and my honorary Chinese daughter, Hazel Huang (Huang Hui). Even though I never joined a Chinese religion, the basic ethics of Confucius and the mystical insights of Taoism have become part of my inner navigation since I first encountered them.

I loved Confucius's many distinctions between big (ethical) and little (small-minded) people. A typical example is—The Little Person asks will it pay; the Big Person, is it right. Confucius's ethical exercise called Rectifying the Name is also helpful. Names like father, mother, husband, wife, eldest brother, younger brother, governor, and king were job descriptions for him. Once a clever student tried to stump him. "Tell me, Master," the student asked. "If my father commands me to do something clearly against the Moral Law, should I obey him or not?" "You must not obey him," Confucius responded. "Aha!" Thought the clever disciple. "I've got the old man this time." Then he continued, "But Master, you said we must always obey our father." "Indeed," answered Confucius. "But the person who commanded you to do something clearly against the Moral Law was in that moment no longer your father." In other words, with fatherhood come certain expectations. Therefore if one is a father and acts in unfatherly ways—for example, by neglecting a child—then the individual must reflect on and correct his failure to fulfill his role as *father*. The same goes for any other role in life. For Confucius, there are certain expectations that must be fulfilled in order to merit a particular title. An equivalent English proverb would be, Handsome is as handsome does.

If Confucius is an ethicist and a good one, Lao Tzu, who was probably a legendary figure—his name means "Old Child"—, was a mystic. Fittingly, the *Tao Te Ching* is one of humanity's great mystical texts. It begins with the famous phrase "The Tao you can name is not the real Tao." One is perhaps reminded of the ancient Jewish practice, still continued in Orthodox traditions, of never saying God's name. In the time of the Temple in Jerusalem, destroyed in 70 C.E., it could be spoken only once a year by the High Priest alone within the Inner Sanctum known as the Holy of Holies. Later, in 18th Century Poland, the Baal Shem Tov, literally "Master of the Good Name," was said to owe his mystical, even magical, powers (like the ability to bi-locate) to his special knowledge of the Name of God. You might even remember how my Grandma Ida would never spell out *God*; she would always write "G – d." So in Taoism, the Ultimate Reality was forever beyond our understanding. The best we could do was an approximation. The worst we could do would be to consider that approximation exact and complete.

Taoism also gave humankind Yin and Yang. The living, evolving world of Reality is in effect a dance between these polar opposites which nevertheless contain something of the opposing partner. The Chinese characters mean light (Yang) or shadow (Yin) on a hill. Light, day, activity, masculinity, and heat are Yang; darkness, night, passivity or receptivity, femaleness, and coolness are Yin. Yet each contains its opposite: Day becomes night; men's seeds can become girl babies, while women can bear sons; and all of Nature sleeps in order to wake up and act. Chinese traditional medicine is based on restoring and maintaining the correct balance in people (and animals) of these two elements. *Feng shui*, the art of placing objects in space for an optimal energy flow, is also based on Yin/Yang, as are acupuncture and acupressure.

Tao (pronounced DAO in modern Mandarin) means "way," as in *pathway*. For late-20th and early-21st Century movie-goers, a better translation would be "The Force," as in the *Star Wars* movies. In the practice of Tai Chi Chuan, literally Great Cosmic-Polarity Fist, individual physical, moral, and spiritual strength derives from learning how to make motions in line with how the Universe turns, that is, with the Great Tao of Everything, that which is unnamable.

In a sense, Confucianism and Taoism comprise a kind of Yang and Yin, the former concerned with worldly wisdom, ethics, and a well-ordered life (Yang), while the latter focuses on inner development and gaining the flexibility of a child versus the rigidity of an old or dead person (Yin). We can contrast the Confucian Gentleman, the well-trained, polite, scholarly, and ethical Mandarin, with the child-like Taoist Sage, who prefers the country to the court, innocence to sophistication, and getting things done by leaving well enough alone and allowing Nature to take its (Its) course. In Western terms, Confucianism is classical, while Taoism is romantic.

Chairman Mao talked about walking on two legs. By that he meant the legs of politics and economics. How Chinese! For traditional China, the two legs are Taoism and Confucianism. In the Sung Dynasty, the two of these were mixed together with a third element imported from India, Buddhism, to create Chinese Buddhism. Nonetheless, one still finds Confucian and Taoist temples in both Taiwan and Mainland China.

Although I have studied Buddhism over the years, it never had the impact on me that Hinduism and the Chinese ways did. For example, I never attended Buddhist services more than once or twice until we moved to Hawai'i and I became active in interfaith affairs. Still, the concept of the Buddha, the Enlightened One, has been significant for me. I totally agree that life is primarily an opportunity for each of us to walk the path of enlightenment, yet we are, as the Buddha said, beset by ignorance in this world of *samsara*, illusion. Our truths tend to be partial and ultimately erroneous. The famous Buddhist teaching story uses the metaphor of the blind men touching an elephant. Each one describes the elephant differently depending on the part he is touching. So each of us with our personal, generational, gender, professional, and cultural blinders on will see things in a certain way and conclude—falsely—that ours is the only take on reality. In extreme cases we may even kill others who do not accept things as we see them.

The Buddha has given us the Eightfold Path, also known as the Dharma (*Dhamma* in the Buddhist sacred language of Pali) and has suggested that we not try to go it alone. Therefore he also invented the Sangha, or sacred community, which in Theravadan, or Old Order, Buddhism is the company of monks and nuns. In Mahayana, or Large-Raft, Buddhism, the kind practiced in China, Japan, and Korea today, one finds religious congregations of laypeople much as in Judaism and Christianity. To be sure, there are still monks and nuns, but the main membership is lay. One of the most famous traditional Buddhist prayers goes, "I take refuge in the Buddha; I take refuge in The Dharma; I take refuge in the Sangha." Basically, if one follows the Buddha's example of striving for Enlightenment—in his case, successfully—by means of the Noble Eightfold Path (Dharma) in the Company of fellow seeker-practitioners (Sangha—although in his case, he found it on his own), then one can hope at the very least for a better incarnation that brings the individual closer to enlightenment the next time around.

For me, the primary and most inspiring Buddhist text is the *Dhammapada*, or Sayings of the Buddha. These short, proverb-like pieces of advice are useful whatever one's formal religion. Wisdom is wisdom regardless of source, just as food is food regardless of its country of origin. Buddhism of course is known as a religion of peace. For one thing, it doesn't send press gangs of missionaries to non-Buddhist countries to convert others. Enlightenment is a matter of karma, after all. So pressured conversions, intimidation, let alone war are big no-nos. One of my favorite sayings from the *Dhammapada* goes, "If people were truly aware of the fact of their own death, they would settle all their differences peacefully." Another saying along these lines is, "The sage lives in the flower of his village without harming either color or scent." Interestingly, one finds Buddhism is a growth industry in the West these days, thanks no doubt to the influence of people like the Vietnamese monk Thich Nath Hanh and above all the Dalai Lama. In fact, more and more of the Buddhist leaders in the West are themselves Occidentals.

Before I conclude this chapter, I want to share just a little about my experiences in Quakerism, Unitarian-Universalism, Unity, Baha`i, and above all Islam. I also want to talk briefly about my interfaith work, especially over the past twelve year in Hawai`i and now abroad.

My parents didn't have much good to say about religion in general or Christianity in particular. For my dad, Christianity was the religion of the gentiles. Still there were individual exceptions like Ilene McHugo, his long-time assistant who was supposed to have become a nun but never did. A dedicated Catholic, she served as Dad's loyal, efficient right hand for years. Once home on vacation from Yale, I remember asking him about Ilene. "She's fine," he responded. Then, with a rather wistful look he added, "She's always fine. She's got Jesus." My mother, for her part, was one of the most secular persons I knew. She wasn't against religion; she just didn't see the need for it.

Yet she always had good things to say about the Quakers. I never got the full story, but apparently once when mother was small and the family was in need, the local Friends Meeting came to their aid—this at a time when Christian charity wasn't much in evidence, she said, when it came to the Jews. For whatever reason, I never became interested in the Religious Society of Friends. I did read the founder George Fox's autobiography, though, and found it quite interesting. I also remember every Wednesday during the Vietnam War how members of the local Friends Meeting in Honolulu would stand for an hour in silent vigil on the University of Hawai`i campus. Everyone knew what they were doing there. Words were superfluous. Their witness was powerful. Later I appreciated what Parker Palmer had to say about the Quakerism he had experienced, especially their clearing committees which seemed like a similar discernment method to our testing in Subud. On a less serious note, I remember my friend Victor's joke about how a Quaker Meeting moved in next door to an ultra-Reform temple, and now "some of my best Jews are Friends."

I did go to a Unitarian-Universalist service on an occasion or two, and although I liked the liberal philosophy espoused, I missed any sense of mystery. It seemed a kind of internationalist ethical society for the head alone. Everything was nice, clear, cut and dried, and rational to a fault. I do however have a warm spot in my heart for the recent UU minister in Honolulu, the Rev. Mike Young, who, besides his ministerial background is trained in Buddhist meditation techniques. He also has plenty of passion, so maybe I just visited the wrong UU congregation—the one in question was in New Haven. What I mainly liked and like about this denomination, if that's what it is, is its second name. I'll explain why in a moment.

I learned about Unity Church from my colleague and friend Loren Ekroth, at the time still in Honolulu. He was an active Unity member, so when Simone and I moved from St. Paul to Honolulu in fall 1996, we occasionally attended services at their little church in Waikiki. The music was good and, like the Unitarian-Universalists, they were theologically inclusive. But, as Simone pointed out, there was no Holy Communion, an important part of church for us both. More than the UUs, there seemed to be an emphasis on personal development, so the church offered workshops and guest speakers from secular, Christian, and non-Western traditions. I even gave a workshop there once on tapping one's personal wisdom. Still, while there was plenty offered for heart and mind, we found there wasn't much for the soul as we understood it.

I first learned about the Baha`i Faith when my family moved to

Chicago from New York in 1955, when I turned 16. On the first family car trip up the Outer Drive to the North Shore, I remember seeing the impressive Baha`i Temple in Wilmette. It came just before my parents' friends the Rosenbergs' house. On my first visit to the latter, I got permission to walk over to the Temple and check it out. Built in the round with a high ceiling, it was impressive to say the least. I also got some brochures and read up on the religion. It was the first one I had heard of that had added religious pioneers from the Eastern line to the more familiar ones of the Abrahamic tradition. Why hadn't others done this? I remember thinking. Later I heard that the Iranian Muslim founders had been very progressive in emphasizing women's rights, universal education, peace, a campaign against smoking, and the use of a universal second language so that everyone worldwide could easily communicate. Later, however, when I attended the service, I found the speaker poor and the whole thing rather head-oriented. It just didn't seem to have the spiritual oomph and sense of mystery that I needed.

For a while when we were living in St. Paul, I joined a group called Lutheran-Universalists led by a retired Lutheran pastor who later came out as gay. We met at his and his wife's town house. Sometimes we were as few as a half dozen. Sometimes we were 15 or 20. What we had in common was our desire as observant Lutherans to embrace our own faith without dismissing the insights of other faiths, Christian and non-Christian alike. To this day, I consider myself a Universalist—in my case now a Catholic-Universalist. Many of my mainstream fellow Roman Catholics may find that a bridge too far. After all, doesn't the word Catholic already mean "all-inclusive"? Yes, but if that is so, why isn't everyone Catholic? Well, they will respond: That's the job of evangelism. To be sure, Jesus was never a Catholic or even a Christian. The religion did not exist by the time of his death. It couldn't have. He lived and died an Orthodox Jew and most likely not a blond-haired, blue-eyed one either. Jesus' religion had a lot to do with being an obedient child to Our Father in Heaven, aka Abba, Daddy; being humble; and practicing compassion (The Golden Rule). If that is the case, individuals of any background, even those not belonging to a religion, could qualify, while clearly, membership in or ritual observance of any religion would not guarantee living up to the high criteria Jesus preached. After all, many of the Jewish religious leaders of his day had failed to do so, and he criticized them relentlessly.

This brings me to my interfaith work. Soon after we moved back to Honolulu in 1996, I learned about a group called Open Table, where information about and even practices from different religions were shared. I began attending each first Wednesday of the month. Soon I found myself on the steering committee, and on occasion I made a presentation, once on Subud and another time on wisdom, while Simone joined two other German women discussing their experiences as children in World War II. Eventually, Open Table made common cause with the more activist Interfaith Alliance of Hawai'i, on whose board I initially sat. But I found civic activism was not for me, so while sometimes supporting the Alliance on specific issues, even to the point of writing a letter or making a donation, I resigned from the board.

One of the people I met through Open Table was a Ph.D. agronomist from Pakistan named Saleem Ahmed. Saleem had served on the staff of Hawai'i's East-West Center for 25 years before being terminated when funding for his program ran out. While his wife worked, Saleem studied to become a certified financial planner, which he is today. His real interest, however, was as advocate of moderate Islam based on interpretation of the Qur'an, not the Traditions of the Prophet Muhammad, and as a leader in the interfaith movement. On the former topic, Saleem has now published two books. In *Beyond Veil and Holy War*, which I edited, he argued from Quranic texts for a more compassionate Islam, the one he believed Muhammad had actually received and promulgated. The second, which appeared in 2009, argues that Islam, contrary to the popular belief in the West, is basically a religion of peace. Concerning interfaith work, he founded the tax-exempt nonprofit All Believers Network, or Belnet, premised on his conviction that all religions rest on certain principles, such as belief in a creator, universal values, and the need to come to terms with life and death. I was involved from the beginning as a board member and think the Belnet Web site, beautifully crafted by The Most Reverend Stephen Randolph Sykes, bishop of the Inclusive Orthodox Church, well expresses the interests and shares some of the products Belnet has thusfar produced. At the moment Belnet is planning for a Honolulu-based international interfaith conference in 2011. Saleem's dream is to have the city named the world's Interfaith Capital. It is true that, like the various races and ethnic groups, the different religions seem to get along quite harmoniously in the Land of Aloha.

Our little nonprofit, Wisdom Factors International (WFI), which Jan and Bithi Rumi and Simone and I founded in 2003, is really an interfaith activity also and the successor to Blue Sky Associates' World Wisdom Project. We saw *wisdom* as a kind of hypo-allergenic word which all kinds of people could accept—religionists, scientists, atheists, anyone. Our point was to transcend the limits of individual faiths—to be universalists.

Earlier I said the only religions I have ever really belonged to were Judaism and Christianity, both in its Protestant (Lutheran) and Catholic forms. Well, technically that's not quite true. In summer 2003, you may remember, I spent two weeks in Morocco as part of the adult group accompanying fourteen youth from Hawai'i to the World Congress of Youth in Bouznika Plage. During the Congress, many of us visited the Muhammad II Mosque in Casablanca. The Muslims in attendance went inside to see this fantastic building which is built out over the Atlantic Ocean and can accommodate 30,000 worshippers at a time. The rest of us non-Muslims were asked to wait outside. My Moroccan friend Ihsan, the member of the Forum of Moroccan Youth assigned to host our Hawaiian delegation, suddenly grabbed my hand and took me and three of her male associates round to the men's entrance. "Now you take him in," she told the young men in French. I should note that Ihsan and I had been sitting together a lot on the bus and had been talking about various aspects of Islam. Her Berber father, moreover, was a *qadi*, or religious judge, so she was quite knowledgeable about her faith. Thanks to my years in Subud, doing the Ramadan Fast many times, reading the Qur'an and books on Islam (including Saleem's), and hanging out with Muslims at the East-West Center and elsewhere, I really did know much more about the religion than most non-Muslims. Ihsan continued, "He's Muslim enough for this place!" So in I went.

Before we got ten paces into that vast structure, an official came up to me and asked in French whether I were a Muslim. I replied by reciting the Shahadah, the Muslim Confession of Faith, in Arabic. The man smiled and said, "*Bienvenu à notre mosqué, Monsieur*!" "Welcome to our mosque, Monsieur!" Technically, by making that statement of faith in front of two or more adult male Muslims, I was now a Muslim. But at that point I wasn't worried about technicalities. I was totally enchanted by the magical space I was in and found myself walking around on my own in a kind of *latihan* state as I repeated over and over again, "Allahu Akhbar!" "God is great!"

Muslim, the word, means someone who has submitted himself or herself to God—in short, a practitioner of *Islam*, surrender and submission to the Almighty. That in fact is my religion, spiritually if not technically. More than anything else, what all my religious and spiritual activities have been about since I was opened in Subud and possibly from my earliest childhood is becoming a true muslim, which I'll write here with a small "m" to distinguish it from membership in the official religion of Islam. As far as I can tell, being a true muslim is all God asks of any of us, whether we join a particular religion or not. When we hit the Celestial Immigration Office after our death, I think that will be the visa the processing angel will be looking for, not our organizational membership or identification. Of course sooner or later we'll all get to know for sure. Right now it remains a leap of faith—one I am willing to make.

22
Wisdom Gained

TODAY IS March 3, 2009, nearly a year after I began this book at a Copenhagen café and a day before what would have been Simone's seventy-eighth birthday. So, what wisdom have I gained? What do I know for sure? What do I regret? What can I share?

First, my life has been an exercise in learning to let go and let God, one of the most familiar and beloved Twelve Step slogans. Am I there yet? I don't think so. Take an example. Bapak had a couple of close calls with death, mainly stemming from his heart condition, before he died at 86. He told us that inevitably his doctors were more scared for him than he was for himself. His attitude was—if I live, I live; if I die, I die. As he would say in his Javanese style of talking in the third person about himself: "Bapak just leaves everything up to Almighty God." On the other hand, when I had a few major high-blood-pressure attacks and it became obvious I could die as easily as live, I was definitely more scared for myself than my doctors were for me. So in one sense, since the time when I first consciously experienced the Voice at age six at a moment when I suddenly realized that, little kid or not, I could die at any time, I have not made much progress. I am still afraid of death. Yet during the two times when I had serious hypertension attacks, there was also something else, a sudden, spontaneous getting quiet and falling asleep. When I awoke, my pressure had already begun to moderate. I also remember the time I caught my left pinky in the closing sections of our pull-down garage door in Lincolnwood and immediately *knew* exactly what to do. Then, when I was campaigning for the late State Senator Vince Yano in Hawai'i to become Lieutenant Governor and was unexpectedly attacked by a large, angry dog, I felt myself growing into a 12-foot giant and *knew* I could kill that dog with my bare hands. More importantly, the dog knew it too, became spooked, and ran away. Or the occasions when disembodied spirits approached me when I was alone or with Simone: After a shudder went down my spine, I *knew* how to respond and resolve the situation.

Point two is thus that the Life Force will absolutely support and guide me if I am able to let it work. This has happened again and again. To be sure, the all-too-human part of me has been slow to understand. That's doubtless why the Voice reminded me a few

Ramadans ago that from now on it would be a sin for me to keep worrying about money.

This leads me to point three. God understands my weaknesses and is willing to intervene when necessary. This is most likely why I don't hear the Voice every hour like a news broadcast. It comes only when required, as that time in Yale's Dwight Chapel when it told me to be baptized with Marianna. Otherwise I am left to figure things out for myself. George Fox, the founder of the Quakers, used to say, "It was opened to me" or "The Lord revealed to me. . . ." The initiator is God, or the Power of God. My experience is that we don't have revelations on demand. But then, what about that testing we do, the Subud discernment process?

So, point four, if I ask for direction out of impatience or some kind of strong emotional need, what I get may lead me astray. My friend the late Ray Owens referred to that kind of forced testing as "voting with your eyes closed." If Bapak said it once, he constantly warned us about the power of our heart and mind, our passions, to lead us astray. In Judeo-Christianity we recall that Satan, though fallen, is still an angel, a spiritual being armed with knowledge and power. It is easy to be deluded like the man in the mental hospital who told everyone around he was Napoleon. When one of the other patients asked him who had told him that, the man replied, "God!" Upon which a third patient piped up, "Now George, I never told you that." I am certain that, like George, I have been sure "God" has told me things which turned out not only to be wrong but which led me up blind alleys from which it was sometimes hard to escape. Nowadays, therefore, I restrain myself from using that frequently invoked Subud verb, *receive*. Once one of Bapak's Indonesian secretaries, a brilliant man with a Ph.D. who taught anthropology and custom law at the University of Indonesia, said to Bapak, "I am sure Bung Karno [Indonesia's founding president, Soekarno] received." (This professor was a big fan of Soekarno.) "Yah," Bapak replied. "But from where?" In retrospect, I am sure I have *received* from that same place many times. I have used hocus-pocus, star dust, and my years of faithfully doing the Subud *latihan* to deceive myself about certain things and sometimes I have deceived others as well. This is one of my regrets, and I am deeply sorry for these mistakes.

Yet point five is precisely that although my mistakes have frequently come at a cost to both me and others, they seem somehow always to have led to new learnings. It is a commonplace of Christianity that without the Crucifixion there could be no Resurrection. Death in this sense is the doorway to larger, more abundant, longer-lasting life. All suffering from God's perspective is like birth pangs, leading to new life. It is not an easy perspective to adopt and live by, but for those who can, it is an immense blessing. I think of my friend the Rev. Dr. Arthur Harvey, a retired American Baptist minister. His motto, adopted from his mentor in the ministry, is "Praise God anyway." Arthur has had an exceptionally hard life in many ways. Yet he is always smiling, happy, and light. People who know his life story inevitably ask him, "Arthur, how do you do it?" As his smile widens, he says, "I just praise God anyway."

This leads me to point six: God is no respecter of labels. Unlike me. Although I am getting better. One of the reasons I like my friend Fr. Philip Chircop, SJ, so much is that he brings in materials from the world's religions, poetry, art, music, history, whatever to illustrate what he is saying. He doesn't just stick to things Catholic. I have at times been a Jewish chauvinist, a Lutheran chauvinist, a Catholic chauvinist and for much too long a Subud chauvinist. God is bigger than all that. All human systems and constructs are inevitably flawed. We do the best we can, but even our best efforts fall short. Infallibility is a property of the Divine, not the human. Therefore, I am learning to find help from a diverse set of sources, Baptist or Muslim, Jewish or Atheist, even from persons and traditions I would normally shun as narrow-minded. We may not be perfect, but it's also true, as the sayings go, that God don't make no junk and all God's chillin' got wings.

Point seven: We have sometimes entertained angels unawares. When I think back on all the helpers in my life, and I don't mean just Subud helpers, I know God has put angels in my path and they have been there just when I needed them. I think of Florine, Miss Sally and Miss Mae, Al Watson, Jim Culver, Alec Witherspoon, Dick Sewall, Sears Jayne, Jaja Kaul, Phillip S.Y. Sun, Jane Parry Tompkins, Muhammad Subuh, Ibu Sumari, Ibu Rahayu, Varindra Vittachi, Sharif and Tuti Horthy, Eileen Rice, Chuck Graham, Simone Zimmermann Feldman, Marianna Levine, Christine Feldman, Halinah Rizzo-Busack, Jim Busack, Doug Olson, Jan Rumi, Aisha Holm, plus others not named here and the cats Bulli, Taji, Winston, and Sita. Then there are all the angels who were there for me through books and music—the authors of the Bible, the Gita, the Tao Te Ching; the Prophet Muhammad, Hafiz, and Rumi; the Greek tragedians; Matthias Claudias, Wordsworth, Whitman, Rilke, Gibran; Carlos Castaneda; Corelli, Vivaldi, Bach, Handel, Haydn, Mozart, Schumann, Schubert, Chopin; jazz; the Beatles. The great artists and architects. The great philosophers. The mystics and saints. And the angels of the moment—those providing glad kindnesses that came at just the right time.

Point eight: Ask and ye shall receive. I don't think I have lived a special life or that I am in any way a special person. Certainly, from the viewpoint of the world, I have not set any records worthy of Guinness. I have not made a lot of money. I am not famous. I am not noted for my good looks or exceptional body. I have not stockpiled notable assets, liquid or otherwise. To quote St. Peter, I don't have gold or silver, but what I do have I will share freely with you. That is, in today's world, the world of spreading democracies, we can't look to the few big people to save us anymore. Those days of the few leaders and many followers are over. Today we all have to be leaders and followers. But to be trustworthy leaders, even just for ourselves, there is only one way: To find and grow into our biggest and best selves, the selves the Great Cosmic Architect had in mind when designing us. Since the beginning of time, hints and techniques for doing just that have been dropped and are as plentiful as public libraries. But public libraries are useless unless used. If all it takes is asking to receive, one still has to ask. Grundtvig, the Danish reformer, took to heart the verse from Deuteronomy where God told Moses and Aaron, "I have put before you life and death, the blessing and the curse. Therefore choose life. . . ." It's the taking to heart and putting into practice that changed Grundtvig and enabled him to change Denmark. It is the taking to heart and putting into practice that constitutes the asking.

The spiritual practice of Subud, which I stumbled on in early 1961 as a 21-year-old Yale graduate, has made it possible for me to meet and begin growing into the real best ME. That growing process, incredibly catalyzed by a simple, twice-weekly half-hour flow of spontaneous energy, has been my bridge to THE GREAT LIFE that somehow exists in me as well as inside and outside everything. Jesus told us, "The Kingdom of Heaven is within." Milton's Satan in *Paradise Lost* glossed that text by confessing, "Myself am Hell." We are children of the earth. Our time here is all about realizing our birthright as children of the sky, of God, also.

Let's be pragmatic. Whatever works, works. I know that many people have entered and left Subud. It was not for them what I have found it to be for me. That is why, 48 years after my opening, I am still faithfully doing my *latihan* two or three times a week, with a group or alone. My advice, adapted from Rodgers and Hammerstein's "Some Enchanted Evening," is—once you have found it, never let it go. So, keep looking until you find that secret of life, that Rosetta Stone, that key to the Universe that works for you. For you and I are fellow human beings, fellow creatures of that which has caused life to be. We can all find the way. And now is the time when we all must. Bon voyage!

Sag Harbor, Long Island, New York
March 3, 2009

Epilogue

I returned to the United States from Denmark February 1, 2009. My first stop was Marianna and Harper's place in Sag Harbor, Long Island, my legal residence. I intended to stay through March 4, Simone's birthday, and complete drafting this book before leaving. After that, I didn't know. My idea at the time was to return to DFL, the teachers college in Denmark, to give a course "Understanding America Through Film" starting in August. Prior to that, in late July, I thought I would accept my student friend Kata's invitation to visit her homeland, Hungary. Still, I would have to petition the college to approve the course. Nothing was set in stone.

After a major snowstorm on Eastern Long Island, I decided on a Southern trip for the next stage of my pilgrimage. The book was now drafted. Marianna and I had duly celebrated what would have been Mom's seventy-eighth birthday. So on March 5 I flew to Palm Beach, Florida, and spent the next two weeks with first my graduate-school girlfriend, Jane Tompkins, and her husband Stanley Fish in Delray Beach; then my sister, Natalie, who turned 78 March 8, in Hallandale; and finally Christine Jax-Castillo and her husband Zeus in West Palm Beach. The Minnesota Commissioner of Education under Governor Jesse Ventura, Christine decided to work with me to develop a wisdom certification program for parents, teachers, and members of the helping professions. The curriculum is being developed at this time (summer 2009).

From Florida I flew to Atlanta for a week, where I stayed with my Subud brother Salahuddin Brownfield, a well-known area artist, and his friend Eve Hoffman. It was a pleasure to be back in a Subud group again. The weather was lovely. And visits to the Carter Center, M.L. King Center, the High Gallery, plus an afternoon of house music at Dahlan and Honora Foah's convinced me by the time I left that Atlanta might be where I should settle. But *should* I settle in the United States at all? After a wonderful week's vacation at Doug and Elsa Felten's winter house on Hilton Head Island, South Carolina, I landed back in Washington, DC, for three weeks, including Easter with the Busacks at their country place near Frederick, Maryland. Here three important things happened: First, I tested with the DC helpers about returning to Denmark or staying in the U.S. The seven of us received unanimously that although spending more time in Denmark would be pleasant, it was now important, even essential, for me to stay in the United States. Second,

I read Gary Taubes' mind-altering study of the politics of dieting, *Good Calories, Bad Calories*, which launched me on my current high-protein, medium-fat, low-carb, no-junk-food diet, on which I've lost 17 pounds. Finally, I had my eating sensitivities tested by a Subud sister in Herndon, Virginia, who specializes in these matters. I was so impressed with Latidjah's insights into areas of my body I knew were stressed that I have been following her recommendations for the last three months. Included in the mix is getting off my blood-pressure medication, which I am now taking every third day with no ill effects thus far.

I left DC in late April to attend my younger daughter Christine's Ph.D. graduation at the University of Pittsburgh. Harper, Marianna, and Sarah flew in from Long Island, and all of us celebrated this huge achievement, sad only that Mom could not be there. From Pittsburgh, after a brief stop at my academic friends' the Fields' in Portsmouth, Ohio, where Michael was retiring as provost of Shawnee State University, I flew to Dallas for three weeks with my honorary Colombian son and Subud brother, Juan (now Felix) Prieto and family. Thirty years ago Juan arrived in Chicago for a conference. An idealistic young man from Bogotá who spoke almost no English, he was clear he wanted to stay in the States and study. I was able to help him do both, and now, the first time we had seen each other in years, he decided it was pay-back time. In the event, refusing to let me pay for anything, he took me to new restaurants for lunch or dinner each day, although as senior health educator for the Parkland (Dallas County) Hospital System, he made sure his "Gringo Papá" stayed on his diet. During this time Juan/Felix, a new Subud member and psychologist from Mexico named Dr. Ramon Cuencas-Zamora, and I cooked up plans to develop franchisable Applied Wisdom Centers, beginning with a bilingual pilot center in Dallas. Our idea was to do broad-gage life coaching using the metaphor of wisdom. So now I became convinced that nice as Atlanta had been, the place where I should settle was Dallas.

Then, on Memorial Day, I flew to Denver. My plan was to spend a week in nearby Boulder exploring a relationship with a Jewish religious educator I had briefly met while attending my friend Jillene Moore's adult *bat mitzvah* in February. And this is where the rest of the story begins.

Boulder really captivated me. However, within a few days it was clear that the Jewish educator and I would be friends but nothing more. Then, while exploring the city, I unexpectedly met another wonderful woman named Cedar Barstow. That was seven weeks ago.

In the interim, on June 22nd, Bapak's birthday, my friend and Subud sister Illène Pevec in Carbondale, Colorado, helped me celebrate the One Thousandth Day since Simone's passing. In this Subud and Sufi tradition, the soul takes its final leave from earth in its journey to the Great Beyond. On September first I'll move to a house in Boulder 15 minutes by foot from Cedar's home so we can pursue our relationship. I intend to continue my wisdom work from my new home base. There's a lot more to be done to help the world wise up. Meantime, my pilgrimage continues. From now on, though, it may become a journey for two. Time will tell.

P.S. I am pleased to present myself to you with my new name—RUSLAN FELDMAN—just confirmed in an e-mail from Ibu Rahayu, Bapak's daughter, today, July 17, 2009. I received this name 38+ years ago and thought it was for Simone's and my second child. Bapak then advised that the names for that child would be Ruslan if a boy and Christine if a girl. It proved a girl, of course, our new-minted Dr. Christine Jacqueline Feldman. Over the years I received from time to time that this name, Ruslan, was actually mine. Since Simone's 1,000 Days, however, I have had whole dialogues in *latihan* addressed to "Ruslan" and clearly meant for me. So I finally bit the bullet and wrote Ibu Rahayu, and today received her blessing. I intend to keep *Reynold* as my legal name but use RUSLAN in Subud and personal circles. For me this new name is a prayer to give me courage in my seventieth year to embrace the new: new book, new directions in work, new place to live, new partner. Please add your prayers. Many thanks.

Reynold Ruslan Feldman

Acknowledgments

IT TAKES a whole village to write a book. This one, though an autobiography, is no exception. Let me begin with my parents who sacrificed to give me the best education money could buy. Then there are my various spiritual mentors, intended and accidental, mentioned in these pages. They helped me learn that we cannot live by either bread or head alone—two fundamental values as I was growing up. My late wife, Simone, showed the way by writing her memoir first and honoring me by having me be her collaborator and editor. If I didn't have the idea of writing a memoir before her death and the appearance of her book, I certainly got it from both those events, the former giving me a certain sense of urgency. After all, I saw how quickly and unexpectedly one's promotion could come.

I owe a debt of gratitude to the various Christian ministers and priests who have served as my pastors over time, with special recognition for Kahu Doug Olson, senior pastor emeritus of Calvary Lutheran Church, Honolulu. Doug has been much more than a pastor to me: He was and is a friend, brother, fellow men's group member, uncle and godfather to my kids, and the one who got me to do the Honolulu Marathon six times. Okay, maybe the last was a bit too much for my knees, but we (especially he) did raise a lot of money for the homeless. All these men of God—and they were all men—put up with my sometimes unorthodox approach to Mainstream Christianity and bore with me without losing their senses of humor. Thank God!

My children, both writers themselves, have encouraged me during my year of living dangerously—20 months, actually—and would occasionally check in with my friends to make sure Dad was doing okay. They understood that in my grief I needed to act out a bit after a goody-two-shoes youth and were more patient with me than I remember having been with them. Another cheerleader for this project, indeed the person who gave me the idea to write an autobiography, is my Danish Subud sister, friend, and sometimes host, Aisha Holm. Many thanks, *lille ven*, for giving me just the push I needed at precisely the right time and for reading through an earlier, much longer version of the manuscript. To Aisha and her brother Rune I also owe my restorative two months at *Den Frie Laererskole,* Ollerup, Fyn, as a guest teacher of sorts. During that time I was encouraged by both the faculty and some extraordinary students, especially Kata, Erik, Michael, and Marianne, and managed to write three or four chapters. Along these lines I would be derelict in my duties were I to forget the many people—you all know who you are—who hosted me during my 20 months on the road as I wrote and rewrote my stories. One special person, without whom this book would have been unthinkable, is my third daughter, Halinah Rizzo-Busack. She has encouraged me in so many ways that I can't even begin to list them. *Millione grazie!*

Coming to the present, I'd like to thank the Board of Wisdom Factors International, M. Jan Rumi, president, and Wisdom Foundation Publishing for "hosting" my attempt at a "personal wisdom narrative." Once again the Most Reverend Stephen Randolph Sykes, bishop of the Inclusive Orthodox Church, has blessed a Wisdom Factors publishing project by bringing his considerable skills as a graphic designer and editor to bear in moving this manuscript from electronics in my computer to the words and pictures, front and back covers, comprising a real book. Along with him I'd like to thank our associates at McNaughton & Gunn printers in Michigan and the individuals who have risked their good names by endorsing this work as worth spending some hours of one's life reading. A bow of gratitude too to the Society for Values in Higher Education's long-standing morning-group seminar "Forms of Autobiography" that, after my presentation at the Summer 2009 Fellows Meeting at Elmhurst College, wondered if I had considered doing "stand-up wisdom." Special *kudos* to Dr. Marianne Gilbert Finnegan, a notable memoirist in her own right and retired academic expert in autobiography, who suggested I retain the full version of this work for close friends and family but craft a considerably abridged one for the general public. If the latter find this book readable, Marianne will deserve most of the credit.

I'm guessing that I never would have written a spiritual autobiography had I not crossed paths with Subud and, later, its founder, Muhammad Subuh Sumohadiwidjojo. That was 1961, when I was 21. Now it is 2009, just a few months before my seventieth birthday. No thanks to him and, before him, Almighty God are adequate but must be made nevertheless.

A final thank-you goes to my newest friend, Cedar Barstow, who has been reading through this manuscript in part as a way to get to know the rest of me. I am grateful for this unexpected opportunity to face life once again as part of a twosome. Beyond wisdom there is faith, and beyond faith there is good fortune. I feel very blessed.